THE WONDERFUL NOVEL

YOU'VE BEEN WAITING FOR

Highly praised by reviewers, adapted into a hit Broadway play and now one of the headline films of the year, this is the hilarious novel about a young American officer and his efforts to impose efficient Western ways on a simple little village on Okinawa during World War II.

The American Colonel in command at Okinawa thought he might win General's stars if Okinawa had modern housing, schools, progressive organizations and profitable business. But the Colonel's plans laid an egg in Tobiki Village. Captain Fisby, in charge there, just couldn't get "American" ideas across. Instead, in a weak moment, he accepted a gift of two geisha girls, who mobilized Tobiki—with explosive results for the Colonel, the Captain, and the community.

This is as delightful a book as you are likely to read this year or in ten years more. You will agree with the critics who say:

"You will enjoy reading it more than once."
—*Hartford Times*

". . . a book rich in passages of verbal beauty, skillful in design and above all, extremely funny."—*Boston Post*

". . . the most entertaining and refreshing book of the season."—*Nashville Tennessean*

". . . a wonderfully humorous and satirical story."—*Library Journal*

THIS IS A REPRINT OF A HARDCOVER EDITION ORIGINALLY PUBLISHED BY G. P. PUTNAM'S SONS.

SIGNET Books Made Into Motion Pictures

TEA AND SYMPATHY *by Robert Anderson*

The poignant drama of a misunderstood adolescent at a New England prep school, and the woman who made a man of him. (#1343—25¢)

BABY DOLL *by Tennessee Williams*

The tender and electrifying drama of a child-bride, her forty year old husband, and a lusty Sicilian immigrant. A screen original by the author of two Pulitzer Prize-winning plays. (#S1334—35c)

THE ROSE TATTOO *by Tennessee Williams*

The famous drama about an earthy woman and her violent reaction when she discovered her husband's infidelity. (#1236—25¢)

MOBY DICK *by Herman Melville*

Here, in its exciting entirety, is the world-famous sea epic about one-legged Captain Ahab and his rough-hewn crew who sailed out to battle the great white whale, dreaded monster of the deep. (#D1229—50¢)

ANASTASIA *by Marcelle Maurette*, English Adaptation *by Guy Bolton*

Was she really a Russian princess, miraculously rescued from the Communist massacre—or was she only an actress, clever enough to fool those who had known Anastasia best? This breath-taking drama of royal intrigue and human heartbreak was a smash-hit on Broadway. (#51356—35¢)

TO OUR READERS

We welcome your comments about any SIGNET, SIGNET KEY or MENTOR BOOK, as well as your suggestions for new reprints. If your dealer does not have the books you want, you may order them by mail, enclosing the list price plus 5¢ a copy to cover mailing costs. Send for our complete catalog. The New American Library of World Literature, Inc., 501 Madison Ave., New York 22, N. Y.

The Teahouse of the August Moon

by VERN SNEIDER

N·A·L SIGNET BOOKS

A SIGNET BOOK
Published by THE NEW AMERICAN LIBRARY

Published as a SIGNET BOOK
By Arrangement with G. P. Putnam's Sons

FIRST PRINTING, NOVEMBER, 1956
SECOND PRINTING (CANADA), DECEMBER, 1956
THIRD PRINTING, DECEMBER, 1956

———

To M. H. And to the people of Tobaru Village, Okinawa—whose homes lay over the blue line.

———

SIGNET BOOKS are published by
The New American Library of World Literature, Inc.
501 Madison Avenue, New York 22, New York

One

D DAY ON OKINAWA, history states, was April 1, 1945. H hour was at 0830. But to the headquarters section of Military Government Camp Team C-147, Colonel Wainright Purdy III commanding, D day was every day, H hour at 0830 each morning.

At a little after eight on an Okinawa morning in early June, Major Thompson, public safety officer of Camp Team C-147, reached for the pistol holster strapped round his ample waist, just to make certain that it was in place, then glanced nervously at his watch. Seeing there were still twenty minutes or so to kill—twenty delicious, relaxing minutes before the problems of the day came pressing in on his not too robust shoulders—he sipped his coffee and smiled.

"Yes, sir, Colonel Purdy," he said, looking out of the window of the officers' plywood mess, "you sure hit it right this morning. Hit it right on the head. It's clear as a bell outside. Not a sign of rain."

There was a ripple of approval among the nine officers gathered along the homemade mess table. And Colonel Wainright Purdy III, with the somewhat weary air of one who was used to being infallible, smiled condescendingly.

Of course it had been clear as a bell every morning for the past month, since the rainy season had ended on Okinawa. It was a safe bet that anyone predicting sunshine every day for the next three months or so would be nearly one hundred per cent right. Yet there was no denying the honest admiration in the eyes of Major Thompson, or in the eyes of the other officers.

"Yes, sir, you certainly hit it," Major Thompson repeated, shaking his head in wonder. Captain Blair, the sanitation officer, nodded. First Lieutenant McEvoy, the engineering officer, nodded. Even Private Gregovich—assigned to permanent K.P. and now surveying the twisted cigarette butts doused in the egg yolk on the plates that he would soon wash—nodded in surprise.

It would have taken a simple soul, indeed, to predict a

rainy day at that season. Private Gregovich, regarding Colonel Purdy, would have laid ten to one that the Colonel would pick rain every time.

But in fairness it must be said that Colonel Purdy had always displayed a marked genius for predicting things. Back in 1924, when Red Grange had scored four touchdowns against a powerful Michigan team in the first quarter, the Colonel had instantly stated that Grange would most certainly make All-American. After the market crash in '29, he had announced, with authority, that there would be a depression. And that fateful day when the Japanese came sneaking in on Pearl Harbor—well, the Colonel had said to Mrs. Purdy, "This means war."

So marked was his genius, in fact, that back in the early twenties during his college days at Indiana, the saying around campus used to be, "Ask ole Purdy, he knows."

In these days of 1945 on Okinawa, the Colonel was bent on making another prediction come true. It was not his own, of course. Mrs. Purdy, herself, had first voiced it to the Tuesday Club back in Pottawattamie, Indiana. "Now that Wainright is going overseas," she had stated to the bosomy little group, daintily picking at their chicken aspic, "I'm willing to wager that he will get his silver star."

The implications were staggering. The number of Reserve Colonels promoted to Brigadier General could be counted on the fingers of one hand. Of the millions of men in the Army of the United States only a few had reached the pinnacle. For the briefest moment the Colonel was hesitant. But then Mrs. Purdy had said, "After all, it's merely a question of ability, Wainright. And you most certainly must admit you have that."

When put in such a logical way, what else could the Colonel do but agree? From that day on he became a man with a clearly defined mission in the Army—he was reaching for the stars.

Now, on this sunny morning, he rose from the table and looked at his watch. He was tall and ramrod-straight, without stomach, as a Colonel should be. The uniform of the day being khaki, his own was starched and sparkling. His thick, steel-gray hair, though carefully brushed, had a rumpled look, and his clipped mustache gave him a somewhat rakish air.

"Gentlemen," he said in that mess-hall tone of comradeship, yet which left no doubt as to where authority lay, "gentlemen, it's 0827."

6

Gone were those carefree minutes of relaxation over a second cup of breakfast coffee. Faces tensed. Major Thompson's shoulders straightened. Major McNeil doused his cigarette and stood up. In brief, this was almost it.

Only Private Gregovich, scraping plates over in the corner, smiled. It was always a pleasure, so he often said, "to get those sad sacks out of here." Then a man could walk around the place without wading up to his knees.

The little group waited at the door, then stepped respectfully aside, giving way to authority. With a flick of his swagger stick, Colonel Purdy led out and the tensed group followed behind on the duck walks.

Headquarters section of Camp Team C-147 was bivouacked in the emerald-green hills between the native village of Goya and the ancient castle of Nakagusuku. In what formerly had been sweet potato fields now stood a neat street of pyramidal tents, connected by wooden walks. At one end of the street was the officers' plywood mess; at the other end stood the enlisted men's mess tent. To one side were the motor pool and supply tents. But the heart of C-147 was perched on a hill, overlooking the rolling countryside. This was the headquarters building itself.

The duties of a camp team, such as C-147, were to operate a native refugee camp. Such things, however, being subject to change, C-147 wound up controlling a section of the little island of Okinawa with eight native villages and 50,000 people under its wing. These were "enemy civilians," so the directives said. They would undoubtedly cause trouble. Being back of the American lines they would cut communication wires, blow up supply dumps, and interfere with ammunition trucks moving to the front. C-147 had to prevent this trouble.

It must be said that the directives were not entirely wrong. There had been a certain amount of wire cutting at first. Now and then a sorely perplexed native would see the black strands running across the open fields and scratch his head. Here was manna from heaven. Here was just the thing. And until Colonel Purdy ordered his village commanders to explain to their people just what a telephone was, every rickety horse cart in the area was held together by American communication wire.

Trucks, too, moving toward the front—or in any direction—were often waylaid. However, a few sticks of gum or chocolate bars tossed to the side of the road would

7

clear the way, and keep it cleared until the smiling, slant-eyed kids finished eating their candy.

But there was one case of sabotage. It happened in head-quarters section itself. After Colonel Purdy put out a "no gambling" order and confiscated all the dice and cards in the outfit, Private Gregovich developed a game. It consisted of standing on the hill at night and tossing a handful of pebbles against the officers' tents—at the same time yelling: "Flak!" The object, of course, was to pick the officer who made the air raid shelter first.

By careful observation, Gregovich learned that Major Thompson could be counted upon to take every heat up until midnight. After that the old legs gave out, and while the Major would "place" occasionally, he was a better "show" bet. Gregovich made a tidy sum on the Major until one night some smart-alecky non-com came prowling around, caught the whole bunch, and turned them in. After that, the officers' sleep was no longer sabotaged.

So with no trouble among the native population, Colonel Purdy was forced to scrap Plan A, which had been drawn up back at the Presidio of Monterey and which covered all possible contingencies. Luckily, C-147 had a secondary mission—to look after the welfare of the native population—or they would have been out of business. Thus Plan B, also drawn up at Monterey, came into effect.

Plan B was a masterpiece, Major Thompson and the headquarters section of C-147 always said. It covered everything from village organization to a distinction between communism and communal living, under which the villages had to operate, the economic system on the island having collapsed. There was even a section written by Mrs. Purdy on the organization of Women's Clubs (specifically a Women's League for Democratic Action) with rules of club procedure and luncheon suggestions for the meetings—chicken aspic, salmon loaf garnished with watercress, fruit compote, and other delicacies.

However, on one of his frequent inspections of neighboring areas, Colonel Purdy made a startling discovery. It seemed as if every team on Okinawa was using sections of Plan B. "An obvious case of cribbing," the Colonel had confided to Mrs. Purdy in his letters. Why, every village on the island had set up a rationing system. Every village had a native mayor, a native police force, an agriculture foreman, plus other officials with similar duties to those outlined in Plan B. They had even cribbed the

Colonel's section on education—they were starting schools.

In fact, a casual observer driving through the half-tumbled villages of reed and bamboo shacks would be unable to distinguish one team area from another. And if the observer happened to be an inspecting general or congressman . . . well, this would never do for a Reserve Colonel with silver stars in his eyes. He must have an area that stood out.

A lesser man would have despaired. But not Colonel Purdy. There was only one solution: prepare a supplement which used Plan B as a basis, and which would raise C-147's area above and beyond anything another team might conceive. It was on this supplement that headquarters section was working at a killing pace.

Promptly at 0829 the group, Colonel Purdy striding briskly at its head and Major Thompson dogtrotting at its rear, entered headquarters building.

The enlisted clerks and draftsmen snapped to attention. Privates Emery and Fannin, the sweeping and mopping detail respectively, stepped aside, like weary subs turning the field over to the first team.

"At ease," Colonel Purdy called and walked between the rows of desks lining the aisle. The group behind him peeled off at their own desks and settled into their chairs. Reaching the head of the aisle, Colonel Purdy turned and looked back. Up by the door Major Thompson sat alert and vigilant. There was no telling when a neighboring team would send someone around snooping, and this supplement was going to be hush-hush. There would be no cribbing here. No snooper was going to get by the public safety officer.

The rest, too, were in position—the engineering officer, the agriculture officer, the planning section. A heavy silence fell over headquarters. All eyes were on the Colonel. This was *it*. Slowly Colonel Purdy looked at his watch, waited, then nodded. "It's eight thirty, gentlemen."

Pencils hit papers. Drawing instruments came down on drawing boards. Major Thompson moved his chair slightly so he could get a better view of the terrain out through the open door. H hour had arrived.

The Colonel settled at his own desk, and as he regarded the group before him, a smile crossed his lips. These were hand-picked men, here in headquarters section. There were no troublemakers here. In fact, they reminded him of his personnel back home at the Purdy Paper Box Co.—of which the Colonel was sole owner by inheritance. Yes, sir, all he had to do was give them a broad general outline, and they would fill in the details. These were hand-picked men.

The secret supplement to Plan B—which was to make C-147's area stand out—had numerous ramifications, and the planning section was busy with one. "I want completely new villages in our area, gentlemen," Colonel Purdy had said. "Those thatched shacks have to go. Mrs. Purdy feels that something of colonial design might be nice, and I'm inclined to agree with her." He had no need to say more.

Captain McPharland, section head, had once visited Williamsburg, Virginia—a little project that had cost the Rockefellers many millions to restore. Now from the drawing boards of the planning section emerged spacious colonial villages with sweeping lawns and box hedges. Villages with spanking-white houses surrounded by picket fences, with broad, tree-lined streets, illuminated at night by colonial street lights set on white posts. But there was one great distinction between these villages and Williamsburg—Duke of Gloucester Street in Williamsburg became Purdy Avenue here.

So thorough was the planning section that they had even made provisions for buried electrical cables. "We don't want any poles cluttering up the place," Captain McPharland always said with a stern nod.

But the bricks, the lumber, the generators to feed the power lines? That was no concern of the planning section. They did the designing. They got things down on paper. The execution wasn't their business.

The engineering section was also busy this morning, even though it had proved quite a problem for the Staff at one time. C-147 was to have new villages, true, but there was no denying that work must be found for the native population, some sort of industry must be set up. Major Thompson had suggested that C-147 build a ricksha factory in each of its eight villages.

"There's about 400,000 people on this island, Colonel," he had announced, "and, by golly, we got a potential market for 400,000 rickshas. Everybody will want one."

After due consideration, Colonel Purdy was forced to reject the plan. Rickshas were fine, he said, but at least half the population would want to ride in them while the other half pulled; so immediately the potential market was

10

reduced fifty per cent. "But on the other hand, gentlemen, if we manufacture bicycles—"

Major Thompson shook his head in admiration. "Colonel, *everybody* will want one."

Then Colonel Purdy laid his trump card on the table, and the Staff was wide-eyed. "When the market is glutted with bicycles, gentlemen," he had said, "we'll convert. We'll make motor scooters. So we really take a limited potential market of 400,000 and increase it to 800,000."

It was sheer genius, the Staff agreed. But Colonel Purdy held up a modestly protesting hand. "Just logical reasoning, gentlemen."

Thus the engineering section was swamped with work this morning. Lieutenant McEvoy, the engineering officer, and half the section were busy at their drafting boards, drawing up plans for the bicycle factories proper. The other half of the section was occupied with the motor scooter conversion problem, while the two enlisted men, borrowed from the agriculture department, dabbled with their water colors, turning out beautiful illustrations of the manufactured products.

There was a sleek number in red called the "Speedster" designed to sell at forty yen, without accessories. There was the "Bantam," a junior model in blue with white trimmings. And, of course, there was the "Purdy de Luxe" model with chrome handlebars, horn, and mudguards— all for eighty-five yen, delivered.

Yes, sir, things were really humming this morning, Colonel Purdy noted, and turned his attention to his own desk. To one side lay a pile of reports, to the other side lay a new copy of *Adventure* magazine. Colonel Purdy smiled. *Adventure* must have just arrived in the morning mail. And they had a good cover this month, too—a three-color job in bright red, yellow, and black. And there was Jean Lafitte, the pirate of the Gulf, a patch over one eye and a dagger between his teeth, climbing over the rail of an about-to-be-captured merchantman.

Colonel Purdy's spine tingled. There was good reading here. He flipped the cover and scanned the title of the lead article, 'I Lived among the Head-Hunters of the Amazon." His eyes brightened. He felt himself already among the head-hunters. They were crowding around him, their spears menacing in the light of the campfire. They were ringing him in, and he was unarmed.

Perhaps he should never have come. They had warned

11

him back in Santarem, back there on the river, of the danger. But he had only laughed at their fears. For he had long heard of this fabulous white woman of the inner country, this queen whom the tribes worshiped as a goddess. And now she was beside him. He could feel her nearness in the night, caught the scent of her hair as she whispered, "I love you, Wainright, and I must go back with you. Do not let them keep me here . . ."

A chair scraped the floor in headquarters. Colonel Purdy looked up. Instead of the lithe-limbed queen of the Amazon, he saw broad-beamed Major Thompson standing in the doorway, surveying the terrain below with a pair of field glasses. His dream snapped, the Colonel glanced at his desk, saw the reports, then frowned. That head-hunter article would be top-notch reading, but— He hesitated, his face solemn. This was war, and duty was duty.

Firmly, he shoved the magazine to one side. He would come back to it tonight. Already he could anticipate the pleasure of sitting in his quarters, a Scotch and soda beside him, Jean Lafitte or the Amazon queen before him. He turned to the reports on his desk. For while the policy and planning of C-147 was developed here in headquarters, the execution of the plans depended on the officers and enlisted men stationed out in the team's eight villages, and there was much to do before all would be well with them.

Of course, the men in the field hardly knew of the supplement to Plan B yet. It was too hush-hush to let past the door of headquarters. But the men in the field had nothing to worry about. As soon as it was completed, Colonel Purdy would shoot it right out to them for execution.

It was generally agreed in headquarters that the village commanders had pretty much of a snap. "Hell," Major Thompson always said a little scornfully. "They don't even have to think, their thinking's been done for them in Plan B. If they get stuck on a point, all they have to do is look it up."

Yet Colonel Purdy kept close watch on these village commanders. He did not want any spoiled apples in the barrel, nor any spoiled villages to hit an inspecting general or congressman right in the eye. The Colonel's method of keeping track of the villages was through a system of spot progress reports—reports that might be demanded daily, weekly, or monthly—the village commanders never quite knew.

"That'll keep them on their toes," Major Thompson said

12

with a knowing nod. "I'd like to see them try ~~~
with that system. They won't have time to sit around ~~
dream up stuff."

The reports, called for the day before, lay in front of
Colonel Purdy now, and he picked up the first one. It was
a five-page affair from Major Enright, commanding Hae-
baru village. Colonel Purdy began to read:

A. Have given the following lectures to the Women's
League for Democratic Action since the last report, one
month ago:
  1. The Theory of Democracy.
  2. The History of Democracy.
  3. Some Great Democrats.
  4. The Four Freedoms.
(Tea and C ration crackers served at all meetings.)

Colonel Purdy smiled. "Democracy in the home through
the women," he told himself, borrowing a phrase Mrs.
Purdy had used often in that section on the creation of
the League that she had written for Plan B. He must in-
clude this in his next letter home. Not only because of
Mrs. Purdy's high personal interest as founder, but also
because she was preparing a paper on the League for the
Tuesday Club in Pottawattamie, and they were awaiting it
with "bated breath."

VERY GOOD. Colonel Purdy was about to write on Major
Enright's report, then frowned, for Lecture 3 was titled:
Some Great Democrats. Quickly, he picked up a pencil.
"What about Republicans?" he wrote. A Republican congressman on inspection would sure raise hell for playing
politics like that. Enright ought to know better. And this
business of refreshments. Tea was all right, but C ration
crackers! His pencil went down again. "See list of luncheon
suggestions Mrs. Purdy has included."

He read on:

B. Education Program:
  1. Have completed construction of a pentagon-shaped
     thatch school.
  2. All classes have been organized up through the sixth
     grade.
  3. Curriculum—First Grade:
     0830—0900 . . . Singing.
     0900—1000 . . . Play period.
     1000—1030 . . . Recess.
     1030—1100 . . . .

...m. Major Enright sure was on ... school would add a nice, homey ... general from Washington should fly ...se, it was only a temporary thing. When the supplement to Plan B was completed, Enright would have to tear down the thatch school and construct one of brick. Naturally, there was bound to be a certain amount of duplication in such matters. But the Colonel did scribble a memo to the planning section, suggesting that all schools be redesigned in pentagon shape.

By the time Colonel Purdy read the curriculum of all grades up through the sixth, by the time he had reached the end of Major Enright's report, he was beaming. Yes, sir, Enright was carrying out Plan B in fine style. Maybe he ought to move the Major up to headquarters. Here was a man who should be doing some planning instead of wasting his time in the villages. Yet C-147 was tremendously short of personnel at the moment, and it would have to wait for the time being.

Colonel Purdy glanced at the next report. "Tobiki village," he read, "Captain Jeff Fisby commanding." The Colonel stirred uneasily. This Fisby was a last-minute addition to C-147 before the unit sailed from San Francisco, and the Colonel had once confided to Major Thompson that he did not believe this Captain was "quite of first-team caliber."

Slowly Colonel Purdy picked up the top sheet, then looked to see where the other pages were. But there was only one page. He looked at the back. It was blank. He looked at the front. It was nearly blank. He began to read.

The roar shook headquarters. Major Thompson, the public safety officer, reached for his pistol, dead certain that a snooper had somehow slipped into headquarters. Then realizing that it might possibly be a sniper, he shoved his chair back from his desk and waited for the first shot before diving under.

But there was no shot, and the Major, certain now that the trouble was American in source, threw caution to the wind. Seeing the Colonel choking, he ran for the Lister bag and a cup of water. "What is it, sir?" he asked.

The Colonel did not answer. For a moment he could only sit there and tremble, his face a royal purple. Then he started shouting. "By God," he yelled. "Imagine a man of his age sending in a report like this. Imagine!" His fist came banging down on the desk.

14

Two

DOWN IN TOBIKI VILLAGE Captain Jeff Fisby was also banging his fist on the desk. He was drawn up to his full chubby five foot seven. One trouser leg had pulled out of his combat boot as usual. And the perspiration stood out on his forehead, way up where his hair had thinned. It could hardly be said that he cut a military figure. Without a doubt, no sculptor would ever ask him to model for a statue to stand in the town square depicting the youth and spirit of America's soldiers in World War II. Yet he was always in great demand around Christmas time back home. The Exchange Club claimed he was the best Santa Claus they ever had.

Now his face was set in unwonted sternness, and he waved a finger at his young native interpreter. "Sakini," he stormed, "this is the last time I'm going to tell you. Now you get those goats out of here."

Sakini scratched his close-cropped black hair. "But, boss, they like it in here. It's nice and cool with the thatch roof. They'll get pretty sore if we make 'em go out in the hot sun."

A goat bleated, as if in agreement, and Fisby slammed the desk again. "I don't care how sore they get. I won't have them lying around headquarters. This is a place of business, not a goatery. You get them out of here."

The uncomprehending Sakini nodded. "Okay, boss." Then he spoke quickly in the Luchuan dialect, and the group of natives gathered in headquarters began shoving the protesting goats out through the front door.

Over to one side of the single room, Corporal Barton raised himself from his cot, looked under just to make certain that no goat had been overlooked, then sank back again.

"Now close the screen door," Captain Fisby ordered. "And keep it closed. And remember, this is a place of business."

Outside, the goats raised pitiful voices in protest, but Fisby hardly heard. In the past few months since he had

15

...age, he had become used to ...erely regarded them through the blind of bamboo, covering the win-...of headquarters. Then, satisfied that they ...outside, he settled his ample waistline com-...rtably in his swivel chair and turned back to the group of natives gathered before his homemade desk. "Now let's see," he said, rubbing his head. "Where were we? Oh, yes, Mr. Motomura, here, wants to move to our village."

Sakini nodded brightly. At the most, he couldn't have been more than twenty-two. This morning he wore an oversized T shirt bearing the name Princeton (a gift from Fisby who had bought the thing for gym classes when in Military Government School there), a pair of Fisby's army shoes, and fatigue trousers with home-sewed pleats. Had there been zoot-suiters on Okinawa, undoubtedly Sakini would have been one of them. "That's right, boss," Sakini said. "He want to move to our village. And see, he even got a note."

Mr. Motomura had a note all right. It was from Lieutenant Fay at Awasi village and addressed to Captain Fisby. It merely stated that Mr. Motomura and his family requested permission to move to Tobiki, and would Fisby approve the deal. That was all, yet it made Fisby frown.

Wryly, he remembered his last dealings with this Lieutenant Fay. They had swapped cart horses, and while Fisby had received ten for five, it hardly took an expert judge of horseflesh to tell who had come out second best on the deal. Now Fisby was certain that Lieutenant Fay was pulling some sort of trick, and he was wary. Yet this little Okinawan, this Mr. Motomura, puzzled him greatly.

Here, obviously, was a man of importance. Mr. Motomura's white linen suit and Panama hat told Fisby that. Previously, all Fisby had seen on the island were worn, faded cotton shirts and nondescript trousers. Here, obviously, was a Captain of Industry. Certainly Mr. Motomura was not in the habit of going into the fields and digging his own sweet potatoes, like the people of Tobiki village.

As Fisby regarded the little Okinawan, Mr. Motormura smiled, displaying a sparkling collection of gold teeth that made Fisby's eyes pop. Never before on Okinawa had he seen so much gold in one mouth. Yes, sir, here was prosperity personified.

The thought of Lieutenant Fay came to Fisby, and he

hesitated. "Sakini," he began cagily, "just why does Mr. Motomura want to leave Awasi?"

Sakini shook his head. "He don't want to leave, boss."

"Then why is he coming here requesting permission to move to our village?"

"Because the Awasi boss kick him out."

"Uh-huh." Fisby nodded. So here was a troublemaker that Lieutenant Fay was trying to palm off. "Uh-huh. And just why did Lieutenant Fay kick him out?"

Sakini scratched his head. "He don't know, boss. But this morning when he wake up, the Awasi boss is standing there. Through his interpreter he say: 'Motomura, pack your stuff. You and your family got to move. Here's a note, now get out of here.' And he send two M.P.'s along to see that Mr. Motomura leave. If you don't let him move here, boss, he don't know what he's going to do. He don't think they let him go back to Awasi."

This threw a little different light on the subject. Fay shouldn't chase people from their homes. Fisby examined Mr. Motomura again, then looked at the group of natives gathered round. His mayor was there. His village secretary was there. In fact, just about every person of importance in the village was before his desk, their faces tense.

"Sakini," Fisby said, "Mr. Motomura must have done something to the Lieutenant."

Sakini shook his head solemnly. "He don't do anything to the Awasi boss. He even make gifts to him. But everyone in Awasi notice how funny their boss act lately. He get real nervous and grouchy. All day long he just smoke one cigarette after another. Then this morning he say, 'Motomura, you got to move.' Don't understand it, boss." Sakini scratched his head.

Fisby, too, scratched his head. He did not understand either. Maybe Lieutenant Fay had just cracked up. He had heard of such cases.

The lanky native mayor whispered excitedly to Sakini. "Boss," Sakini explained, "the mayor say we sure need a man like Mr. Motomura around this place."

Fisby saw his village officials nod.

"And the mayor say Mr. Motomura can even live down at his house."

"Is that a fact?" Fisby's eyebrows shot up. Indeed, here was a man of importance. The mayor was asking him to live at his home when the village was so crowded that it was next to impossible to squeeze another person in.

17

Usually the whole village kicked up a fuss over new arrivals.

Besides, a little plan involving Mr. Motomura was forming in Fisby's mind. Here was a man with great potentialities. Frankly, Fisby was having trouble with his village officials of late. It was due to a peculiar affliction of the Okinawan gentry, namely that they liked to sleep, especially when there was work to be done.

During the first few weeks of the Occupation, Fisby had gotten into the habit of going around to all the houses in the village and routing them out when they were needed. But just when he had their homes nicely spotted, they had rigged up some secret place to sleep that he could not find. Now he could only catch them home at mealtime.

But with Mr. Motomura in the village . . . Fisby smiled. Mr. Motomura did not get that white linen suit and gold teeth by sleeping. No, sir. Here would be a club to hold over the heads of his officials. If Hokkaido Yamaguchi, the agriculture foreman, failed to bring in the harvest, Fisby would simply say: "Uh-huh. Well, you just report for the sweet potato digging detail tomorrow morning, Hokkaido. From now on Mr. Motomura is foreman." Or if the construction chief . . . Fisby shook his head and smiled again. With a man who could fill in at any position, he would get some action around the place. Those officials were too proud of their jobs to take any chances if they knew he had a substitute handy.

"Boss," Sakini said slowly, "you think maybe Mr. Motomura can move here?"

Fisby saw the group around his desk tense. "Well, Sakini, I think Mr. Motomura has great potentialities."

Over to the side of headquarters, Corporal Barton raised himself on the cot and propped his head on his hand. "Captain," he said. "I think you better watch out for this guy. Here's a railroad deal for sure."

Fisby smiled. "I think Lieutenant Fay just got a little upset."

Barton shrugged. "You're the boss." He sank back on the cot. "But don't forget I told you."

"Then Mr. Motomura can move here?" Sakini asked breathlessly.

"Well, I can't see any objection—"

Sakini let out his breath sharply, a smile crossed his bronzed face. "Good, boss. Good." And when he explained, the group, too, seemed relieved. Mr. Motomura wiped his forehead, and the bowing started. Fisby nodded a few times by way of acknowledging those tossed in his direction.

Then Mr. Motomura conferred with Sakini, and Fisby saw the group of natives go wide-eyed. The village secretary whispered to the mayor. They looked at Mr. Motomura, then at Fisby, and began whispering again.

"What did he say, Sakini?" Fisby asked.

"Huh?" Sakini was a little dazed. "Oh, he say he would like to make to you a gift in appreciation for letting him move to our village."

Now Fisby's eye widened. Never before had the natives offered him a present, and he was pleased. "Tell him I thank him."

"Okay, boss. Then you accept the gift?"

Fisby considered. Mr. Motomura, with all his obvious prosperity, certainly looked as if he could spare a few gifts. Besides, it would be pretty nice to take some souvenirs from the Orient back home to Ohio. When the gang dropped into the drugstore after supper, as they usually did, he could bring them out and show them around. The gang would get a kick out of that. He might even be able to use them as a window display. "Well, I wouldn't be averse to a few souvenirs, Sakini," he said with a smile.

Sakini nodded vigorously. "Good, boss. Good. Now Mr. Motomura ask to be excused. He go get the souvenirs."

As the group paraded out, Fisby leaned back in his swivel chair. He told himself that this Motomura was going to be a good man to have around the village. Here was a man with potentialities.

The phone rang and absently Fisby picked up the receiver. "Tobiki village, Captain . . ."

The roar from the other end made him snap to attention in the swivel chair. "Fisby," Colonel Purdy roared. "I sent you down there to build up a village. What kind of a progress report is this—six kids born last month!"

Fisby rubbed his head. Running his own drugstore back in Ohio was never like this. "But, Colonel, I thought—"

"I don't care what you thought," Colonel Purdy exploded. "Besides, you ought to know that births are entered under population increases, not progress."

Fisby brightened. "Oh, but they weren't children, sir. They were kids—goats. So you see we are increasing our livestock herds, and—"

"Goats! Fisby, suppose some congressman flies in to

inspect us. Suppose he says, 'Let's see, Colonel, and just what is your team doing on Okinawa?' Do you think I'm going to say: 'Oh, we're letting the goats copulate.' Now you listen to me!"

The force of the blast made Fisby wince. He could see the Colonel's gray mustache bristling, could see the Colonel towering over the phone, and his own chubby five foot seven slipped lower in the swivel chair.

Across the desk, a breathless Sakini signaled briskly to draw Fisby's attention. "Boss," Sakini said, "tell that guy to hurry up. Mr. Motomura has sent the souvenirs."

But Fisby hardly heard.

"Look, Fisby," came the Colonel's voice. "Now think hard. You must have made some progress during the past month, besides the goats."

Fisby thought hard. "Well, sir, we started building the new school for the education program, as directed in Plan B."

"You started that six weeks ago, Fisby."

"Yes, sir. Well, we established a home to take care of the old people."

"You did that two months ago."

"Yes, sir. Let's see—oh, we set up a ration system."

"You did that on D day." Colonel Purdy's voice was like steel. "Fisby, let me ask you a question. What are you doing right now?"

"Now, sir? Just sitting at my desk."

"So I thought. And what have you accomplished this morning?"

Fisby considered. "Well, one of the natives gave me some souvenirs, Colonel, and—"

"That's all you've done—accept some souvenirs! Fisby, don't tell me you haven't even been giving your lectures to the Women's League for Democratic Action lately."

Fisby hesitated. He remembered the night back in the Officers' Club at the Presidio of San Francisco when the formidable Mrs. Purdy had cornered him, had given him a stern little lecture on the importance of the League. "You most certainly cannot overlook the feminine viewpoint on this Occupation, Captain," she had said. Fisby tried to point out that as a bachelor he hardly understood the feminine viewpoint. But Mrs. Purdy paid no attention. She just went on and on. By the time she had finished they were closing the Club, and he never did get into a game of nine ball that night.

"Well, answer me, Fisby," the Colonel demanded impatiently.

"Beg pardon? Oh, yes, sir. Well, we almost had a meeting of the League a couple of weeks ago."

"What do you mean—you almost had a meeting?"

"We just got nicely started, sir, when some kid came running in, saying that one of Miss Higa Jiga's . . ."

"Miss who?"

Fisby pronounced the name slowly and distinctly. "Miss Hee-ga Gee-ga. She's the president. Anyway, this kid said that one of her pigs had broken loose. Well, Miss Susano, the recording secretary, made a motion that the League adjourn to catch it. The executive council seconded the motion, so . . ."

Fisby heard the gasp. It was a moment before the Colonel caught his breath. "You mean to say, Fisby, that catching a pig was more important than your lecture?"

"Oh, no, sir. But Miss Higa Jiga says it was her best pig and she sure didn't want to let it get away." Fisby felt the storm brewing, and went on quickly. "Anyway, sir, I haven't had much time for meetings. You see, I've been pretty busy lately."

"Busy. You've been busy." Disbelief was evident in the Colonel's voice.

"Yes, sir. I've been having trouble with the sanitation program in the village. Someone is always blocking off the drainage ditches to wash their feet, so I have to go around kicking the dams out."

"You what?" Colonel Purdy was horrified. "Fisby, right at this moment you should be organizing your nurse's aide program, as directed in Plan B. And here you are—going around kicking the dams out of drainage ditches. Why don't you utilize your native police for that. Why do you think I organized them?"

"But, sir, the police like to sneak over to the airstrip and watch the planes land."

"I don't care what they like!" In the middle of the blast, Sakini, his bronzed face set in a puzzled frown, tugged Fisby's sleeve. "But, boss. Mr. Motomura left the souvenirs."

Absently Fisby waved him away. He was caught between "Don't you have any control over that village?" and "Just what the hell do you think you're doing down there?" Frankly, he did not know.

"Now look," Colonel Purdy said, "if you had mastered

21

Plan B, you'd know how to handle the police in such a situation."

"But I followed the Plan, sir," Fisby said quickly. "I threw the whole bunch in jail. Only they liked the meals so well, and they could sleep all day—well, sir, before I knew it everyone in the village wanted to get locked up, including the mayor, so I had to throw them all out and close the place down.

"You know, sir, I think if we made going to jail a sort of a bonus, it would certainly pay dividends."

"Make going to jail a bonus," Colonel Purdy's voice was a horrified whisper. "Fisby, would you put a blot like that on a man's character? Would you have people walking around saying, 'See, there's a jailbird.' "

Fisby squirmed. "I didn't mean it that way, sir. Only they seem to like the place pretty well."

"And you don't get the implication, Fisby? You don't know what that means?"

"No, sir."

"Well, you failed with your indoctrination. You haven't fired the people with the spirit of the Occupation. Here they want to lie around all day in jail when all the time they should be willing to work twenty-four hours a day, if necessary, to put it over." The Colonel's voice grew stern. "I can't say that I'm pleased with your work, Fisby. Not one bit!"

Fisby, visualizing a big UNSATISFACTORY on his efficiency report, wiped his forehead in desperation. "But, sir, things just don't seem to go right."

"You better make them go right," Colonel Purdy warned. "Fisby, do you realize what Major Enright is doing over in his village? Why, already the fourth-graders know the alphabet through 'M,' and the sixth-graders are singing 'Auld Lang Syne' in English. Now isn't that quite impressive?"

Fisby had to admit that it was.

"Now listen," Colonel Purdy snapped. "I want you to finish that school and get the education program started. I want you to follow every section of Plan B to the letter. And I want those people fired with the spirit of the Occupation. Understand?"

"Yes, sir."

"Now get out of that swivel chair!"

Captain Fisby jumped, was in the middle of a salute before he caught himself. "Yes, sir!" But the phone had

22

already clicked dead. He let himself down easily, then remembering Colonel Purdy's words, stood up quickly.

Raising the improvised Venetian blind, he settled his chubby frame on the homemade desk and looked out of the windowless window of headquarters.

About him, Tobiki village dozed in the heat of the June morning. Down the narrow, bamboo-lined main street, a goat lazily nibbled at the half-tumbled thatch roof of a mud and reed shack, unbothered by the group of natives sipping their tea on the weathered stoop. Here and there a pig, surrounded by a covering squadron of flies, wallowed contentedly in the cool mud of the textile banana groves, ringing the houses.

And as the breeze from the Pacific, just beyond, blew in over Tobiki village—bringing the not so spicy odors of the Orient—Captain Fisby shook his head sadly.

The place could certainly do with some progress, all right, he had to admit that. But how anyone was going to fire the people with the spirit of the Occupation, as Colonel Purdy directed, or how anyone was going to fire the people with the spirit of any thing, for that matter, Fisby did not know.

Three

"HEY, BOSS." Sakini was becoming impatient. "Here's the souvenirs that Mr. Motomura leave for you."

Fisby nodded absently and continued to look out through the window. "Just put them on the desk."

Sakini's dark eyes became puzzled. "Okay, boss, but I think maybe they don't like it."

"They? Who's they?"

"The souvenirs."

Captain Fisby heard the tinkling laughter. Turning, he saw the short white boots, the blue, flowered kimonos, and was afraid to look further. "These—these are the souvenirs?"

Sakini nodded enthusiastically. "Yep, boss. Two geisha girls. Nice, eh?"

Fisby stole a glance at the pretty, smiling faces, and his

balding head turned crimson. Geisha girls! Back at the Military Government School at Princeton, Fisby recalled, his class had spent an entire two-hour seminar period discussing them. And while the official status of the geisha was never quite made clear, Colonel Purdy, with his usual crushing logic, had pointed out, "And why, gentlemen, would the Japanese government levy a monthly tax on these girls if they weren't legalized prostitutes?"

Fisby cringed. A man couldn't go around owning prostitutes. They had names for people like that. What if Colonel Purdy found out about this! It would mean a court-martial for sure. Suppose the papers back home picked it up. Suppose it should come out in headlines: *Captain Jeff Fisby dishonorably discharged from the Army* . . . A man's reputation would be ruined in no time. They would kick him out of the Business Men's Association immediately; the Business Men kept a pretty sharp lookout on the practices of their members. He swallowed hard.

"And now, boss," Sakini announced proudly, "this is First Flower, geisha girl first class."

First Flower, her dark eyes twinkling, did a little bow. She couldn't have been more than twenty at the most. And Fisby, furtively regarding her small, delicate features and jet-black hair piled high in the elaborate coiffure of the geisha, edged back from the desk; edged back from this—this tainted woman. Then she tilted her pretty head coyly, questioned Sakini as to the proper form of introduction in English, and said: "Hello, boss."

Fisby's semibald head lit up like a stop light. "Sakini, you tell her not to call me 'boss.'"

"Don't understand." Sakini scratched his head. "Mr. Motomura give 'em to you."

Fisby, seeing Corporal Barton on the cot across the room snicker, drew himself up in what, to him, was a military position.

"And, boss," Sakini went on, "this is Lotus Blossom." She, too, did a little bow, and Sakini leaned across the desk. "She only second-class geisha, boss," he whispered confidentially. "But she study real hard to pass her first-class exams."

Helplessly, Fisby glanced at the smiling Sakini. "But, Sakini, I never said I'd accept geisha girls." He turned. "Corporal Barton, did I say that?"

Corporal Barton, who was enjoying this immensely, propped himself on an elbow. "Well, Captain, I just know what I hear. Now, this guy comes in here and says will you accept some souvenirs, and you said okay, Captain."

"That's right, boss," Sakini agreed.

The two smiling geishas moved closer to the desk, and Fisby moved back. "Sakini, you give these girls back to Mr. Motomura."

Sakini shook his head. "We can't do that, boss."

"We can't?"

"No, Mr. Motomura lose much face."

"That's right, Captain," Corporal Barton said. "And remember what Colonel Purdy wrote in Plan B: 'Never make anyone lose face.'"

Captain Fisby remembered all right, but at the moment he was worried about his own neck.

"Besides, boss," Sakini said, "Mr. Motomura isn't in the village any more."

"He isn't?"

"No. The Awasi boss got him pretty upset by kicking him out, so he thinks he ought to have a long rest. He go up to Kunigami country to see an old friend."

Fisby flinched. So Motomura had pulled the same thing on Lieutenant Fay over in Awasi, but Fay wouldn't stand for it. Now Motomura was taking a powder before Fisby kicked him out. Well this Motomura certainly showed his true colors, Fisby told himself, but what could you expect from a man who made a profession of owning—well, what could you expect? Still, Corporal Barton had no right to be wearing that smirking I-told-you-so look on his face. Everyone made a mistake in judging character now and then. Fisby began to simmer a little. Then realizing he still had the girls on his hands, he turned to Sakini. "But I can't own geishas," he protested.

Sakini scratched his head. "Don't understand, boss. A very honorable profession."

Fisby groped for words, tried to think. Then he smiled. "Well, it's just not allowed, Sakini. You see, once there was a great man in our country. We called him the Great Emancipator."

"The great who?"

"Emancipator. And he said that people can't own other people, so—" Fisby shrugged and eased himself back into the swivel chair, pleased with his explanation.

Sakini considered carefully. "Boss, did the Great Emancipator say you can't own geishas?"

In self-defense, Fisby edged forward on the chair. "Well,

not exactly. In the first place, I don't think he knew about geishas."

Sakini nodded slyly. "Everything all right then, boss. You own."

There was a certain finality about Sakini's words that made Fisby's shoulders slump.

First Flower tugged at Sakini's sleeve, whispered quickly. "Boss," Sakini explained, "she want to know where they stay."

"Stay?"

"Yep, boss. Just a little while ago the mayor tell me to remind you that he ask Mr. Motomura to live at his place, and that he mean Mr. Motomura's family, too, so—"

Horrified, Fisby banged the desk. "No!" He wasn't going to allow anything like that to go on.

"But, boss, the mayor say he always likes to think of all the people in the village as his children. And he say he'd be pretty worried if he knew some of his daughters were out in the rain, and the dark, and—"

"No!"

Sakini considered, then edged forward hopefully. "Well, boss, there's plenty of room at my house. Just me and my grandpa."

"No!"

Though a little disappointed, Sakini smiled. "Understand, boss. Understand. They stay at your house."

Fisby was a picture of uprighteous indignation. "They will not!"

Sakini scratched his head. "But where do they stay then, boss?"

Fisby supposed he ought to at least find them temporary quarters. "For the time being, they'll stay . . ." He tried to think. "Let's see. They'll stay at the old folk's home. That's it. They can help out around there. They can be— well, nurses."

When Sakini explained, First Flower's dark eyes flashed. She broke forth excitedly in the Luchuan dialect. With great display, she and Lotus Blossom brought out papers, waved them indignantly before Sakini.

Sakini regarded Fisby. "Can't be nurses, boss. Got papers from the geisha guild." His voice grew confidential. "The guild say they got a right to work, and the guild gets pretty sore when somebody starts monkeying around, boss. Maybe they even have people walk up and down with signs, saying you aren't fair to geisha girls."

26

Captain Fisby sank lower in his swivel chair. "All right. They can still be geisha." He saw the girls smile happily. "But get them out of here, Sakini. Take them down to the old folk's home."

The girls giggled and bowed. Then learning the proper English words from Sakini, they chorused: "Good-by, boss." And the flush swept up into Fisby's face. At the door they paused briefly, waved, then turned to the smiling, bowing mob outside headquarters. Though the native police were still panting from their run from the airstrip, the whole crew was there, all grins and shining red helmet-liners, as they opened a path for the girls to sweep through. And as Captain Fisby watched, he had the uneasy feeling that here were a lot of little country boys seeing the big city for the first time.

There was Hokkaido Yamaguchi, his roly-poly agriculture foreman. "The life line of the village," that's what Colonel Purdy called the agriculture foreman in Plan B. "Get a good man here, a good dependable man," the Colonel warned. "Someone who can shoulder the responsibility of planting and harvesting. Someone who can get the food from the fields into the village."

At the moment, Fisby sadly reflected, the "life line" hardly seemed interested in digging sweet potatoes. He was busy slicking down his hair, busy brushing off his trousers, which barely covered his knock-knees. And as Lotus Blossom passed, Hokkaido's cherubic face was wreathed in smiles. He just stood there grinning like a jackass eating cactus.

And there was the construction chief, who was supposed to be building the new school. And there was that coordinator of village activity—the mayor, himself. In fact, all the village officials were there, elbowing their way up into the front rank to get a better look.

As the geishas swept through the crowd, Fisby heard them draw in their breaths sharply. Though they spoke in the Luchuan dialect, still it sounded suspiciously like "You nice." And never had Fisby seen so much bowing and scraping in all his days in the village. Somehow, he hated to think of what effect these girls were going to have on future progress.

Progress! The thought of the word made Fisby jump, for he could hear Colonel Purdy roar: "So the minute I hang up you sit down in that swivel chair again, eh, Fisby? Uh-huh, and you get mixed up with two geisha girls. Well, what of the education program? What of—"

Fisby paled and could see the court-martial charge sheet right before him: Failure to obey a direct order; conduct unbecoming an officer and gentleman; bringing discredit upon the military service by— Well, first he had to get rid of those girls, then those village officials of his were going to work. They were going to get this place fixed up or he'd know the reason why.

For a moment he considered, then picked up a printed form and scribbled quickly:

To: All Village Commanders, Okinawa.
Subject: Family Reunion.
Motomura—First Flower and Lotus Blossom—request permission to join their grandfather, your village. Request reunion your village immediately.
                    Signed: Jeff Fisby, Capt., C.A.C.

He couldn't just turn the girls out to roam the country-side even if they were—well, calloused. But slipping them into another village was a different matter. He held out the card. "Corporal Barton, take this around to every village you can think of. Nobody will bother checking through their entire village for Grandpa Motomura. They'll assume he's there and automatically give permission for the girls to move. But in case they should object, you just head for the next village."

Reluctantly, Corporal Barton rose from the cot.

"When you find someone who will take them," Fisby continued, "you come back and pick them up. By golly, I don't care if it takes the rest of the morning and all afternoon, you get rid of them. Understand?"

Barton nodded absently and scanned the card. "Oh, just one thing, Captain. You left a blank here, under occupation."

The flush started in Fisby's throat and crept up to his forehead.

"Well, let's see," Barton went on, "they're staying at the home for the aged. I'll just put them down as 'At home.' How's that, Captain?"

"All right. All right," Fisby said quickly, then hesitated. "Barton," he began slowly, confidentially, "this business about the geisha girls—you really don't believe I own them, do you?"

28

The Corporal considered, rubbed his stubble of beard. "Well, I just know what I hear, Captain. Now this guy says . . ." Fisby's look made Barton retreat quickly toward the door.

It was a long morning and a longer afternoon for Captain Fisby, peering out the windowless window of headquarters, hopefully waiting for Corporal Barton to come driving in. And at five o'clock it was a worried Captain who walked up to his quarters on the hill. He only picked at his supper, even though he liked C ration. And afterward he sat on his cot, puffing his evening cigar, but tonight it didn't taste good.

Usually by sunset he had his bedroll unfolded; by twilight he had his mosquito netting down; and by darkness he was snoring happily. Now he ignored these things, and when night closed in he took to pacing the floor.

Below him, the village looked the same. The half-tumbled shacks and sties nestled at the foot of the hill, their thatched roofs reflecting the pale light of the moon, rising slowly out of the Pacific. Here and there a flickering candle cut the darkness, just as every night. But tonight, instead of silence, a new sound came from the village.

Fisby recognized it as the strains of the *dahisen,* the Okinawan ukulele. And he recognized certain other sounds. There was no mistaking the laughter of his mayor and the police chief. And once, when he heard something that was a cross between the braying of a donkey and the bleating of a goat, Fisby knew that Hokkaido Yamaguchi was singing a song. There was an awful commotion, the shouting of the mayor and police chief carried way up the hill. Then the singing stopped, and another voice rose to take its place—a high-pitched, feminine voice that sent quivering notes floating out into the night.

Fisby stirred uneasily. Something was going on down there and all his village officials were mixed up in it. All right, he told himself, let them sing, let them laugh. But tomorrow they were going to work. They were going to get that village built up. Yet, looking at his watch, he was worried. It was way past nine o'clock, and he wondered how they were ever going to get out of bed in the morning.

When Corporal Barton finally returned, Fisby rubbed his hands and smiled. "Well, Barton, you got rid of the girls?" he asked hopefully.

Barton eyed him, then began opening a K ration. "I went around to every village I could find, Captain."

"Fine. But what did they have to say? How about Lieutentant Green at Takaesu?"

"Oh, Lieutenant Green says to tell First Flower hello."

"You mean he knows her?"

"Captain, every village commander on this island knows her."

"Is that a fact. Well, what did Lieutenant Smith at Maebaru say?"

"He says if he ever finds Grandpa Motomura, he'll make sure the reunion takes place in our village."

Fisby sat on his cot. "What about Major Enright?" he asked hopefully, never having considered the Major quite bright.

"He got pretty sore, Captain. He says those girls wrecked his village once, and it's not going to happen again."

Alarm crept into Fisby's face. "What does he mean—they wrecked his village?"

"Don't know, Captain, but everywhere I went they said the same thing. And they told me to warn you not to try sneaking them in, because they were going to put up road blocks."

Fisby was visibly shaken. He could stand no village wrecking now, not with Colonel Purdy riding herd on him. "Wouldn't anyone give permission for the girls to move to their village?" he asked desperately.

"Captain, those gals lived in every village on this island. This is the end of the line. You're stuck."

Fisby's shoulders slumped. He sat on his cot, chewing his dead cigar. And somehow—somehow the prospects for the morrow hardly seemed bright.

Four

IN THE MORNING when Fisby reached the village, no one was up; so he went from house to house, routing out his village officials. It was almost eight thirty before he got the harvesting crews started on their way to the fields. By nine he had the warehouse open and sleepy ration clerks busy with the day's distribution of food. By nine thirty he had the carpenters at work on the new school building.

Satisfied for the moment, he started for headquarters to make a cup of coffee before going on.

Entering headquarters, he was a little surprised to find the Women's League for Democratic Action crowded round his desk. Briefly he thought of the formidable Mrs. Purdy, its founder, for whenever he faced the League he always had the uneasy feeling that there she was—all chintz and flowery summer dresses—looking right over his shoulder, beaming her best clubwoman smile.

Fisby smiled, too. "Well, well, good morning, ladies," he said, rubbing his hands. Then he surveyed the barefooted members, clad in their knee-length brown kimonos of home-woven banana cloth, and his smile faded. Before him, the bronzed faces were sullen. Miss Susano, the recording secretary, was pouting. The executive council was pouting.

Fisby eyed the pug-nosed Miss Higa Jiga, the League president. Frankly, he could not tell if Miss Higa Jiga was pouting or not, for she always looked as if she had just finished sucking a lemon, yet her dark eyes were filled with danger signals. He shuffled uneasily on his feet. This Miss Higa Jiga was indeed someone to be reckoned with. True, she could hardly be called a pretty girl. In fact, with her pushed-in face, hunched shoulders, and bowed legs she bore a faint resemblance to a baboon. But she was sturdy. What other person in the village could carry half a pony load of kindling wood on her head, like she could?

Fisby glanced at his interpreter. "There's something wrong, Sakini?" he asked cautiously, regarding Miss Higa Jiga.

Sakini nodded solemnly. "Yep, boss, something's wrong. Do you know what Miss Higa Jiga say we have in the village?"

"What?"

"Discrimination."

"Discrimination?" Fisby was horrified.

"Yep, boss. Miss Higa Jiga say the Women's League wait in line this morning for rations. They take their turn, then geisha girls come along, and do you know what the ration clerks do?"

Fisby didn't have the slightest idea.

"They say, 'Oh, how do you do. Don't stand in line. Come in the warehouse and have a cup of tea.' And the Women's League have to stand there while everybody else sit around and sip tea."

"Is that a fact?"

"Uh-huh, boss. That's right. Then do you know what the ration clerks say?"

"What?"

"They say to geisha girls, 'You want some sweet potatoes? Oh, never mind the ration, just take all you want. What? You have to carry them yourself? Well, we can't let that happen.'"

Miss Higa Jiga nodded angrily. Miss Susano, the recording secretary, nodded. The League, en masse, nodded, their dark eyes flashing.

"Then, boss, the ration clerks pick up the sweet potatoes, lock up the place, and everybody go to have another cup of tea with the geishas. And there's the Women's League, standing in the hot sun again."

Through Captain Fisby's mind flashed the picture of Mrs. Purdy, her mouth drawn in a thin, straight line, her jaw thrust forward. Quickly, he banged the desk with his fist. "Discrimination, indeed." He pointed sternly toward the door. "Corporal Barton, you go down there and get that warehouse open. And you stay there. See that everyone gets regular rations. See that everyone takes their turn in line." He nodded reassuringly to the Women's League. "Sakini, tell them we'll have no more of that around here."

Sakini scratched his head. "But they don't talk about that, boss."

"They don't?"

"No, boss. They say they like tea, too, but the ration clerks never ask them to have a cup once in a while. Now they want some democratic action."

Fisby rubbed his head. Somehow he felt that there had been a misunderstanding of certain basic principles. "But, Sakini, the ration clerks can ask whom they please to have a cup of tea. I can't make them, well, I can't do anything if—"

"Yes, you can, boss."

"I can?"

"Yes. Miss Higa Jiga say if you get the Women's League pretty silk kimonos, like the geisha girls have, then maybe once in a while somebody will say, 'Oh, how do you do.'"

Fisby sank into the swivel chair. "Where will I get fifty silk kimonos?" he protested. Since D day, all he had seen on Okinawa were fields of sweet potatoes and soy beans, shacks, and goats.

"She don't know, boss, but they want 'em. And they want some face powder, too."

Fisby felt a serious supply problem developing, a problem that was best to shut off here and now. "Well, if they want face powder, tell them to go down to the warehouse. I'll tell the ration clerks to issue a little extra flour."

"No, boss. Miss Higa Jiga say they don't want that. They want real powder that smells pretty."

"Where will I get powder?" Fisby demanded.

But Sakini hardly heard. Miss Higa Jiga was whispering excitedly to him. "And, boss, she say they want some of those silk things that go around—"

Fisby blushed. "All right. All right," he said quickly.

"And they want some . . ."

"Now wait a minute," Fisby banged the desk. "You just tell them that I'm not going to get those things. In the first place, there's nothing like that on Okinawa. In the second place, it's not my job." He leaned back in the swivel chair.

When Sakini translated, there was an excited stirring among the Women's League. But Miss Higa Jiga seemed to have the situation well in hand.

"Boss," Sakini said slowly, "do you know what Miss Higa Jiga thinks maybe she's going to have to do if they don't get some democratic action?"

"What?" Fisby asked warily.

"She thinks maybe she's going to have to write a letter to this Uncle Sam you always talk about."

Fisby ran a finger along his collar. By golly, she'd do it, too. He mopped his forehead. If Colonel Purdy ever got hold of such a letter—well, this was a village affair. There was no sense in letting it get up to higher headquarters. Fisby forced a smile. "Sakini, just tell her I'll think it over. We shouldn't be too hasty about these things, you know."

The Women's League nodded happily; Miss Higa Jiga even showed all her gold teeth in a grin. "And here's the list, boss," Sakini said.

"What list?"

"The rest of the things they want. Miss Higa Jiga copy it in English so you won't forget."

Cautiously, Fisby examined it:

1. The red stuff you put on your lips.
2. The stuff that smells pretty you put behind your ears.
3. The silk things that match the silk things that go around . . .

It went on for pages, and gingerly Fisby flipped the list on the desk.

"Now, boss," Sakini said, "the Women's League ask to be excused."

Frankly, Fisby was more than glad to see the barefooted members go trooping out. But at the door, Miss Higa Jiga stopped, whispered to Sakini. "Boss," Sakini smiled brightly, "she say she sure like this democratic action. She only wish she know about it before. And she say not to worry. If they think of any more things they want, they let you know."

Fisby's shoulders sagged, and he leaned back in his swivel chair. These geisha girls were starting a trend he didn't like, not one bit. But, he told himself, Plan B never stated that a village commander had to get underwear for a bunch of women. He would just pigeonhole this list, just forget about it.

His thoughts were interrupted by Hokkaido Yamaguchi, his roly-poly agriculture foreman, and Asato Kiei, his construction chief, entering headquarters. Curiously, Fisby regarded the bare-footed, knock-kneed Hokkaido, for now the tears were streaming down Hokkaido's cherub face.

"Sakini, what's the matter with him?" Fisby demanded.

"Him? Oh, boss, he say he can't do his job."

The novelty of someone in the village crying because he couldn't do his job made Fisby sit up. "Why not?"

"Well, boss, Hokkaido claim as agriculture foreman he is in charge of all horse carts."

"That's right."

"Well, just a little while ago when they load sweet potatoes out in the field to bring to the village, the police chief come along. 'Hokkaido,' he say, 'unload all the carts, we need 'em. Lotus Blossom leave all her things over at Awasi, and we have to send for them.' "

"The police chief did that?" Fisby could hardly believe. He had visions of 5,000 hungry people storming headquarters, demanding sweet potatoes. "So the police chief won't let Hokkaido use the carts for hauling food, eh? Well, we'll just take care of that."

Sakini scratched his head. "Hokkaido don't say nothing about hauling food, boss."

"Well, what's all this about not being able to do his job?"

"Oh, he say since the horse carts belong to the agriculture department, he must supervise moving Lotus Blossom's things, not the police chief."

Fisby brought his fist down on the desk. "When is he going to haul those potatoes into the village?"

"I don't know, boss."

"Well, ask him."

After a lengthy conference, accompanied by much head scratching, Sakini smiled brightly. "Boss, he say they haul potatoes tomorrow, maybe."

"Oh, he does. And I suppose the whole village is to go hungry just because the police chief is beating his time?"

Sakini considered carefully. " 'Beating his time'—means what, boss?"

"Never mind," Fisby indicated Asato, his construction chief. "I suppose he can't do his job either?"

"That's right, boss." Sakini nodded. "How did you know?"

"Go on," Fisby said wearily, "why can't he do his job?"

"Well, this morning the mayor say to him, 'Asato, you look tired. Take a vacation for three or four years. I'll supervise the carpenters.' "

"Yes?"

"Asato say he promise First Flower that the carpenters do a good job remodeling the old folk's home where she stay. Now every time he goes down there to supervise, the mayor chase him home. So he can't do his job either."

"Remodeling the old folk's home!" Fisby exploded. "The carpenters are supposed to be building a school."

Sakini smiled brightly. "Oh, but we change priorities, boss."

Fisby's jaw dropped. "And you're not even working on the school," he could hear Colonel Purdy roar. For a moment Fisby regarded the group severely. It was evident that someone around here needed straightening out. "Sakini," he said, "call the village officials together. Get every last one of them. We're going to have a meeting."

Five

As the twelve officials, hats in hand, came trooping into headquarters, Fisby noted that the group was definitely divided into two major factions. One, he assumed, was the First Flower faction; the other, the Lotus Blossom faction. And while these two major divisions seemed to be on speaking terms with each other, still it was evident that within each division things weren't going so well.

Hokkaido scowled at the police chief, a fellow competitor for the favor of Lotus Blossom. The sanitation foreman scowled at both, and threw a couple of dirty looks at the ration chief. On the other hand the mayor and construction chief, leading candidates in the First Flower faction, were eyeing each other coldly.

"Gentlemen," Fisby said. "Be seated." Then he sank into his swivel chair and regarded them sternly. "In meetings with your officials," Colonel Purdy always warned, "ask them direct questions. Put them on the spot. It's more forceful." And Fisby was certainly in a mood to be forceful.

"Sakini," he said, not turning his head. "I want you to repeat my exact words. Repeat my same tone of voice. Understand?"

"Understand, boss."

"Okay." Fisby drew himself up, leveled a stern finger at the group. "Gentlemen," he said, "do you want to be ignorant?"

He heard the words come forth in Japanese, which Sakini always used for meetings, caught the steel-like quality in Sakini's voice. And Fisby looked at the group, waited for the terrible impact to sink in.

There was a moment's hesitation, then Hokkaido said: *"Hie."*

Now Fisby did not know many words of Japanese, but he did know that *Iie* meant no. *Hie* meant yes. He dropped his finger. Perhaps there was some misunderstanding here. "Sakini, I'll repeat the question." He brought his finger

36

up again, the sternness returned to his face. "Gentlemen, do you want to be ignorant?"

Hokkaido nodded brightly. *"Hie!"*

Fisby's mouth flew open. "Sakini, he—he wants to be ignorant?"

Sakini shook his head. "He don't say that, boss."

"He said yes."

"That's right. Only he mean no."

"Then why did he say yes?"

"He say—yes, he don't want to be ignorant. In English that means—no, he don't want to be ignorant. You see, boss, yes and no in English, and Japanese, and our dialect don't mean the same thing at all." Then Sakini had to explain to the village officials, and there were understanding nods.

"Okay," Fisby said. "Well, let's get on. Now ask them this: Gentlemen, do you want the children of the village to be ignorant?"

When Sakini translated, there was a mingled chorus of *Hie's* and *Iie's*. Fisby felt the perspiration break out on his forehead. Apparently some were using the English version of no, and some were using the Japanese version. Yet a new thought struck him: maybe they did want the children to be ignorant.

"Boss," Sakini said, "do you want to ask any more questions?"

"Questions?" Fisby was a little afraid to take chances. First thing you know they might twist this thing around and he, not they, would be on the defensive. "I think we'll dispense with questions for the time being. That's all."

Bowing, the group stood up and began walking toward the door. "Sakini," Fisby demanded, "where are they going?"

"You say that's all, boss."

"I said that's all the questions. You tell them to come back here and sit down. We haven't started the meeting yet."

"We haven't?"

"No!"

Slowly, the group came back; and as they sank onto the benches, Fisby noted their uneasiness. So they were trying to pull a fast one on him. So they thought they were going to get off as easy as that. All right, he'd show them. He'd make them squirm.

Without taking his eyes from Hokkaido and the police

37

chief, Fisby shamefully pointed out how the sweet potato crop was left in the fields, how the people were left hungry while the horse carts went chasing over to Awasi to get Lotus Blossom's things. Then, in great detail, he carefully outlined the duties and responsibilities of each official, just as listed in Plan B. "So you see, gentlemen," he said, "it is you who must see that the people are fed. It is you, the leaders, who must look after the welfare of the population."

Hokkaido glanced at the police chief. The mayor glanced at the village secretary. The group twisted uneasily, and Fisby permitted himself an inward smile.

"And the carpenters were taken off the new school." He feigned great shock. For a long while he went on—extolling the merits of education. Here and there he saw an official whisper excitedly. Then he painted a horrible picture of a village without a school, of a people reduced to ignorance because their leaders were "more interested in chasing girls, and geisha girls at that, than in education." By the time he had finished, the group around him was hardly able to sit still.

That's getting a point across, he told himself, as he regarded the squirming mayor and nervous Hokkaido. Pleased, he leaned back in his swivel chair. "And now, Sakini, do they want to ask me any questions?"

Sakini nodded. "Yep, boss. What time is it?"

"Time? 1145. Why?"

"Well, boss, we suppose to have dinner with First Flower and Lotus Blossom. We sure don't want to be late."

Fisby slumped. For a long time after the meeting broke up, he sat there. "No sense of responsibility," he told himself. "No sense of responsibility whatsoever."

Even by midafternoon he was not fully recovered. He just slumped listlessly in his chair; and it was not until the strains of the *dahisen* came drifting down to head-quarters that he perked up. Then he eyed Sakini uncertainly.

But Sakini nodded reassuringly. "The Women's League for Democratic Action has a meeting, boss."

"With music?"

"Sure, got to have music."

"Is that a fact?"

"Uh-huh." Sakini leaned across the desk and whispered confidentially. "You see, boss, this noon when we have dinner with the geisha girls, everybody talk about what

38

you say to us. We tell the girls how you like education. And do you know what First Flower say?"

"What?"

"She say, 'The boss is right. We sure need some education around this place.' And everybody agree, so we get the education program started right away."

Fisby smiled. Maybe he had misjudged his village officials. Maybe they just needed a little time to discuss it. "Oh I see. And now the Women's League is having a meeting. They're going to do the teaching, eh, and they're making plans?"

Sakini shook his head. "No, boss. They don't teach. They get educated."

"Educated?"

"Sure. I tell First Flower how nobody ever ask 'em to have a cup of tea once in a while or anything. Then do you know what she say?"

Fisby was afraid to ask.

"She say, 'Sakini, I always like to help the boss. Tell you what I do. I'll start the new education program with the Women's League. I'll teach them to sing and dance.' And Lotus Blossom always likes to help the boss, too, so she teach them to play the *dahisen*. But I don't know." Sakini scratched his head. "First Flower claim geisha girls start training when they're seven years old, and she thinks the Women's League get started about twenty-five years too late. She don't know if she can get 'em papers from the geisha guild or not, but she try like the dickens."

Fisby gripped the desk. "You mean the Women's League wants to become—uh—geishas?"

"Well, boss, they notice that all the men follow First Flower and Lotus Blossom around. Miss Higa Jiga thinks it would be pretty nice if once in a while they got some democratic action, too."

The picture of Mrs. Purdy, with mouth agape, flashed through Fisby's mind. He was positive that this was not what she had in mind when founding the League.

"Now, boss," Sakini said, smiling, "if you just get the League kimonos, and powder, and stuff, it's going to be pretty nice."

"Pretty nice?"

"Sure. You get 'em those things and set 'em up in business, well, you're the boss. Have fifty, maybe sixty geisha girls. All you have to do is just sit back and collect presents, and—"

The flush started in Fisby's throat, spread to his cheeks, and up to his head. "Sakini," he said firmly. "Let's get this straight, once and for all. I'm not setting anyone up in business."

Sakini scratched his head. "Don't understand, boss."

Fisby heard the excited whispering over by the door and turned; then he peered through the Venetian blind. Outside, a huge crowd of women was milling around. "Sakini, who are all those people?" he asked.

"Them?" Sakini smiled brightly. "Oh, the eligible ladies of the village hear about the new education program. Now they all want to join the Women's League."

For the briefest moment Fisby considered dissolving the League, but Colonel Purdy's voice came to him: "Dissolve the League for Democratic Action! What do you want to do, Fisby. Get us investigated by Congress?" Fisby winced. He could think of nothing he wanted less than an investigation, of any kind.

One of the women whispered to Sakini. "Boss," Sakini explained, "she want to know when you start the new classes?"

"Classes!" Fisby could only run a finger·along his collar, could only mop his brow helplessly.

And that night as he sat in his quarters on the hill, the singing drifted up to him. He resigned himself to the high-pitched, trained voices which he recognized as belonging to First Flower and Lotus Blossom. But it was the singing of those little practice groups, which seemed to be meeting all over the place, that put the wrinkles in his forehead. A man had a certain moral responsibility. A man had to live with his conscience. He lit a cigar, even inhaled.

Sleep was slow in coming this night. For hours he twisted and turned on his cot. But when sleep did come, it was troubled sleep, punctured by the strains of the Okinawan ukulele. From his dreams came the dancing, singing Women's League, led by Miss Higa Jiga. And from his dreams came the whisperings, "Mr. Captain Fisby? He's the biggest operator on Okinawa."

Six

AGAIN NO ONE was up in the morning. No one was up to go into the fields and dig sweet potatoes; no one was up to distribute them to the people of the village. And Captain Fisby, determination written on his face, strode through the narrow streets, searching for the house of Hokkaido Yamaguchi, his agriculture foreman. At length he found it and banged on the unpainted shutters, forming the walls as well as the doors.

"Hokkaido," he called. There was no answer. "Hokkaido!"

"*Hie*—yes," came a sleepy voice.

"This is the boss. Get up."

"*Dare* . . . who?"

"The boss. Now get up!"

"Hokay. Hokay."

Fisby heard the rustling. A wooden shutter was pushed back, and the sleepy Hokkaido stood there in a brown kimono. Fisby spoke firmly. "We got to have some sweet potatoes around this place. Now you get your digging crews out."

"English I can no," Hokkaido said, and his cherub face lit up in a smile.

Fisby knew that Hokkaido fully understood his meaning, yet was more interested in getting back to bed than in going into the fields. Quickly, he brought out his GI issue Japanese-English phrase book, paged through it. "*Imo* . . . potatoes. *Ima* . . . now. *Wakarimaska* . . . understand?"

Hokkaido's smile faded. "Ah, *imo*. Hokay. Hokay, boss." For a moment Hokkaido regarded him, then, resigned to the inevitable, slipped on his clothes, and picked up a potato hoe. When Hokkaido banged on a number of doors and began rounding up his digging crews, Fisby was temporarily satisfied. He ought to get the ration chief up next and get the village rolling, but decided to go to headquarters first and make a cup of coffee.

There was quite a delegation waiting for him when he entered the door. In fact, it looked as if the entire old folk's home had turned out. Fisby regarded the group, saw their sullen faces, and turned to the sleepy Sakini. *"Now* what's the matter?" he demanded.

Sakini rubbed his eyes and pointed to an ancient grandfather, who apparently was their spokesman. "Boss, Oshiro say he's mad at the damn fool mayor and ration chief; damn fool Hokkaido and Asato; damn fool construction and sanitation chiefs." Sakini scratched his head. "Oh, yes, and damn fool me."

Oshiro drew his worn blue kimono about him and slammed his cane on the floor. "I tell the boss," he warned Sakini, his old eyes flashing. "I speak the English."

"Okay. Okay, Oshiro," Fisby said, easing into his swivel chair. "Go ahead."

Oshiro drew himself up. "Boss, last night . . . night before last, all the officials come down to old folk's home where you tell the geisha girls to stay. 'Oho,' the damn fool mayor say, 'let's cook *sukiyaki*. Have chicken *sukiyaki* party.' "

Sakini bent over and whispered confidentially. "He just mad because we don't ask him to eat any."

Oshiro slammed his cane on the floor again. "I tell the boss." He glared at Sakini and went on. "Everybody laugh, boss. Ha! Ha! Everybody sing." Oshiro sang a little. "Sixty years old, seventy years old, geisha party all right. Eighty years old, want to sleep." He fixed Sakini with a critical stare. "Don't like damn fool *sukiyaki* anyway."

"I see," Fisby said with an understanding nod. "So they won't let you sleep, eh, Oshiro? We'll just take care of that. Sakini, you tell the mayor and other village officials that from now on there will be no more geisha parties at the old folk's home."

Sakini's eyes widened in alarm. "No more geisha parties, boss?"

"That's right. I won't have anyone keeping those people awake."

"Not even me, boss?"

"Not even you. Those people need their rest. I don't want any more carrying on down there. Understand?"

"Understand, boss. Understand." But as Sakini went off to tell the officials, he scratched his head and his dark eyes were puzzled.

"Don't worry, Oshiro," Fisby said reassuringly. "Now you'll be able to get your rest."

Oshiro bowed. "We thank you, boss."

42

"That's perfectly all right."

Then the group in headquarters began to confer and Fisby caught the excitement in their voices. "Boss," Oshiro began hesitantly, "do you think maybe we could have some extra sweet potatoes?"

"Extra sweet potatoes." Fisby sat up quickly. "Isn't that ration chief sending you people down there enough to eat?"

Oshiro moved uneasily. "Sure, boss. But sometime First Flower and Lotus Blossom get pretty hungry at night. Everybody think it would be nice if once in a while we made some sweet potato taffy, and——"

"I thought you said when you're eighty years old, you just wanted to sleep."

"I was talking about Kanemoto, not me, boss. He didn't come down to the meeting with us. I'm only seventy-nine. Won't be eighty until next year, maybe."

What's the use, Fisby told himself. What's the use. He looked out through the window. A delegation of some sort was lining up outside. Quickly, he picked up his helmet-liner. By golly, maybe he ought to inspect the village. He eyed the delegation again. He hadn't been through the village in a couple of days. Yes, sir, he ought to do a little inspecting.

Slipping out the side door of headquarters, he took a back path leading into a narrow, twisting side street. The village was beginning to awaken now. The goats were bleating for their breakfast of sweet potato slips, the pigs added their squeal, the children shrieked, and the symphony of Tobiki rose on all sides of him.

Rounding a corner by the old folk's home, he found every horse cart belonging to the agriculture department parked along the path. Curious, he edged along the coral wall, surrounding the ramshackle building where the aged lived, and peeked into the opening of the courtyard.

On the veranda, running in front of the building, was a long line of shoes and sparkling red helmet-liners marked "Native Police." Fisby guessed maybe the entire male population of the village had dropped in for breakfast with First Flower and Lotus Blossom. He inched forward and saw the group gathered over their teacups, saw their solemn faces. For a moment he was tempted to break in and put the whole bunch to work. Then he realized that Sakini was announcing the "no more geisha party" edict.

Maybe Oshiro and the aged only wanted to get the
43

younger competition out of the way; maybe they weren't interested in sleep after all, still Fisby decided to let the edict stand. By golly, it was about time he put an end to the goings-on around the place. His face grew stern. It was about time there was a show of authority. They had to learn just who the boss was.

He regarded the solemn, silent group. "We'll just let them think it over," he told himself. Cutting through a boggy grove of textile bananas, he came across a group of women washing their feet in a blocked-off drainage ditch. He reached for his phrase book. "Ka . . . mosquitoes," he said, pointing to the stagnant water. "Netsu . . . fever."

The little group regarded him curiously, as if trying to get the connection between mosquitoes and fever.

Fisby indicated the earthen dam and gestured. "Out!"

A certain light crept into their faces. Smiling brightly, they kicked away the dam. But as Fisby passed the street, they shrugged uncomprehendingly and built it up again.

Rounding a corner, Fisby saw Miss Higa Jiga, president of the Women's League, in the distance. He ducked back just in time to avoid her, cut through a yard, and promptly ran into Miss Susano, the recording secretary. "Kimono, you get?" she asked hopefully.

Fisby grew stern. He wasn't going to get any kimonos and he wasn't going to set anyone up in business. He was about to tell her, too, only he didn't have Sakini with him. Besides, he caught a glimpse of Miss Higa Jiga coming his way. "Wakarimasen . . . I don't understand." He shrugged helplessly. "Sakini, no." Tipping his helmet-liner, he beat a hasty retreat, for the executive council of the Women's League was coming up from the other direction and they nearly had him pinned in.

Come to think of it, he had had no breakfast yet. He started for headquarters by a roundabout way to throw the League off. A man couldn't be expected to do any work on an empty stomach; he ought to have some breakfast. Seeing there was no one around headquarters but Sakini, he slipped in the side door and eased into his swivel chair. Then noticing the things piled on his desk, he regarded them curiously. "What's all this, Sakini?" he asked.

"That? Oh, Hokkaido think maybe you get tired of eating that stuff that comes in the cans all the time."

"C ration?"

"Uh-huh. So he brings you some nice fresh eggs for breakfast."

"I see."

"And look." Sakini held up a pair of chopsticks. "I think, maybe the boss got to have something to eat the eggs with and I bring you these. Made 'em myself out of ebony wood."

"Say, these are all right." Fisby examined the black, polished wood, and started to smile. So they were trying to get in good with him again by bringing gifts. They couldn't put anything over on him. He knew what was going on.

"Boss," Sakini said, "Asato make you the *geta*."

"What?"

"*Geta*." Sakini pointed to a pair of native wooden sandals.

"Oh." Fisby picked them up, regarded the curious bridgelike clogs. Then, unbuckling his combat boots, he slipped on the sandals, and was teetering experimentally across the floor when Miss Higa Jiga entered headquarters.

Quickly, Fisby sat down at his desk and assumed a professional air. "Yes, Sakini," he began hesitantly, "what docs she want?"

"Oh, she want to add to the list, boss. The Women's League decide if they are going to be geisha girls, they got to have a lot of things besides kimonos. First, they want some perfumed fans."

"Perfumed fans! Where would I get those?"

"She don't know, but they want some."

"Now just a minute." Fisby stood up. "You tell her I'm not going to get . . ." He caught a glimpse of Miss Higa Jiga's eyes and hesitated. After all, you had to be a little tactful with a girl who could carry half a pony load of kindling wood on her head. He sat down again. "Just tell her I'll think it over."

"Okay, boss. And she say they want some stuff that you burn to make the place smell pretty."

"Incense? But, Sakini—"

Miss Higa Jiga was pouting. "Boss, she say you better write it down or you forget."

Reluctantly, Fisby brought out the previous list of Miss Higa Jiga's requests from a drawer and began to scribble: Perfumed fans, incense, rouge. In fact, the Women's League wanted quite a few additional things. And after Miss Higa Jiga left, Fisby regarded the paper with alarm.

Where would a man ever be able to pick up these things on Okinawa. It would be impossible. Why, the whole economy of the island was shot now. This was like being stranded somewhere in the woods, a couple of thousand miles away from the nearest department store. He flipped the list back into the drawer, determined to forget it.

As the day wore on, when the Women's League wasn't in headquarters with some new request, certain other visitors were bringing in gifts. Fisby regarded the fast-growing pile on his desk. There were bamboo bird cages and bamboo flower baskets. There were reed sandals and things he had never seen before, and he had absolutely no conception of their use. Secretly, he was pleased. Apparently they saw the error of their ways and were getting back in line.

It was late in the afternoon when Sakini returned. "Here's the list for tonight, boss."

"What list?" Fisby asked in his innocence.

"The invitations for First Flower and Lotus Blossom. You say we can't have any more geisha parties at the old folk's home, so everybody want the geisha girls to come over to their house."

Fisby shuffled uneasily. "But I don't have anything to do with that."

"Yes, you do, boss."

"I do?"

"Sure. Mr. Motomura give First Flower and Lotus Blossom to you, so as their boss you have to decide who they go to visit tonight."

Fisby drew back in alarm. "Now wait a minute, Sakini." He didn't want any part of this. "In the first place, I don't own those girls—"

"Oh, but you do, boss. Don't you remember Mr. Motomura say he want to make to you a present."

The look on Sakini's face fully convinced Fisby that it was useless to argue. He felt the list being shoved into his hand and scanned it nervously.

Sakini	1 pair of chopsticks.
Hokkaido	3 eggs.
Asato	1 pair of *geta*.
Yamashiro	1 Panama hat.
Nakamura	2 cricket cages, without crickets.

It went on for pages. "And all you have to do, boss,"

Sakini explained, "is decide who give you the nicest presents and let the geishas go see 'em."

Fisby shuddered. A man couldn't go plunging these girls into iniquity even though they were . . . well . . . already calloused. He glanced at the tainted gifts and shrank back from them in horror.

"Boss," Sakini said slowly. "I think maybe it might be nice if they come over to my house. My grandpa don't feel so good lately. Maybe some singing and some dancing will cheer him up."

"But, Sakini, I couldn't send these girls to anyone's home like that."

Sakini scratched his head. "You can't, boss. Why not?"

"Because—" Fisby groped for a reason that Sakini might be able to understand. "Because, well look. Suppose the girls go to see the police chief, then all day tomorrow Hokkaido will sulk. He won't dig any sweet potatoes. And if they visit the construction chief, then the mayor will get sore. Before you know it, everyone will be mad at everyone else."

Sakini considered carefully. "I never think of that, boss."

Fisby drew himself up with the firm conviction of a man who knew that he was morally right. "Sakini, there will be no visits tonight. And you give those presents back. I don't want them."

That his order was carried out, Fisby had no doubts. For as he lay on his cot in the dark, only silence came from the village below. He settled himself for a good night's sleep, yet sleep would not come. Somehow he kept listening for the strains of the *dahisen* and the high-pitched, quivering songs to float out into the darkness.

Propping himself on an elbow, he looked down on the village. Without the music, without the singing, it seemed lonely down there. One by one the flickering candles in the shacks below were extinguished, and the night closed in. Only in one house did a candle burn long and steadily. Watching it, Fisby grew uneasy.

That was in the home of his mayor. He strained, listening for laughter, dead certain that the mayor was violating his order. But no sound came. Nine o'clock faded into ten, and ten into eleven. Still the candle burned. There was something going on down there. They were cooking up something. Fisby was certain of that. And when he finally dozed off, the candle still burned.

Seven

IT WAS BARELY DAYBREAK when Fisby was awakened by
the shouting. Sleepily he sat up, looked out the open door,
then shoved aside his mosquito netting and hopped from
bed. All around him, the hillsides were alive with long lines
of workers streaming down into the village. Some carried
huge bundles of thatch. Some, rocks and bushes. And some
—Fisby's eyes popped—some were manhandling quarter-
grown pine trees down the narrow hillside paths.

Down in the village itself, Fisby could see people and
horse carts everywhere. And all seemed to move toward
a spot out in the middle of the sweet potato fields. Dressing quickly, he ran down into the village, bumped into a
procession of carts loaded with lumber, and followed it
along, out past the last houses, until he came to an open
field. Then, curiously, he looked around.

Every kid in the village seemed to be there, digging some
kind of hole in the dirt. Over to one side, a great pile of
thatch, and rocks, and bushes was growing, brought down
by the men from the hills. And there in the middle of all
the shouting and grinning was First Flower, a fan in one
hand, calmly directing the operation.

Seeing him, she waved and called, "Hello, boss." A
smile played on her pretty face.

Flushing, he waved back—but not very enthusiastically
—then quickly looked up Sakini. "What are you doing
there?" Fisby asked, pointing to the hole the kids were
scraping in the ground.

"There?" Sakini smiled. "Well, boss, First Flower say
we got to have a lotus pond."

"What for?" Fisby demanded.

"For the *cha ya*. First Flower say any *cha ya* she builds
has to have one."

Fisby edged forward, his eyes narrowed suspiciously.
"What's a *cha ya?*" he asked.

"That's a place, boss, where everybody sit around and
sip tea, and geisha girls sing and dance. And everybody
laugh. Ha. Ha."

It was exactly as Fisby suspected, only he felt there was more to the story than singing and dancing. By golly, he wasn't going to set up an immoral establishment like that in his village. "So you're building a *cha ya,* eh?" He grew stern.

"Yep, boss." Sakini nodded. "Yesterday you say we can't have any more geisha parties at the old folk's home. And last night you say if geishas go to somebody's house to visit, everybody get sore."

Fisby did remember saying that.

"So when I tell First Flower about everybody getting sore at everybody else, do you know what she say?"

"What?"

"She say, 'Sakini, the boss is right. I never think of that before. What we need around here is a place where everybody can go, where everybody can sit around and sip tea.' "

Fisby straightened. It was hard enough to get any work out of the village as it was, but with such an establishment, well . . .

Beside him, Sakini looked out over the workers. A smile crossed his lips, and he shook his head in wonder. "You know, boss, we never have a *cha ya* in the village before."

Fisby winced, for he could hear Colonel Purdy roar, "Do you think I'm going to have the Military Government remembered on this island for building a *cha ya* in each village, Fisby? Think! What will Congress say!"

Fisby was afraid to think. Then his eyes narrowed and he turned. "Sakini, you listen to me. By golly, I'm not going to have these   these bad girls ruining the morals of the people."

"Bad girls?" Sakini questioned.

"That's right. These geisha."

Sakini shook his head. "But they're not bad girls, boss. They're nice."

"Maybe you think so, but I don't."

"You don't?"

"I certainly do not."

Sakini seemed puzzled. For a moment he considered, then his eyes widened. "Boss, do you think, maybe, that geisha girls are——"

Blushing, Fisby admitted that he thought they were——

"Oh, no, boss," Sakini said, shaking his head solemnly. "You make a mistake. You think of some other kind of girls. Geishas not that way at all. They're ladies."

"Ladies?" Fisby was suspicious.

"Yes, boss. They just sing and dance. Now the other kind of girls—"

"All right. All right," Fisby said quickly. "Just tell me about the geisha."

"Well, they go to all the big *cha yas*." Sakini scratched his head. "See, boss, *cha* means tea, and *ya*—well, that means shop or house. Anyway, they go to the teahouses, I guess you call 'em that. Maybe a bunch of guys are sitting around, so the geisha sing songs, and the guys give 'em money for it."

"You mean they're sort of like night club entertainers?"

"Night club entertainers—means what, boss?"

"Well, they're people who—well, sing songs and tell jokes. Go on, tell me more about the geisha."

"Okay, boss. The geisha sing all kinds of songs. Sometimes the old songs from long, long time ago. Everybody say if the geisha don't sing 'em the people forget, and the people wouldn't know about what happened when our grandpas, and our grandpas' grandpas were just little boys."

"Is that a fact? Folk songs, eh?"

"Yep, boss. And sometimes the geisha write new songs, too. They might even write a song about Military Government and four, five hundred years from now some other geisha will sing all about it to the people, then the people will know what happened."

"I didn't know that, Sakini."

"That's right, boss. They do the same with dances. And do you know what else they do?"

"What?" Fisby asked curiously.

Sakini considered a moment. "Well, boss, suppose some afternoon a guy don't feel so good. Suppose he's all mixed up down inside. Then he go to a *cha ya* to see a geisha girl. And do you know what she say?"

Fisby had no idea.

"She say, 'Now you just sit there, and we'll have a cup of tea. Go on now.' Then she smile at him, and fold her hands in her lap, and say, 'Now tell me all about it.' "

"Does he tell her?"

"Sure, boss. He tell her everything. Every once in a while she shake her head and say, 'Now, isn't that too bad.' And pretty soon he start to feel good again, and she talk to him real soft, and after a while he can't remember what his troubles are."

Fisby nodded. He rather liked this arrangement even

though, he imagined, the geisha listened only for a price. He could see a real need for someone who would extend a little sympathy now and then, someone who would share problems—even though the extender was a professional sympathizer. Still they must know their business if fellows went to them, as Sakini said. "Tell me, Sakini," Fisby asked, "did you use to go to the teahouses very often?"

Sakini looked down at his shoes. "Maybe once or twice a year, boss, when the sweet potatoes get ripe and me and my grandpa take 'em into market at Naha, the capital."

"You always took your potatoes into Naha?"

"Oh, yes, boss. Grandpa would rent a horse cart, and we would start before it was daylight even."

"Everyone from the village would do that?"

"Sure, boss. If you turn, sometimes, and look back along the road, all you can see is horse carts and people carrying potatoes in big baskets on their heads. Then where the roads come together, you would meet other people from the other villages. And pretty soon, by gosh, there would be people everywhere going into Naha."

Fisby was curious now. "What did you do when you reached Naha?"

"First, boss, we use to go to the market. They have a big square with trees all around it. Then everybody would line up their carts, and we would wait for the guys to come along who buy sweet potatoes."

"And then?"

"Then? After we sell our potatoes, grandpa would pay the guy we rent the cart from. Maybe if grandpa make a little money, he'd say, 'Here, Sakini, you been a pretty good boy. Go buy yourself something.' So I'd go get Hokkaido."

"Oh," Fisby said, "was Hokkaido there, too?"

Sakini nodded. "And he'd be all dressed up, boss. He always wear his Panama hat, and his best shirt. And he would even make a rope of new straw to wrap around his waist to hold his pants up."

"Is that right?" Fisby looked around. "Just a minute, Sakini. Let's go over and sit on that four by four." They walked a few paces to where a horse cart had just finished unloading lumber. "Now," Fisby said, "after you got Hokkaido, what happened?"

"Well, then we start for the *Tsuji* quarter."

"*Tsuji* quarter?"

"That's where all the *cha yas* were, boss. There was a

whole big block, nothing but teahouses. Sometimes, maybe, we'd buy a mandarin orange at one of the food stalls to eat along the way." Sakini stopped suddenly and regarded Fisby. "Boss, do you know what to do with an orange peel down in Naha when you're finished with it?"

"What?"

"You just step over to the gutter and drop it in. The water comes right along and carries it away." Sakini's eyes were wide, and he nodded solemnly.

"That was quite an arrangement," Fisby said. "Running water in the gutters and everything, eh?"

"And you should see the buildings in Naha. Some of 'em have five floors, one right on top the other. I use to stand on the corner and look and look."

"Would Hokkaido stand on the corner, too?"

"Sure, boss, but he never look at the buildings. He just stand there and watch the girls go by."

Fisby rather suspected that Hokkaido wouldn't be much interested in buildings. "Well, what happened when you reached the teahouse, Sakini?"

Sakini's face lit up in remembrance. "Everybody would be there, boss. Guys from Kunigami country, even, way up north. You see people you don't see, maybe in a whole year. We have a cup of tea and a bowl of noodles. Everybody visit, talk about the crops, talk about the harvest. Tell jokes, laugh. Have a good time."

"And would the geisha girls sing for you?"

Sakini shook his head. "We never have enough money for that, boss."

Fisby was silent for a moment. "I see. So you didn't know First Flower and Lotus Blossom before they moved here."

"I don't know 'em, but I see Lotus Blossom once when she ride by in a ricksha," Sakini declared proudly. "Never see First Flower though. They have over three hundred geishas in Naha, and she's the most famous of all, boss. If the governor have a big banquet or something at his house, she go to dance and sing. Or she go to the big *cha yas*, but never to the small ones like us."

"So she was quite famous, eh?"

"Oh, yes, boss. Everybody, everywhere on Okinawa hear about her. She have lots of money, too. She even have her own ricksha and a boy to pull it. And do you know what?"

"What?"

"They say she eat rice three times a day, for breakfast even." The awe was apparent in Sakini's voice. "And some guy tell me she have people to cook it for her, and people to make her tea and sweep up the place. And I hear all her kimonos come from the *Ginza*."

"From where?"

"The *Ginza*. That's a big street in Tokyo where they sell only the best things. The mayor say the other night he hear some of her kimonos cost two thousand yen. And she drinks only the good tea from China and the *ginseng* tea from Korea."

Fisby considered. So she bought all her things on the Japanese Fifth Avenue and drank only imported stuff, yet he was puzzled. "But, Sakini, if she had all that money, how come Mr. Motomura owned her and Lotus Blossom?"

Sakini scratched his head. "Don't know how to explain, boss. I guess her papa don't have much money, and he have to sell her."

"Sell her?" Fisby was horrified.

"Yes, boss. Maybe Mr. Motomura or some guy who owns geishas comes around to her village when she was just a little girl six or seven years old. Well, he sees that she's real pretty, and he says to her papa. 'Say, tell you what I do. I buy her. She make a good geisha.' So he buy her and send her to school."

"School?"

"That's right, boss. She got to learn how to sing, and dance, and play the *dahisen*. She got to know manners, and how to arrange flowers, and drink tea, and how to talk to guys to make them feel good inside. Then when she know all that, the geisha owner buy her nice kimonos and stuff. And he set her up in business."

Fisby nodded in understanding. "So then the girls have to pay him back for the money he spent, plus interest, of course?"

"Yes, boss. Only sometimes they never get him paid back, because he always keeps remembering something else they owe him for."

Fisby's eyes narrowed, and he looked out at the Pacific, just beyond. "Well, tell me, what else did you use to do down in Naha?"

"We'd stay in the *cha ya*," Sakini said, "until our money was gone. Then we'd walk around, look in the stores, look in the food stalls, maybe go out to see the tombs that the rich guys build. And when we get tired, we'd go to the Golden Dragon."

"The Golden Dragon?" Fisby questioned.

"Uh-huh, boss. That was the biggest and best *cha ya* in all the *Tsuji* quarter." Sakini's eyes had a faraway look. "We use to sit under a tree across the street, boss, and watch the big guys in the government come up in rickshas. The geisha girls would sing, then; we could hear 'em all the way across the street. And we could smell the rice and pork cooking." He smiled and shook his head.

"So the big guys in the government used to spend a lot of time in the teahouses, eh, Sakini?"

"They have to, boss. Sometimes big problems come up. They don't know what to do. Then they have to go there and have a cup of tea and talk it over, maybe ask the geisha girls to help 'em solve it."

Fisby smiled, for he remembered reading how Jefferson, and Monroe, and the other members of the House of Burgesses after a stormy session with the royal Governor of Virginia would retire to the Apollo Room of the Raleigh Tavern in Williamsburg, and there—over their cups— make plans for the yet unborn American nation. Then he remembered something else, and his face clouded. "And you liked sitting across the street from the Golden Dragon like that, Sakini?"

"Oh, yes, boss." Sakini smiled, as if remembering. "It was nice. But my grandpa always use to come around, and say, 'Come on, Sakini. We go home now.' I didn't like that."

"Why not?"

Sakini shrugged. "Well, we don't have any *cha ya* here in Tobiki, boss."

"What did you use to do in the village, then?"

"Do?" Sakini scratched his head. "Plant sweet potatoes, hoe sweet potatoes, dig sweet potatoes. Sometime in the evening I use to go see Nakamura San. You don't know him, boss. He die before you come. But he live thirty, maybe forty years in Hawaii; work on a pineapple planta- tion; learn to speak English. So in the evening he would teach me some. Then when it got dark—" Sakini shrugged. "Well, I go to bed, boss."

"And dream, maybe, of going into Naha again?"

Sakini grinned and nodded. "Maybe, boss." Then he shook his head. "But now we have a teahouse here. First Flower say it's going to be better than the Golden Dragon even, because the *Tsuji* quarter was too crowded. Here we got lots of space." For a moment Sakini seemed lost in a dream, then a frightened look appeared on his face. "Boss, you don't care if we build a *cha ya,* do you?"

"Care?" Fisby regarded the activity about him, watched the sweating workers bringing the pine trees down from the hills. And he could visualize Sakini and Hokkaido standing on the street corners down in Naha. Somehow, Fisby was a little ashamed of himself for misjudging these girls and the people of the village. Here he thought his officials were just interested in—well, chasing bad girls— when all the time they were simply impressed by the fame of First Flower, who only went to the big *cha yas* and danced for the governor, and Lotus Blossom, whom they had only caught a glimpse of as she rode by in a ricksha. "Why no, Sakini," Fisby said slowly, "I can't see any objection to a *cha ya* here in the village."

Sakini let out his breath sharply. "Good, boss. Good." Then he tugged Fisby's sleeve. "Come on, boss. I show you what First Flower is going to do. See, that will be the lotus pond," Sakini explained excitedly. "Then all along the edge and one side of it, she is going to have a veranda with a roof over it."

Fisby eyed the smiling carpenters, busy sinking piling so that the L-shaped veranda of the teahouse would overhang the water of the lotus pond. "I see. But, Sakini, what are those ditches they're digging over in that potato field?"

"Those aren't ditches, boss. They're streams that wind from the pond all through the garden."

"What garden?"

"The one First Flower make for the *cha ya*. See, she have those guys bring pine trees down from the hills, then she plant them all around. She plant shrubs, too, and there's the stones for the paths." Sakini regarded Captain Fisby. "Boss, First Flower say it's pretty nice to sit in the garden and listen to the wind blow through the pines. You ever try it?"

Fisby shook his head, and they walked along a winding stream, out among the sweet potato slips. "What's this thing going to be?" he asked, pointing.

"That's going to be a bridge, boss. It's going to curve up over the stream. We build 'em everywhere in the garden."

Fisby regarded the bridge, then was curious. "Sakini,

55

where are you getting the lumber for the teahouse and these bridges?"

Sakini smiled brightly. "Oh, we tear down Hokkaido's house, boss."

"You what?" Fisby's jaw dropped. "Doesn't Hokkaido care?"

"He get pretty sore for a while," Sakini admitted. "But then we promise him that whenever we have a geisha party, we won't let the police chief sit next to Lotus Blossom."

"And that made him feel better?"

"Uh-huh, boss. And when we make him President, too, everything was all right."

"President of what?"

"The Men's League for Democratic Action."

Fisby flinched. He had the uneasy feeling that something was developing here, something he didn't care to face. "What's all this about a Men's League?"

"Well, it's going to be kinda like the Women's League, boss."

That was enough for Fisby. He had his fill of Leagues, all kinds of Leagues, and decided to get out of there.

"Now, boss," Sakini went on, "the Men's League is supposed to—"

Fisby held up a protesting hand. "Tell me about it later." He was firmly convinced that he was going to meet up with this new organization soon enough, and there was no sense in rushing the meeting. Turning, he started for headquarters, but he took a roundabout route, a route which took him near First Flower. When she looked in his direction, he smiled and waved. After all, he told himself as he regarded her, the least a man could do was to show a little common courtesy. After all, not every girl was the most famous geisha in Naha, or on all Okinawa for that matter.

Eight

When Fisby reached headquarters, his groaning stomach told him that it was time for breakfast. Dolefully, he regarded the stack of rations, over in the corner, to see what was on the menu. There was C ration, and there was K ration. Rummaging through the pile, he came across a can or two of sardines, of his own purchase, but tossed them aside—never having had a particular fondness for sardines for breakfast.

Finally he settled on a concentrated egg-and-bacon mixture of a K unit, laid it on the desk, and decided to splurge. None of that powdered coffee for him this morning. From his musette bag, he brought out a can of real coffee, unwound the metal seal; and as the delicate fragrance rose, a smile crossed his lips. There was nothing like a good cup of coffee to start the day right, he always said.

He had just put his twenty-five-cent percolator on and settled back in the swivel chair, anticipating the heady aroma of new-made breakfast coffee, when Sakini, followed by the roly-poly Hokkaido, entered headquarters.

As usual, Hokkaido was wearing the cut-off trousers that barely covered his knock-knees, but this morning Hokkaido was also wearing something that made Fisby sit up in his chair. "Sakini," he demanded, "where did Hokkaido get that white suit coat?"

"That?" Sakini regarded Hokkaido. "Oh, that belongs to the mayor, boss. You see, when we make Hokkaido President of the Men's League, we have to promise him that whenever he acts as President he can wear the mayor's white coat."

Fisby shuffled uneasily, not only because he knew Hokkaido was now acting as President, but also because the coat looked suspiciously familiar. He pointed. "And where did the mayor get it?"

"Oh, do you remember when Mr. Motomura come in and ask permission to move to our village?"

"Yes."

"Well, Mr. Motomura say if the mayor put in a good word for him, he'll give the coat to the mayor."

"Just as I thought." Fisby's eyes narrowed. He had little use for Mr. Motomura and his kind, these big syndicate operators who never gave an honest, hard-working geisha girl a chance to get out of debt. And that mayor certainly showed his true colors—putting in a good word for someone like Motomura just to receive a present for himself. Fisby straightened. "So the mayor gave me the business, eh?"

"The business?" Sakini scratched his head. "Means what, boss?"

"The works."

"The works?" Sakini was definitely puzzled.

"Never mind. I'll explain some other time." Knowing he had to face it, Fisby made himself as comfortable as possible in the swivel chair. "Well, what does Hokkaido want?"

Carefully, Hokkaido brushed the shoulders of the coat, adjusted the lapels, and stepped forward proudly—a big smile on his cherubic face. "Boss, he say as President of the Men's League, he brings you the list."

"What list?" Fisby demanded.

"The list of things the Men's League needs. First, they want some reeds. Next, they want some thin rice paper for the sliding doors of the *cha ya*—"

"Now wait a minute," Fisby said quickly. "You're not going to give me the business again. Don't bring any lists in here, because I'm not getting those things. I'm going to sit right here and eat my breakfast. Understand?"

Sakini scratched his head. "But, boss, you get kimonos and things for the Women's League."

"I didn't get anything for them."

"Yes, but you say you get 'em. You promise Miss Higa Jiga."

"I didn't promise anyone. I said I'd think it over." Unwilling to be drawn into further discussion, Fisby decided to change the subject. "Now look. Hokkaido is agriculture foreman. He's supposed to bring food in here for the people. Has he harvested any sweet potatoes this morning?"

"I don't know, boss."

"Well ask him."

After a lengthy conference, Sakini smiled brightly. "Boss, Hokkaido say with building the *cha ya* and being made President, and all, he get so excited he forget about that."

"Oh, he did. Now you just tell him I want him to go out there and dig those sweet potatoes."

When Sakini translated, Hokkaido's lip trembled, then slowly the tears began to slip down his face.

Fisby shuffled uneasily. "What's the matter now?"

"Boss, Hokkaido wish you don't say that. He claim whenever he wants to sing a song at a geisha party, or whenever he wants to sip a cup of tea with Lotus Blossom, somebody always say, 'Oh go dig your sweet potatoes.'"

Hokkaido nodded, his nostrils quivering. "And, boss, he wants to know how you think that makes him feel?"

"But I didn't mean it that way," Fisby said apologetically.

"Boss, Hokkaido say when we have the big meeting and everybody see all the things we need for the *cha ya,* right away the mayor say, 'You know, Hokkaido's just the guy to get 'em.' Now if he don't get 'em, maybe they won't let him be President any more."

Fisby's eyes narrowed. "So he got the business, too." The strong, tantalizing odor of his breakfast coffee came to Fisby and his stomach rumbled. Yet there was Hokkaido's tear-streaked face before him. He considered carefully, then shrugged in resignation, and rose from his swivel chair. "Now about that stuff, do you have any idea where I can get it?"

Sakini pointed to a strip of land jutting out into the Pacific. "You can get reeds for the *tatami* out there on the Chinen Peninsula, boss."

"Reeds for what?"

"*Tatami.* See, we take rice straw, maybe two inches thick, then we fix a mat of reeds over it. And we put 'em on the floor of the *cha ya.* The *tatami* are real pale green and they smell good, too."

"I see."

"We'd send horse carts for reeds," Sakini went on, "but the M.P.'s say, 'You guys got to stay out of here.' "

Fisby nodded. That was a military area, closed to the native population, unless they had an American along. "Well, get a detail together," Fisby said. "I'll hook the trailer up to the jeep, and we'll get a load." He leveled a warning finger. "But step it up. I'm not going to run around all day."

It took Fisby quite some time to get started. First, there was an argument between Hokkaido and the lanky mayor. "Boss," Sakini explained, "the mayor say if Hokkaido wear the coat in the jeep, he's going to get it all dusty."

Fisby regarded the ill-gotten coat, gave the mayor a scorching look, and made a pontifical decision: namely, that when Hokkaido was going after reeds, he most certainly was acting as President, and he should wear the coat.

Then Sakini and Hokkaido promptly got into an argument—Hokkaido claimed that the President should sit in the front seat of the jeep, and Sakini stated that if he, the interpreter, didn't sit in front how would the boss know which way to go?

While they were squabbling, a little fight broke out in the police department. All the native police wanted to go for a trailer ride, with those who couldn't squeeze in objecting loudly. When Hokkaido, as President, rose to quiet the police, Fisby heard something in the Luchuan dialect that sounded suspiciously like, "Oh, go dig your sweet potatoes." And Hokkaido started sobbing.

Wearily, Fisby took the reins in his own hands. "Sakini, you tell those police to get out of that trailer. Where are we going to put the reeds if they all jam in like that?"

The introduction of this new idea caused quite a bit of head scratching, but finally Fisby got under way with the President firmly enthroned on the front seat beside him, Sakini in the back seat. And six grinning native police, holding onto their sparkling red helmet-liners for dear life, bouncing along in the trailer behind.

Fisby settled down for the slow, jarring ride along the Okinawan cart trails. But as they neared little Koza, Hokkaido carefully brushed his coat and pointed to the cluster of thatched shacks set in a grove of dwarfed pines. "Boss," Sakini explained, "Hokkaido thinks it might be nice if we stop off and have a cup of tea with the mayor."

Fisby turned. "Sakini," he said tartly, "you tell him this is a business trip, and we don't have time to monkey around with social calls." Stepping on the gas, he skirted little Koza and headed for the road atop the seawall.

Passing Maebaru village, the police in the trailer behind set up a clamor. "They want to stop and see some guys they know," Sakini said. Fisby pretended not to hear and speeded up. In every village they passed, someone would want to stop, and Fisby kept brushing them off. But finally, when returning with the loaded reeds, they cornered him. "We got to stop at Takaesu," Sakini said, indicating the village ahead.

"Why?" Fisby demanded. He was getting hungrier now.

"To get the loom, boss."

"What loom?"

"The one to weave the reeds into mats."

Fisby groaned and eyed the six police perched precariously atop the reeds in the trailer behind. "Where we going to put it?"

"Up there." Sakini pointed to the hood. "The police hold it."

"No room," Fisby said, and could see Hokkaido's lip begin to tremble.

"But, boss," Sakini protested, "reeds are no good if we can't weave 'em into a mat."

Fisby tilted back his helmet-liner. Hokkaido was dangerously close to tears now. "All right, we'll get the loom, but tell him not to start crying." Reluctantly, Fisby pulled into a narrow, twisting side street as directed by the beaming Hokkaido.

They stopped before a low building that resembled a small home factory. Fisby, Hokkaido, and Sakini, leading the native police, entered, and the three natives inside greeted them with deep bows. When they were seated, at what Fisby assumed to be a conference table, the teacups came out, the pale, golden tea was poured; and Fisby found himself wishing it were inky-black coffee. How could a man drink tea for breakfast?

Evidently, it was a deep discussion. Sakini talked. Hokkaido talked, and every once in a while would give the police a dirty look for butting in when he, the President, was speaking. Fisby hardly knew what was going on, except now and then the Takaesu group would look at him questioningly and nod. He would nod back and glance distastefully at his cup of tea.

When the cups were filled for the fourth time, he had to give it up. "Sakini," he said, "let's go. I want some breakfast."

After another cup of tea, the group arose. Everyone bowed to everyone else, and Fisby nodded a couple of times when the bows were directed his way. The native police picked up an ancient wooden loom, one of the three setting over in a corner of the room, carried it out, and placed it on the hood of the jeep.

"All set?" Fisby asked, slipping behind the wheel.

"Yep, boss," Sakini replied. "Just one thing. These guys from Takaesu want to know when you bring the salt."

"What salt?"

"The salt we just traded 'em for the loom. They don't want to give it to us at first, then Hokkaido tell 'em all about the Men's League and Democratic Action, and you nodded, so they said okay. But they make us promise you get salt for 'em."

Fisby took off his helmet-liner, ran a hand through his thin hair. "Now look, Sakini. I'm not going to start supplying every village on Okinawa. Unload that loom!"

61

"But, boss," Sakini protested, "it's not hard to make salt. Just take sea water, let it stand in the sun, and you got salt. Not hard."

Fisby considered. "If it's that easy, all right. But you got to make it and deliver it, not me."

"Sure, boss," Sakini pledged.

Fisby got the jeep under way, started along a narrow, dusty street, and had passed an intersection by a good fifty feet when Sakini called, "Boss, you go the wrong way. Supposed to turn back there."

As patiently as he could, Fisby backed up, followed the indicated road, and found himself in Maebaru village. "I didn't want to come here," he protested to Sakini.

"But we got to get the saltmaker, boss," Sakini said.

"What saltmaker?"

"The one to make the salt we promise the guys in Takaesu for the loom."

"I thought you were going to make the salt," Fisby exploded.

"Oh, we are, boss." Sakini nodded brightly. "But we don't know how. Got to have special sand to put in the pits. We get someone to show us."

Before Fisby could speak, half the police force was off the jeep and disappearing behind a high coral wall, leaving the loom all by itself on the hood. Quickly, Fisby stopped, and the rest of the police disappeared. Then Sakini and Hokkaido were gone.

He waited perhaps twenty minutes, then two women with three children and a goat came out. Smiling, they began to load bundles of tattered clothing, iron cooking pots, and a varied assortment of bottles into the jeep.

"What are you doing?" Fisby demanded.

One of the women smiled brightly, nodded, then industriously went about lifting kids, and the goat, and herself into the back seat of the jeep.

"Now wait a minute." Fisby got out and regarded the group. They smiled, nodded once or twice, and settled themselves as comfortably as possible. Fisby glanced at the sagging jeep, then blew the horn. "Sakini!"

Ten minutes later Sakini and the rest came trotting out. "Sakini, who are all these people?" Fisby demanded.

"Them? Oh, that's the saltmaker's wife, and those are his kids, and that's his goat." Sakini turned and pointed to a wizened little Okinawan. "And that's the saltmaker, boss. We move the whole bunch to our village."

"We do? Well, who's the other woman?"

"Don't know, boss. Never see her before."

"Well ask her who she is."

It was some time before Sakini looked up. "That's Mrs. Watanabe, boss. She go to visit her Uncle Yoshimitsu in little Koza and decide to ride with us."

Fisby considered throwing the whole bunch out of the back seat, yet the way they sat there had a certain air of permanence about it, and he was in no mood for argument. Besides, the police were loading up now, and he figured it was too late. "Well, let's get started for home," he said.

After the saltmaker chased his wife out of the back seat, and settled himself comfortably, she climbed up on the hood beside the two police, firmly gripping the loom. The remaining four police were already on the trailer. Hokkaido and Sakini squeezed in front with Fisby. Then Mrs. Watanabe handed the goat over for Hokkaido to hold on his lap.

Fisby threw the jeep in first, and Sakini promptly pointed. "That way, boss."

"We just came from that way!" Fisby couldn't hold his temper.

"But we got to go back to Takaesu." Sakini held up a large roll of thin rice paper. "See, we got the *shoji* for the sliding doors of the *cha ya*. Now we got to get the fish nets in Takaesu."

"Fish nets! What for?"

"To catch the fish to pay the guy for the paper."

Fisby adjusted his helmet-liner. They could keep a man running around for weeks. If he got fish nets, then they would have to go somewhere to get a fisherman to show them how to fish. Then they would think of something else. He glanced at the already overloaded jeep. "We're going home," he announced firmly. "I want my breakfast today."

But driving was a little more difficult than he thought. With two police, a loom, and the saltmaker's wife on the hood he had to half stand to see anything at all. Every time they hit a bump the kids in the rear would throw their arms around his neck, knocking the helmet-liner down over his eyes. Then Hokkaido, loosening his grip on the goat, would grab the wheel; and the goat, making a break for freedom, would scoot across Fisby's lap, only to be stopped by the obliging Mrs. Watanabe, reaching over from the back seat.

He crept through the outskirts of Maebaru village on

63

hand signals from the police on the hood, avoiding wallowing pigs, horse carts, and shrieking kids. By the time they reached open country and began skirting the green, finger-like hills, his shirt was sticking to his back.

Somewhere between Maebaru and little Koza, the police on the hood began gesturing wildly, and Fisby couldn't see a thing. It was a moment before he could slam the brakes, but then it was too late. A jeep, coming from the opposite direction, was already run off the road and into an open potato field. The kids in the back seat started screaming, threw their arms around his neck, knocking the helmet-liner over his eyes.

"Fisby!" He heard the roar. "What the hell do you think you're doing?"

Struggling, he got the helmet-liner back on his head and saw Colonel Purdy.

The Colonel was in no mood for trifling this morning, for a case of sabotage had developed. And up in head-quarters, itself. On the preceding evening just as he had settled down for a few hours of good reading, he found that he didn't have the latest issue of *Adventure* after all. Someone had torn off the new cover and pasted it over last month's contents. And though every man in the outfit had stood an immediate shakedown inspection, it was feared, in official circles, that Jean Lafitte had gone the way of rural editions of Sears and Roebuck catalogues.

Now, striding toward Fisby, the Colonel's jaw was hard, his eyes narrowed, and his mustache bristling. And to Fisby, looking up, he seemed at least eight feet tall. "Fisby," he demanded, surveying the jeep. "What are you doing? Joy riding?"

Fisby pried the arms of the kids loose from around his neck. "No, sir. We were just out cutting reeds."

"Cutting reeds! Don't tell me you were picking flowers, too." The Colonel waved a stern finger in Fisby's face. "I just came from your village. Do you realize that Corporal of yours was still in bed at ten o'clock this morning?"

Fisby didn't realize.

"And what's that hole in the ground you're digging down there?"

Fisby considered. "Oh, that must be the lotus pond, sir."

The veins in Colonel Purdy's temples stood out. "Wonderful, Fisby. Wonderful. Here I send out every available man to help drain off stagnant water, and you're collecting it. So now you're raising mosquitoes as well as goats. And what about that new school building?"

The Colonel seemed to grow another foot, and Fisby gripped the wheel. "By golly, sir, I've been so busy lately it slipped my mind."

"You forgot about the education program!" Colonel Purdy was horrified. "Fisby, if I had a replacement to spare, you'd be doing the laundry up at headquarters this very minute."

Just then Sakini tugged Fisby's sleeve. "Boss, Mrs. Watanabe says to tell that guy to hurry up."

"I beg your pardon." The Colonel's mouth flew open, and Fisby forced a smile.

"I guess Mrs. Watanabe is in a hurry, sir," he said. You see, she's going over to visit her Uncle Yoshimitsu in little Koza, and we're giving her a ride."

"Very interesting. A regular taxi service, eh? I can see you're awful busy, Fisby." The Colonel regarded him. "Well, since you're not building anything up over at Tobiki, what's that thing you're tearing down?"

"Tearing down, sir?" For a moment Fisby was puzzled, then remembered. "Oh, that must be Hokkaido's house, Colonel. You see, we need the lumber to build a teahouse."

"You're tearing down a man's home, his castle, for something like that?" The blood rushed to Colonel Purdy's face.

Fisby nodded reassuringly. "But it's all right, sir. We made him President."

At the word "president" Hokkaido perked up, shifted the goat on his lap, and smiled brightly.

"And besides," Fisby went on, "whenever there's a geisha party, we don't let the police chief sit next to Lotus Blossom."

The Colonel regarded Fisby closely and seemed confused.

"And when Hokkaido acts as President, sir," Fisby continued, "we always let him wear the mayor's white coat." He smiled and leaned back, satisfied with this complete explanation.

But Colonel Purdy edged forward, bewilderment in his eyes. Carefully, he looked Fisby over. "Captain," he said, "have you been taking your Atabrine regularly?"

"Oh, yes, sir."

"You haven't had chills or anything like that?"

"Not that I know of, Colonel."

"And this morning you're just out cutting reeds?"

"Yes, sir."

"And digging a lotus pond?"

"That's right, Colonel."

The Colonel was definitely puzzled. For a moment he was silent, apparently thinking the situation over, then he began slowly, "Well, Fisby, I think you and the President, there, better be getting back to Tobiki."

Saluting, Fisby threw the jeep in gear, crept off. But he kept looking back. The Colonel was standing in the middle of the road, scratching his head. And all the way to little Koza, Fisby could see him standing there, watching.

Nine

ONCE BACK IN TOBIKI VILLAGE, Hokkaido, with great ceremony, supervised the unloading of the reeds, and the crowd smiled happily. Then when Hokkaido proudly held up the roll of thin, almost transparent, paper for the sliding doors of the teahouse, Fisby heard the crowd gasp in astonishment.

But of all the crowd, only the wizened little saltmaker seemed unhappy. "Boss," Sakini said, "he want to know when you get him the white coat."

"White coat?" Fisby questioned.

"The one like Hokkaido's wearing. We promise you get him one if he move here and make salt for us."

It seemed to Fisby as if someone around the place was pretty free and generous with their promises. "I'm not getting any white coats," he said sternly.

Sakini shook his head. "But, boss, those guys from Takaesu come and say: 'Uh-huh, and where is our salt? Oh, you don't have any. Well, we'll just take back our loom.'" Sakini's eyes clouded. "Everybody get pretty sore, boss, if we don't have a loom to weave mats for the *cha ya*."

Fisby eyed the smiling crowd. "But where will I get a coat like that?"

"I don't know, boss. I think Mr. Motomura buy that one on the *Ginza* in Tokyo."

"Tokyo!" Fisby slapped his forehead. "Sakini, do you

think those bombers flying over here every day are dropping greeting cards on Japan? What am I supposed to do—parachute in, buy a coat for the saltmaker, and swim back?"

Sakini shrugged. "Well, boss, he say he can't make salt until he gets his pay."

At that moment, the lanky mayor came dashing up, peeling the coat off Hokkaido, and the tears began to stream down Hokkaido's cherubic face. "Now what's the matter?" Fisby asked wearily.

"Oh, the mayor say one of the police tell him that all the way to little Koza Hokkaido hold a goat on his lap. He say if Hokkaido wants to hold goats, let him get a coat of his own."

The tearful Hokkaido stepped forward, and Fisby mopped his brow. "I know. I know, Sakini. Now he wants a coat, too."

"That's right, boss. Hokkaido say if he don't have one, how is everybody going to know that he's President?"

Fisby searched for a way out. "Well, couldn't he just tie a cloth around his arm and mark it?"

"No, boss. Hokkaido say the President's got to be all dressed up."

"I'm going to eat breakfast," Fisby said and stalked off toward headquarters.

He eased into the swivel chair, then noticing that the gifts were still piled on his desk, he slipped off his heavy boots, and slipped on a pair of *geta,* the native wooden sandals. Outside, a new group of native police were crowding into the trailer. "Boss," Sakini said, "they ready to go for another load of reeds now. It's their turn."

Fisby leaned back in his chair. "Sakini, if you think I'm going out with that crew, you're crazy. I owe somebody fish, and somebody salt—" He shook his head. "You're not going to entangle me in any more obligations."

"But we don't have enough reeds," Sakini protested.

"Well, that's just too bad." Fisby hesitated for he remembered something, and regarded Corporal Barton, lying on the cot across the room. "Barton, Colonel Purdy says you were still in bed at ten o'clock this morning."

"I didn't hear the alarm," Barton hedged.

"I see. Well, you just get in that jeep and start hauling reeds until I tell you to stop."

A little surprised, Barton stood up.

"Boss," Sakini whispered, "you have to get some fish nets to catch the fish to pay the guy for the rice paper."

67

"Okay. Barton, stop off in Takaesu and get those nets." Fisby held up a warning finger. "But don't make any promises to anyone."

After his late breakfast, Fisby, teetering inexpertly on the native wooden sandals, walked toward the far end of the village. He was attracted by the grove of small pines rapidly rising in the middle of an open potato field.

"First Flower double the tree planting crews," Sakini explained. "Goes fast, huh, boss?"

Fisby had to admit that it was going fast. And he was surprised to see that the lotus pond was scraped out now. The new-cut streams, winding between the pines, were also completed, as well as the high, arched bridges. He walked along a path of newly laid stones. It was cool here, and he took off his helmet-liner.

"Look, boss," Sakini said. "Here's the edge of the garden. See, First Flower have 'em put a bamboo fence all around it. Nice, eh?"

Fisby nodded. For a moment he looked at the open fields of sweet potato slips, then turned back to the coolness of the pines. "Come on, boss," Sakini said enthusiastically. "I show you the *cha ya*."

From the way they had the foundation posts laid out, Fisby could see that it was going to be a sprawling thing with five or six wings. The wide veranda, overhanging the lotus pond, was almost completed now, and they were rubbing it with bits of broken glass to smooth the wood. Off to one side, Fisby saw the huge pile of thatch for the roof, but he also saw something else—they were not going to have enough lumber.

He backed away. Ahead, Hokkaido, reduced to a temporary expedient, was busily fastening a white arm band with printed characters, which Fisby assumed to mean President. And Fisby knew the Men's League was ready to go into action. "I have to inspect the village," he said quickly, and looked around for a back path.

But Hokkaido caught him just as he started through the garden. "Now I suppose he wants lumber," Fisby said, a little irritated.

"He don't say anything about lumber, boss," Sakini announced. "Do you want me to ask him?"

"No. No, just let it go," Fisby said quickly. "Forget I mentioned it."

"Okay, boss. But now Hokkaido wants some water to fill the lotus pond."

"Water!" Fisby sank on a stone bench. "Where will I get water?"

"He don't know, boss. But tonight we have a party on the veranda, and the Men's League say we got to have water in the lotus pond. The paper lanterns don't make pretty lights unless they shine on water."

Fisby looked at the blue, cloudless sky. "Well, maybe it'll rain."

Sakini shook his head. "Hokkaido don't think so, boss. He say this is the dry season and it never rains."

Fisby rubbed his hands on his trousers. What did they expect him to do? Pass a miracle? Then he regarded the new-cut streams and had an idea. "Look," he said slowly, "why not just run the streams up toward the village?"

"But First Flower don't want 'em that way."

"Yes, but you could tie them in with the drainage ditches in the village. See, all the water will run down into the pond. If you ever get those banana groves drained, you'll need a couple more ponds besides this one."

Sakini consulted Hokkaido, and Hokkaido nodded enthusiastically. "By gosh, boss, he say he never think of that. Do you know what he's going to do?"

"What?"

"He's going right over and get the Women's League. He's going to put 'em to work digging streams. They just sit around all day anyway."

Fisby felt the President was overstepping his authority. In fact, he thought the President was sticking his neck out, and could see a squabble developing between the Men's and Women's Leagues. At once, he decided to make himself scarce. Besides, he noticed there were no lotus plants in the lotus pond. First thing you know, they would want some.

As he skirted the garden, Fisby noticed a jeep pull up near headquarters. He paled. Maybe Colonel Purdy was checking back on him. Maybe the Colonel wanted to know if he had started the new school. Fisby snapped his fingers. By golly, he had forgotten all about the education program again. He would have to get that under way just as soon as he found out who was in the jeep.

Cautiously, he edged through a banana grove, keeping well out of sight. He peered out, looking for headquarters markings on the jeep; but it bore the insignia of some field hospital, so he walked boldly forward. Colonel Purdy always warned to be on the lookout for snoopers. "We're not going to let those other teams prowl around and pick up our ideas," the Colonel always said. "If you catch them, just throw them out of your village."

Fisby barely glanced at the driver, sitting behind the wheel, reading a comic book. But the gimlet-eyed little Captain inside headquarters made him quicken his step. The Captain pretended to be standing at Fisby's desk, waiting; yet Fisby could see that he was glancing curiously at the papers in the half-opened drawer.

The Captain was taken by surprise when Fisby walked in on him, and held out a hand rather sheepishly. "So you're Captain Fisby, well, my name is McLean."

Fisby noted the insignia of the Medical Corps. "Glad to know you, Doc." He hesitated. "You know, Doc, I hate to do this, but anyone visiting in the village has to have a pass. Orders from headquarters."

The Doc had a pass all right. Not only was it signed by Colonel Purdy, but also by Major Thompson, the Public Safety Officer. Fisby smiled, failing to note the Doc's piercing eyes regarding him carefully. "Well, in that case just make yourself at home, Doc. Just kind of looking around, eh?"

The Doc nodded. "Yes, I just ran in for a quick look, Captain. You see, I'm making a little study."

"A study?" Fisby was interested. "What kind of study, Doc?"

"Ah—" The Doc cleared his throat. "Sort of a study of the ethnological aspects of the—the native population."

Fisby considered. "Well, Doc, I don't know a thing about ethnology myself, but if there's anything I can do, perhaps show you the village, maybe introduce you to the gang—"

The Doc was interested in meeting the gang, so he said. Yet as they walked along the narrow streets, his eyes seemed to be only on Fisby. "Captain," he said at length, "do you always wear native wooden sandals?"

Fisby glanced down and smiled. "Gosh, Doc, I forgot I had them on. You know, once you get used to that strap between your big toe, why—"

"They just sort of grow on you?"

Fisby nodded. "Come to think of it, Doc, that's right."

"I see." The Doc rubbed his jaw thoughtfully. "And how are things going in the village, Captain?"

"Well, we did a pretty good day's work so far, and it isn't even noon yet, Doc. We finished the lotus pond, and in a little while, I think, we're going to fill it with water."

"Oh, you're building a lotus pond?"

"We have to have one, Doc. You can't build a first-class *cha ya* without a lotus pond."

Every first-class *cha ya* ought to have a lotus pond, the Doc agreed, then regarded Fisby carefully. "This idea of the lotus pond, was that yours, Captain?"

Fisby shook his head. "No, First Flower thought of it."

"First Flower?" The Doc was like a bird dog picking up the scent. "Is she a good friend of yours?"

Fisby's voice grew confidential. "Well, I wouldn't want you to mention this, Doc, but she's a little more than a friend. You see, Mr. Motomura gave me a couple of geisha girls, and she's one of them. In fact, before the invasion she was just about the most famous geisha in Naha, the capital, and, of course, that means on all Okinawa. Never went to the small teahouses or anything like that. Governor's parties and that sort of stuff."

The Doc nodded. "As long as you're owning geisha, you might as well own the top flight. That's what I always say, Captain."

Fisby was beginning to like this gimlet-eyed little Captain of the Medical Corps. "Doc, what say we go up to headquarters, and I'll rustle up some coffee?"

But the Doc begged off. "I have some business to attend to, Fisby. If you have no objections, though, I'd sure like to spend a few days here in the village to—to complete my studies. I thought I could do it in an hour or two, but I fear there's more to it than I originally believed."

Fisby had no objections. "I suggest you contact Colonel Purdy, though," he said. "The Colonel's pretty strict about visitors."

Strangely enough, the Doc, himself, at that very moment was thinking about contacting the Colonel.

That night as they sat on the hill looking down on the village, the Doc displayed a keen interest in Fisby's quarters. "But why did you build it up here?" he asked.

Fisby regarded his aftersupper cigar. "I don't know, Doc, but I like sitting up here in the evening and just watching the village down there."

The Doc gave him a sidelong look. "It sort of makes a man feel like the great white father, doesn't it, Fisby?"

"Now that you mention it, Doc, it does." Something below caught Fisby's attention, and he leaned forward to see better. "Look, Doc, there's the President."

The Doc straightened quickly. "Roosevelt?"

71

"No. Hokkaido. You see, they're having a party on the veranda of the *cha ya* tonight, and I guess he's going over early to arrange things.

The Doc thought he better write some letters then, so Fisby just sat there, watching the village. Occasionally, however, when he glanced around, he would catch the Doc regarding him. Nodding, the Doc would turn back to the pad of paper on his knee, and Fisby would turn back to the village.

Twilight faded into darkness, and the moon rose, new and red, out of the Pacific. One by one, in the village below, lights began to appear. They were more than mere flickering candles in half-tumbled shacks tonight, however. They were paper Japanese lanterns strung throughout the dark island of pines, casting their soft glow on the arched bridges and the still water of the lotus pond.

Soon the strains of the *dahisen* reached Fisby, and the high-pitched, quivering voice of First Flower floated out on the night. At first, he merely hummed along, then began to whistle. But the music of the East was strange to his Western ear, and his whistling became rather tuneless. He tried again, only to see the Doc staring at him. Flushing, he gave it up.

For a long while as he lay on his cot in the dark, Fisby regarded the lanterns below. He could hear the laughter and the voices raised in song, and a smile spread across his face. He lay there watching as the candles of the lanterns burned lower and lower, until the laughter ceased, then sleep came.

Ten

IT WAS BARELY DAYLIGHT when Fisby was awakened by someone shaking him vigorously. He tried rolling over, but the shaking continued; and he looked up into the not so pretty face of Miss Higa Jiga.

He rubbed his eyes. "Sakini no," he said drowsily.

"Sakini yes!" Miss Higa Jiga flashed and pointed to the sleepy Sakini, shaking his head as if to clear it.

Fisby sat up on the cot and looked about. The morning

was clear and fresh, the breeze off the Pacific cool. But Miss Higa Jiga's eyes were flying storm warnings. Not only did she have Sakini in tow, but also Asato, the construction chief. "Sakini, now what's the matter?" Fisby asked.

Sakini shook his head a couple more times. "Well, boss, Miss Higa Jiga's pretty sore. Yesterday afternoon Hokkaido come around to the Women's League. 'Ladies,' he say, 'we need somebody to dig streams so that the water all drains down into the lotus pond. You help us out, and we might invite you to a party down at the *cha ya* sometime.' "

"So?"

"So they dig the streams, boss. Then last night Miss Higa Jiga, and Miss Susano, and the executive council decide to go to the party on the veranda. Miss Higa Jiga say they wash their feet and everything, but do you know what happens when they get there?"

Fisby wouldn't even attempt to guess.

"Well, everybody say, 'Oh, so you want to come to the party, eh? Uh-huh, and where is your papers from the geisha guild?' Well, they don't have any papers, boss, so everybody chase 'em home."

Fisby glanced at Miss Higa Jiga. "I certainly don't see why a few ladies of the village can't attend a party in the village teahouse," he said tersely.

"But, boss," Sakini protested, "women can't go to a *cha ya* unless they're geishas. The guild's pretty strict about that. They say they don't want any nonguild members hanging around the place."

While Fisby certainly had no desire of interfering with a union shop, still he felt that the ladies of the village were entitled to a few privileges. "Couldn't First Flower issue them papers?" he asked.

"No, boss. You see, yesterday afternoon First Flower have a long talk with the League. She say she and Lotus Blossom do their best to teach the League to sing and dance like geisha, but she don't think they can make it. They can sing pretty good and all that, First Flower say, but all the guys around the place are supposed to want to sit around and sip tea with the geishas."

Fisby glanced cautiously at the pouting Miss Higa Jiga. "And no one wants to sit around and sip tea with the Women's League?"

"That's just the trouble, boss," Sakini said. "First Flower notice that whenever the League comes down the street, all the guys duck around the corner."

"That's too bad, Sakini." Fisby imagined that not making the geisha guild must be quite a blow, indeed, to the Women's League. "But what am I supposed to do about it?"

"Well, boss, First Flower thinks as long as the League isn't going to get any democratic action, they better get a pastime. Maybe drinking tea or arranging flowers."

It sounded sensible to Fisby.

"So, boss," Sakini continued, "Miss Higa Jiga wants you to build her a *cha no yu* house."

"What's that?"

"That's a little teahouse, boss, that you put in your backyard. Miss Higa Jiga say she use to see 'em down in Naha when she carry sweet potatoes to market."

"You mean she wants her own private teahouse?"

"Yep, boss. Then she can sit around all afternoon like the ladies in Naha use to do and practice the tea drinking ceremony. She say it's an esthetic pastime. Besides, if she happens to ask some guy to have a cup of tea with her, he can't say no."

"But we don't have any lumber."

"I tell her that, boss. She say you build a teahouse for the Men's League, but you don't do anything for the Women's League. You know what she thinks maybe we have in the village?"

"What?"

"Discrimination. And she bets Uncle Sam would be pretty interested in hearing about that."

Fisby winced. "Sakini," he said quickly, "do you know where we can get some lumber?"

"Sure, boss. They got some over in big Koza. All we have to do is tell 'em that you get 'em anything they want, and . . ."

"Now wait a minute." Fisby grew stern. "I'm not going to start supplying big Koza, too." He caught a glimpse of Miss Higa Jiga's flashing eyes, and rubbed his jaw thoughtfully. "Sakini, do you think big Koza would swap with us? We'll give them salt for lumber. How's that?"

"Good, boss. But where will we get salt?"

"What about that saltmaker we carted in here yesterday? Isn't he making salt?"

"No, boss. He say we promise him a white coat. He can't make any until he gets it." Miss Higa Jiga tugged Sakini's sleeve. "Boss, she wants to know when you'll have the *cha no yu* house done?"

"I didn't say I'd build it," Fisby hedged, but a glance at Miss Higa Jiga convinced him that she was in a mood to write letters to Uncle Sam via Colonel Purdy. "That is, I have to think it over. Maybe if I can get a white coat, then the saltmaker will make salt, and maybe we can swap for lumber. See, there's a lot of things to be worked out."

Sakini nodded in agreement and pointed to the construction foreman with his head on his arms, asleep on the stoop. "Besides, Asato don't know how to build one."

Fisby ran his hand over his eyes. "Well don't ask me anything about it. I never even saw one."

"Boss," Sakini said, "Miss Higa Jiga don't know anything about it either. The only time she see 'em is when she peek in the backyards down in Naha."

Fisby shrugged. "See, there are a lot of things to be worked out. Tell her I'll think it over." He leaned back. "I'm going to sleep a while yet."

But Miss Higa Jiga was tugging at Sakini's sleeve again. "Boss, she claim First Flower knows all about *cha no yu* houses."

"That's nice." Fisby shook his pillow. "Tell them to talk it over and let me know about it sometime."

Sakini shook his head. "She can't do that, boss. First Flower is pretty sore at her. Last night Hiyoshi break loose again, and when First Flower come home from the party on the veranda he is sleeping in her room."

"Who's Hiyoshi?"

"That's Miss Higa Jiga's best pig. By gosh, First Flower sure raise the dickens. She even get all the police out, and now she won't talk to Miss Higa Jiga. So Miss Higa Jiga wants you to ask First Flower about the *cha no yu* house, because you're the boss."

"What's that got to do with it?"

"Well, First Flower always likes to help the boss. Maybe if you ask her, she'll teach the construction chief how to build it."

"All right." Fisby sank back on the cot.

"And, boss, Miss Higa Jiga wants you to ask First Flower to teach her the tea drinking ceremony and how to fix flowers real nice."

At that moment Fisby noted that Miss Higa Jiga was staring at his pajamas. Blushing, he pulled the army blankets up around him. "Okay, when I get around to it."

"Boss," Sakini said, "she say those things you got on are

pretty. She never see red and white stripes like that, and she just think of something."

Self-consciously, Fisby wrapped the blankets tighter around him. "She can tell me later when I get to headquarters."

But Miss Higa Jiga couldn't seem to get her mind from the pajamas. "Boss, she thinks if those things were cut up into pieces and wrapped around the straw rope of the *geta,* it would look nice."

"Now just a minute," Fisby said. "These are my best pajamas. I'm not cutting them up to decorate wooden sandals."

"But, boss, she say if she's going to drink tea like the ladies down in Naha use to do, she ought to have some sandals. They never walk around barefooted." Miss Higa Jiga nodded, her lower lip sagging, her nostrils quivering.

"Well, tell her to go cut up her own pajamas."

"But she don't have any, boss."

"Well . . ." Fisby was stymied.

"And, boss, she thinks it would be nice if you made some sandals for all the ladies in the League. Then they could practice walking around in them, and by the time the *cha no yu* house is finished, they could walk real good."

Fisby's one idea was to get her out of there. He pointed to the dozing construction foreman on the stoop. "Can he make *geta?*"

"Sure, boss, but I think he's going to need some guys to help him. The Women's League is pretty big."

"Tell him to use the men he needs. I'm going back to sleep."

Miss Higa Jiga pouted. "Boss, she wants those red and white things now so she can start cutting 'em up. If you don't give 'em to her now, you might forget all about it."

In desperation, Fisby sat up. "All right. But tell her to get out of here so I can take them off."

After he was dressed, Fisby rolled the pajamas and started down to the village, carrying them under his arm. Miss Higa Jiga was waiting in headquarters and accepted them with a smile. But Miss Susano, the recording secretary, and the executive council of the Women's League were also waiting. "They want *cha no yu* houses, too," Sakini explained.

Looking out through the windowless window of headquarters, Fisby could see quite a delegation lining up to put in their orders. He didn't know how much lumber big

Koza had but knew if he built one of those things, he would need plenty. The best thing to do, Fisby decided, was to just disappear, and maybe they would forget the whole affair. He picked up a K ration breakfast unit. "Sakini, I think I'll take a little ride."

Sakini nodded in understanding. "You go to get the white coat for the saltmaker, eh, boss?"

"I didn't say that!" Fisby flashed.

But Sakini was already explaining the situation to the Women's League, and they were enthusiastic, indeed. "It's good, boss," Sakini said. "Then the saltmaker make salt, and we swap for lumber, and we have *cha no yu* houses all over the place."

As Fisby drove away from headquarters, Sakini called, "Boss, don't forget to get a white coat for Hokkaido, too. And maybe if you get three——"

Fisby speeded up. How could he get white coats? He glanced at the fields of sweet potatoes. They stretched up the hill before him, on both sides of him. And over the hill, he knew, there was nothing but more sweet potatoes.

Stopping in a grove of pines, he leisurely ate his breakfast. Yet his mind played on the coats and it worried him. It would be hard going back to the village without them. But what could he do? He wasn't running a clothing store.

For nearly an hour he drove aimlessly before sighting something that looked like the Grand Hotel going up on a hilltop, and went up to investigate.

"What do you think it is, Mac?" a grizzled old Sea Bee Chief told him. "An Officers' Club, naturally."

Fisby was curious. "For what outfit, Chief?"

"It beats me." The Chief pointed to a downy-cheeked young Ensign in work grays. "Golden Boy, over there in the presalted uniform, is in charge. Ask him."

Fisby decided to look around a little. If things became too pressing in the village now and then, here might be a hangout.

"Yes, it's an Officers' Club," the young Ensign in charge told him after the introductions. "And you really have no idea what a problem it is to furnish, Mr. Fisby. They haven't even sent us chairs from the States. Imagine!"

"Why, that's too bad, Ensign."

"In the Navy, Mr. Fisby," the Ensign said quickly, "we don't use rank as a form of address. Perhaps you better call me Mister."

"I'm sorry, Mr. Van Druten," Fisby said, and at the

moment noticed the bolts of coarse white cloth lying over in the corner.

"It's dreadful," Mr. Van Druten went on. "Why, Mr. Fisby, we have to improvise everything out here. I really don't know how they expect us to get anything done at all. Why at Plattsburg they told us—"

Fisby tried to appear interested, yet his eyes kept straying to the cloth. Then he scratched his head and looked around the bare room. "You know, Mr. Van Druten, maybe I can help you out," he said thoughtfully. "How would you like to fix up the place native style. Say, throw some *tatami* on the floor?"

"*Tatami?* I beg your pardon, Mr. Fisby."

"Oh, that's a kind of mat the natives make out of reeds."

The young Ensign's eyebrows arched. "I really don't know, Mr. Fisby. Do you think it would be sanitary? I hear there's so much disease over here—flukes, and dengue fever, and—"

"Well," Fisby confided, "we're building a little club over at our place, and that's what we're using."

"Oh, you are?" Mr. Van Druten hesitated. "Would they be new mats?"

"Brand-new. And I'll tell you what I'll do. Doc McLean came over to our place yesterday. I'll ask him to inspect them and give his okay."

"That would be splendid," Mr. Van Druten said.

Fisby eyed him carefully, then remembered some of the gifts that had poured in when Hokkaido and the rest wanted him to give permission for First Flower and Lotus Blossom to visit their homes. "And maybe I could get you some bamboo flower baskets. It'd be pretty nice to have flower baskets hanging all around the place, Mr. Van Druten."

Mr. Van Druten had to admit that it would.

"And how about some bamboo for a bar," Fisby went on expansively, remembering a place he had once seen in San Francisco. "You might hang bamboo on the ceiling. Might even make Venetian blinds out of it."

Mr. Van Druten smiled. "It would make a splendid atmosphere, Mr. Fisby. Almost like going native."

Fisby edged close. "Tell you what. Give me a day or two and I'll get the stuff ready. How's that?"

It was splendid. "And if I can do anything for you, Mr. Fisby, don't hesitate to call on me."

Fisby regarded the coarse cloth. "Come to think of it, Mr. Van Druten, I could use a little target cloth." He saw the Ensign's puzzled look. "That's the stuff they make targets out of for the rifle range. That stuff over in the corner."

"Oh, that. I often wondered what it was for. Just help yourself, Mr. Fisby. They sent us plenty of that from the States."

When Fisby drove back into Tobiki village, he had the jeep loaded down with bolts of the coarse white cloth. And when he faced the wizened little saltmaker, he had a bolt spread out on his desk. "Sakini, there's his coat." He held his breath. "All he has to do is make it up."

"Lots of tailors in the village, boss," Sakini said. "Even got Gushi, the best tailor in Naha, here now." And Fisby breathed easier.

Still his eyes were on the little Okinawan who critically inspected the cloth, felt it between thumb and forefinger, and held it up to the light.

"Isn't it all right?" Fisby asked nervously.

"Sure, boss. He says it's fine, be nice and cool, only—"

"Only what?"

"Only he wonders if he could have an extra piece. Ever since he can remember, his wife say, 'Miyagi, you never get me anything. Nakamura gets his wife lots of pretty things, but you—' " Sakini shook his head. "Boss, he say she drives him crazy as the dickens."

Fisby considered. "Well, in that case—"

"Boss," Sakini said quickly, "he say he work hard every day. Make all the salt you want. Make more even. Get fifty, maybe sixty guys to help him if you give him some extra cloth. Please, boss, he say he's got to have some peace and quiet."

"It's a deal." Fisby unrolled an ample amount, then gave the bolt an extra tug. "Here, this is for his kids. And he might as well have a pair of pants made to go with the coat while he's at it."

The little saltmaker was all bows. "He thanks you, boss."

Fisby waved his hand. "Don't mention it. But have him get busy making that salt."

Sakini nodded absently, his eyes on the cloth. "Boss, you think maybe I can have some, too?"

"Don't see why not." Fisby unrolled a generous piece. "Here, make yourself a couple suits." Then he remembered. "And take some along for your grandpa."

By late afternoon, Fisby had Hokkaido, president of the Men's League, fitted out, had every family in the village fixed up, sent some cloth down to the old folk's home. And he even supplied First Flower and Lotus Blossom with a generous amount. "Just tell them it's a little present from the boss," he instructed Sakini.

The entire village accepted the cloth with smiles and bows, and the ancient grandmothers insisted on squeezing Fisby's hand, their old eyes sparkling as they whispered, "*Arigato gozaimas, Taicho San* . . . we thank you very much, Mr. Commanding Officer."

Only Miss Higa Jiga and the Women's League hardly seemed enthusiastic. "They say it's nice, boss," Sakini explained. "But they claim you promised 'em silk kimonos that are real fine and soft."

"But look, Sakini. It's a good serviceable material. Nice and cool. You heard what the saltmaker said."

"I know, boss. But Miss Higa Jiga say it don't look pretty like the geisha girls' kimonos. It don't have flowers on it or anything."

Fisby eyed the Women's League carefully, then began rerolling the bolt. "Well, if they don't want it, I think I'll just send their share over to little Koza."

There was an excited buzzing in the Women's League. Miss Higa Jiga's lower lip dropped. Miss Susano's nostrils began to quiver. "Boss," Sakini said slowly, "they claim they don't say they don't want the cloth. They just say they want the kimonos, too."

"So I thought." Fisby nodded. "All right, I don't have time to argue. Come on, Sakini." His hand swept the bolts. "I have to get the stuff together to pay for this."

Eleven

As THEY WALKED FROM HEADQUARTERS, Fisby pointed to the bamboo growing on both sides of the narrow street. "I need a big pile of that, Sakini."

"What for, boss?" Sakini asked.

"I swapped bamboo for the white cloth. You see, they're building an Officers' Club, and I promised to help fix it up."

"What's an Officers' Club, boss?"

"Well, it's sort of—sort of a *cha ya*."

Sakini smiled. "Oh, a place where everybody sit around, and sip tea, and sing songs, huh, boss?"

"That's about it. Anyway, I promised them some bamboo, and some bamboo flower baskets. Can you make them?"

"Sure, boss. Everybody can make baskets."

"Good. And let's see, I promised them some mats for the floor. How's the mat weaving coming?"

"Fine, boss. We almost got one finished."

"One! How long did it take to make that?"

"Maybe a day."

With the *cha ya* needing mats and the Officers' Club needing mats, Fisby could visualize weeks and months before the project was completed. "I guess we need more looms," he said.

"Could use two or three more," Sakini agreed. "But we don't have those guys in Takaesu paid off in salt yet."

"You mean that saltmaker hasn't started working," Fisby exploded.

"Oh, sure, boss. But it take a while to dig the pits and get ready. We'll pay those guys pretty soon."

Fisby calmed. "That's all right. But when we do pay them off, do you think they'll give us more looms?"

"Don't think so, boss. They only got a couple left."

"I see. Well, where can we get more?"

"Don't know. They're pretty hard to get. Not many on Okinawa. They use to make 'em on Amami O'Shima, but now I don't know."

Fisby was worried. Suppose in the future he needed more target cloth? He'd have to see this Ensign Van Druten again. And if he didn't pay off in mats now . . . well, no future target cloth. "Sakini," he said, "let's take a look at that loom."

For a while, he and Sakini stood watching the woman weaving the mat. It was a slow process, all right. First she had to press a foot pedal to carry a single reed through the vertical reeds. Then she had to press another pedal to stamp the reed in place. And though she worked fast, still her progress was barely noticeable.

"Sakini," Fisby said, "if we had a hundred of those looms, we could turn out a hundred mats a day, couldn't we?"

"But where we get a hundred looms?" Sakini asked.

Fisby hardly heard. He was inspecting the ancient wooden frame, examining the foot pedals and armlike slat

81

that flew back and forth, carrying the horizontal reed over. "Sakini," he said. "I guess we'll have to tear it down."

Alarm showed in Sakini's eyes. "But, boss, that's the only one we have. Then we can't weave any more, and we won't have mats for the *cha ya.*"

"Huh? Oh, I just want to—never mind. Get me about twenty men. And see if they have some two by fours, and four by fours down by the *cha ya* that I can borrow."

Fisby hardly saw Sakini run off through the village. He was too busy knocking out the wooden pegs, tearing the loom apart. Nor did he see the fear in the eyes of the twenty men Sakini brought back as they gazed at the dismantled loom.

"Here, Sakini," Fisby said, picking up part of the frame and laying it on a four by four. "Tell them to watch." With a pencil, he carefully traced the outline of the frame part. "See, they can do that, can't they?"

"Sure, boss."

"All right. Now let's give each one a certain section to trace." Fisby looked up. "And get me about fifty men to saw these sections out. I want to set up fifty frames this afternoon yet."

As Sakini ran off through the village again, Fisby picked up a piece of wood. They were going to need pegs, so he might as well start whittling. Seating himself on a four by four, he brought out his pocketknife and began.

So intent was he on his work, that he failed to notice Doc McLean approach through the banana grove. "Oh, there you are, Captain," the Doc said, "where did you disappear to this morning? I looked all over for you."

"I took a ride, Doc. By the way, how's your ethnological study coming?"

"Fine. Of course, I didn't get much done this morning. I, uh, I slept in." The Doc regarded Fisby. "What are you doing there?"

"Just whittling." Fisby leaned forward. "Doc, offhand, what are some of the traits you noticed in the people?"

The Doc's skinny head jerked around. "Offhand, Captain," his eyes fell on Fisby, "I would say they don't have much of a sense of responsibility."

Fisby whistled. "Is that a fact?"

"Now that's just a first impression, Captain. I don't doubt that they are well meaning, but they seem to let things slide. Perhaps they are unable to distinguish the important from the nonimportant. Of course, that's not a comprehensive analysis."

Fisby considered. "Well, Doc, from my own observation I'd say they'd like to have things around here just like it used to be down in Naha, the capital. After all, this was just a little country village, and Naha seemed to be the quintessence of everything worthwhile in life."

"Ah, yes." The Doc cleared his throat. "Incidentally, Captain, have you ever thought of trying to instill a sense of responsibility in—in the people?"

"No, Doc, I hadn't. I suppose I ought to, but . . ." Fisby held up the piece of wood. "Well, you can see I'm pretty busy."

"Of course, Captain. Of course. Now I wouldn't want to take you away from your whittling, yet I think you should seriously consider it."

Fisby agreed to do that. First, however, he had quite a pressing problem. "I need some rubber bands, Doc," he said. "Something good and heavy like they use for slingshots."

"Slingshots!" The Doc's beady eyes popped.

"Yep, Doc. Do you know where I can get some inner tubes?"

The Doc was cautious. "Well, Captain, I certainly wouldn't go cutting up the tubes in your jeep. Destroying government property is a serious offense, even under the circumstances." He stood up. "I think I better make some notes now for my study."

After he was gone, Fisby turned back to the loom. Springs would be best to snap that armlike slat back into place after it carried the reed across, but where would he get springs? Rubber bands would have to do. If he could get bands, that is. As he whittled, he thought over the situation. With all the trucks on the island, there were bound to be blowouts, hence useless tubes. He snapped his fingers. "Sakini!"

Sakini walked over from the other side of the grove. "What, boss?"

"Run up to headquarters and tell Corporal Barton to find the Army salvage dump. Tell him to bring me all the old inner tubes he can get."

Fisby lost track of time, and when next he looked up, Sakini was tugging at his sleeve. "Boss," he indicated the group tracing out parts and sawing. "These guys want to know when you let 'em go home and eat supper."

"Supper?" Fisby hadn't noticed that it was nearly dark. He regarded the stacks of newly cut parts for the looms. "Okay, they can go home now. But I want this same bunch back in the morning, early. Tomorrow I'll show them how to put the looms together."

Twelve

IN THE MORNING Fisby showed his workers how to assemble the looms. He had to put three or four together himself before they caught on. At first they worked slowly, but then speeded up. And in less than two hours twenty new looms stood in a neat row in the banana grove. "Now get someone to run them," he told Sakini, "and let's start turning out mats."

"We'll need a lot of reeds, boss," Sakini said. "Some rice straw, too. See, boss, we need a couple inches of straw for the bottom of the *tatami*."

Fisby didn't know about rice straw, but up in the hills he could see the wild grass waving in the morning breeze. "Isn't that the stuff you use for thatched roofs?" he asked.

Sakini nodded.

"Well, why can't we use that in place of rice straw?"

"We can, but rice straw is better."

"We'll use that," Fisby promptly decided. "Look, we'll turn this thing over to the agriculture department. Tell Hokkaido to round up a couple hundred kids. They're not doing anything except bumming candy out on the roads. I want Hokkaido to have them bring plenty of thatch down. I don't want production held up."

"What about reeds?" Sakini asked.

Fisby considered. "I'll send Corporal Barton out on the Chinen Peninsula for them. Round up some police to do the cutting."

After Corporal Barton pulled out in the jeep, Fisby stood before headquarters. For a while he watched the long line of children making their way up the hillsides. When they fanned out into the fields of grass, he nodded with satisfaction, then turned. A cup of coffee would go good now.

He had just put the pot over the portable gasoline stove

when he looked up and saw First Flower in the doorway watching him. This morning she wore a rose kimono, her hair in the usual elaborate coiffure, and she was even prettier than he last remembered.

Fisby was a little flustered and felt himself blushing. "Well, well," he said, trying to cover his confusion. "Is there something I can do for her, Sakini?"

"No, boss."

Somehow Fisby was a little disappointed. "Are you sure?"

"Yes, boss. She was down supervising the building of the *cha ya,* but it's time for *kobiru.*"

"For what?"

"Kobiru. In the middle of the morning everybody like to stop work for a cup of tea, and maybe eat a baked sweet potato."

"Oh, sort of a midmorning snack?"

"I guess so, boss. Anyway, it's time for *kobiru,* so she decide to come up here to thank you for sending her and Lotus Blossom the white cloth yesterday."

"Is that a fact?" Fisby regarded her fine silk kimono, thought of the coarse target cloth, and was a little ashamed. "But it wasn't much, Sakini."

"She say it was, boss, and she thanks you."

Fisby was embarrassed, for she stood there in the doorway smiling at him. "Well—" He glanced at the coffeepot. "Sakini, I was just about to take time out for *kobiru* myself. Will she have a cup of coffee?"

When Sakini translated, her dark eyes twinkled. "She never drink coffee, boss, but she like to try it."

Fisby smiled and rubbed his hands. "Well, well. Tell her to come right in. You know, I'm just about the best coffee maker in northern Ohio."

Sakini's eyes widened. "You are, boss?"

"There's none better. Back in Napoleon I own a pharmacy."

"A what?"

"A place where they sell drugs."

"You mean like powdered shark's tooth and ground-up horns of the blue sheep?"

"Not exactly. But that's the general idea. Anyway, everybody always says that Fisby's has the best coffee in town. Why in the morning all the businessmen drop in."

"What for, boss?"

Fisby shrugged. "You know, *kobiru.* Coffee and a dough-

85

nut, maybe a sweet roll. Things like that. You tell First Flower she has to try a cup of Fisby's coffee." He looked around for a chair. There was none. Then, spying his own swivel chair, he moved it over for her. She sat on the edge, folded her hands on her lap; and to Fisby, regarding her small, pretty features, she seemed a tiny doll come to life.

He busied himself with the coffee for a moment, but it wasn't near percolated—a fact which made him happy. Somehow, he wanted to talk with her. He sat on the edge of the desk, and in that instant caught the slight frown on her face. "Sakini," he began hesitantly, "is something the matter?"

She looked up at him and smiled. "No, boss."

"Oh. For a moment I thought—well, she seemed worried about something."

Now Sakini hesitated. "I guess, boss, maybe she is worried. You see, none of the guys around here have got any money. When she sings and dances at parties, she just do it because she likes to. They can't pay her, and—"

"And what?"

"Well, when the guys from the Military Government come around and say, 'Uh-huh, and did you pay your geisha tax?' she don't know what she's going to do." Sakini regarded Fisby. "Boss, she wants to know if you think the taxes are going to be high?"

Fisby scratched his head. "Offhand, Sakini, I don't think there's going to be a geisha tax."

When Sakini translated, First Flower's mouth flew open. "No taxes, boss? She can't believe."

Fisby smiled benevolently. "Tell her to just forget about them, Sakini."

First Flower was wide eyed. "Boss, she say she never hear of anything like that before."

Fisby assured her that it was really nothing at all.

"But she wants to know about you, too, boss," Sakini went on. "She thinks maybe you're pretty sore because she and Lotus Blossom aren't making any money. Usually, by gosh, the boss wants fifty per cent of the profit each day, and—"

Fisby held up a hand. "Tell her not to worry. I don't want a single cent—that is, a single *sen*."

"You don't?" Sakini scratched his head. And when he explained, Fisby saw a very confused girl there before him, who could only shake her head in wonder. "Boss, she say at first she didn't like this Military Government because they chase her from village to village. But now, no taxes, the boss don't want any of the profits, and he even send her gifts—boy, she sure likes it around this place."

Fisby was about to explain what might be termed extenuating circumstances, but refrained. Not only because he didn't know how to begin such a complicated explanation, but also because he liked the look in her eyes as she regarded him. It was a look of wonder, and awe, and, perhaps, a look of hero worship.

Beaming, he straightened his shoulders, and sat there grinning.

The lull in the conversation, however, brought him back to reality, and he began conversationally, "Sakini, ask her how things are going down at the *cha ya*."

"She say pretty good, only they're almost out of lumber." Fisby smiled. "Tell her not to worry. I think I can arrange a deal with big Koza. Now as soon as the saltmaker makes enough . . ."

"Oh, she already knows about that, boss," Sakini interrupted. "This morning Lotus Blossom went over to big Koza to do the swapping, or else she would have come down to thank you, too. You see, First Flower say the mayor of big Koza is all right, but you got to watch him pretty close, or he try to give you wood with knots in it. Lotus Blossom makes sure the wood is good, with a nice grain, and real pretty."

"I see." Frankly, Fisby was glad to get the swapping off his hands, though he would have preferred a little more glory.

"So while we're waiting for the lumber," Sakini went on, "First Flower is going ahead with the kitchen."

"Oh, you're going to have a kitchen, too?" Surprise was evident in Fisby's voice.

"Sure, boss. First Flower ask Mrs. Kamakura to move to our village, so yesterday she did. You know her?"

Fisby couldn't recall ever having met the lady.

"She use to cook in the *cha ya* of the Golden Dragon," Sakini explained. "That was the best in Naha."

The coffee was ready then. Fisby poured a canteen cup for First Flower. She accepted it with a bow, holding the cup in both hands. And Fisby watched as she sipped it, watched the moment of indecision on her face, then she smiled. "She say it's good, boss."

Pleased, Fisby sat down on the desk again, then decided they ought to have a little something to eat for *kobiru*.

Opening a can of C ration, he arranged the candy and biscuits on a sheet of typing paper. "Tell her to try a biscuit, Sakini," he said.

First Flower tried one. She smiled again; but this time, Fisby could tell, the smile was forced.

"I show her how to do it, boss," Sakini, an old hand at the game, explained. Fisby saw him teach her to dip the biscuit in coffee and let it get a little soggy. "I tell her they're not so bad that way," Sakini said brightly.

Fisby had to agree that they weren't so bad that way. Yet they weren't so good. He eyed his own biscuit. "Now about this Mrs. Kamakura, who used to cook at the Golden Dragon," he said. "What's her specialty?"

"Specialty, boss?"

"What does she cook best?"

"First Flower say she make *unagi no kabayaki* real good."

"What's that?"

Sakini scratched his head. "I don't know. I never eat it. Just a minute, I ask her."

Unagi no kabayaki, it developed, was eels with soy sauce, brown sugar, and sweet *sake*. The eels were impaled on a bamboo skewer, broiled on both sides, after which the sauce was poured over them.

"That sounds good," Fisby said. "What else does she make?"

"She make *tempura,* boss. That's shrimp, or sometimes fish, that Mrs. Kamakura dip in batter and fry in oil."

"Shrimp. Sakini, when I was at the Presidio of Monterey, that's in California, I used to go down on the wharf every night for fried shrimp."

"Boss," Sakini said, "First Flower wants to know if you like sea food?"

Fisby nodded. "I was the best customer Christie's had."

"She say that's good because nobody can cook sea food like Mrs. Kamakura. You know what? First Flower is going to have her fix you some *ebi no unigarayaki*. That's little pieces of lobster with the shells on, First Flower say. And you boil 'em in soup made of bonito fish, sweet *sake,* and soy sauce until the shells get all red."

Fisby patted his ample stomach. "Sakini, when does this kitchen open?" Then he thought of something and frowned. "But where is she going to get all the food to cook?"

"Oh, First Flower say she get sick and tired of sweet potatoes, boss, so she have some guys put those nets we

IDENTIFICATION CARD

AN Elaine Peters PRODUCT

name... Jody Kay Olson

address..3095 Main St.

city...Waupaca... state...Wis.

social security no...

in case of an
accident or
serious illness,
please notify

name...Mr. or Mrs. Steve Olson

address...309 S. Main St.

telephone no...337R

PRINTED IN USA

got in Takaesu out in the sea. Catch a lot of fish and stuff. Besides, she know where there's a lot of food."

"She does?"

"Sure, boss. Before you guys come here, the Japanese officers sometimes don't feel so good, so they come around to talk with her. They tell her how they hide food all over the place. She thinks the Japanese aren't going to need it any more, so we'll just go out to the caves with horse carts and get it."

Fisby was curious. "What kind of food was hidden?"

"Soldier food, boss. Lots of rice and pickled plums. Shrimp, clams, and crab meat in tin cans for the officers. Maybe canned oranges and tangerines. First Flower say now if she can teach Hokkaido to grow something besides sweet potatoes and soy beans, everything will be all right."

"Grow something?" Fisby questioned.

"Sure, boss. Things like Chinese cabbage, and eggplant. They make nice pickles. She say when she eats, she likes to see the seasons of the year there on the dishes before her. In the spring she likes to see the little green peas, and they make her think of the whole earth coming to life, and the birds singing in the blossoming cherry trees. Then she is happy because the breeze of spring brushes her cheek, and the dishes before her are offering the treasures that come only after the winter's snow.

"And, boss, when the purple grapes are there before her, she sees the October moon, high and white in the heavens. She feels the chill of the October night when the gray clouds drift before the face of the moon. And within her heart comes the aching loneliness of the autumn, for then the world is dying . . ." First Flower shook her head, and Fisby saw the remote, distant look in her eyes. "Boss, she say she's got to teach these guys how to grow something besides sweet potatoes."

Fisby considered. He had never quite thought of seeing the seasons of the year there on the dishes before him. While he enjoyed food, usually he ate to get it over with. But now he rather liked First Flower's way of thinking. "It would be nice if we could grow all those things here in the village," he said. And his mind was on the Japanese military rations hidden in the caves. While he appreciated this windfall, still it worried him. For they reminded him of the Christmas baskets passed out to the needy during the Yule season. For one day the hungry feasted, but after Christmas what?

He glanced out at the Pacific, just beyond. The sea would always be there, supplying its proteins. Yet the land, too, ought to produce the grains and vegetables in variety to help relieve the monotonous diet of sweet potatoes and soy beans.

When First Flower arose, Fisby looked up quickly. "Boss," Sakini explained. "She have to go now."

"Oh." Fisby was genuinely sorry to see her rise. "Well, maybe she would like another cup of coffee. There's plenty left, and it's still hot."

First Flower bowed deeply. "She thanks you, boss, but she has to send for some guys now that we need in the village."

Fisby was a little surprised. "Do we need someone in the village?"

"Yes, boss. First, we need Kiei. He's an old friend of hers who knows how to work with clay. First Flower say he makes dishes so thin and so clear you can almost see through them. We need him to make dishes for the *cha ya*."

Fisby nodded. "I guess we do need Kiei in the village. Where is he at?"

"In Kishaba. She's going to send someone over for him. And she's going to ask Seiko to move here, too."

"Who's Seiko?"

"She say he's a guy who's kind of crazy, but he can sure paint like the dickens."

"Paint?"

"You know . . . pictures. First Flower claim that he can just make one or two lines on a dish, but in those lines you can see the delicateness of a flower. And it makes something catch in your throat."

"Is that a fact? But what did she mean . . . he's kind of crazy?"

"Well, boss, she use to know him down in Naha. All day he sits around the teahouses. He wouldn't paint. He wouldn't do anything. He just want to sit and talk with her."

Fisby caught the faint flush in her cheek. "I see, he was her boy friend."

She flushed just a little more. "Maybe."

Fisby smiled. "Well, I certainly think we ought to send for Seiko then."

But First Flower's eyes clouded and a frown appeared on her pretty face. "She don't know if he'll come, boss."

"No? Why not?"

"Well, she and Seiko don't get along so good."

Fisby leaned forward. "They had an argument?"

"She guesses so, boss. She don't like to have him just sit around and waste his time talking with her, even though he tells her some pretty nice things already." Fisby saw the concern in her dark eyes. "She wants him to paint and paint, for she knows someday he could be court artist, if he wants to. And she wants people from all over to come and say, 'Seiko painted that picture.'"

Fisby regarded her. "Did she tell him that?"

"Yes, boss. But he just shrug and say all he ever wants to do is just talk with her."

"And what did she do about that?"

"She thinks and thinks, and then she has a plan. There's a lot of rich guys in Naha who want Seiko to paint pretty pictures on silk screens for them, but Seiko won't listen. So she decide to make him work."

"How?" Fisby asked curiously.

"One day, boss, she tell him it costs money to sit around and talk with geisha girls. And from now on—since she is the most famous geisha in Naha—if he wants to talk with her, he's going to have to pay double the price."

"And what did Seiko say?"

"He say—oh, she's just interested in money. All right. He don't care. He'll go talk with some other geisha girls. And that makes her pretty sore. She say, 'Go ahead. Make a fool out of yourself chasing girls.' She claim it don't matter to her. He should go right ahead."

"Did he?"

"No, boss. She don't give him a chance. None of the other geishas will talk with him, because she warns them that she don't want any monkeying around. So now she thinks if he moves here and paints dishes, it will be good practice for him, and . . ."

"And that's the only reason she wants him to move here?" Fisby asked, and smiled as the color crept into her cheeks.

"Yes, boss," Sakini said, then whispered confidentially: "But I think maybe she's fibbing a little bit."

Fisby thought so, too, but refrained from mentioning it. "Well, does she think he'll move here?"

"She don't know; but just before the Americans come and all the people are hurrying to get out of Naha, because they know the Japanese are going to defend it and there will be a big battle there, he comes up to her in the crowd for a minute. 'First Flower,' he whispers, 'if ever you need me, send the half-opened bud of a chrysanthemum and I will come.' "

"Why the half-opened bud of a chrysanthemum?" Fisby asked.

"Because Seiko say he always thinks of her heart as a flower, and the bud will tell him that her heart is opening, maybe not all the way, but maybe half the way for him."

Fisby smiled. "Is she going to send a bud?"

"She don't think so, boss. Maybe if she had one, she would. But she don't have time to bother looking around." Her dark eyes flashed. "She say a guy who makes a fool of himself chasing girls don't deserve nothing."

It was evident to Fisby that Seiko had made a tactical error in walking out on the most famous geisha girl in all Naha. She wouldn't stand for that business. "But what is she going to tell him to get him to move here?"

"She's just going to send a message that there's a tea-house here, and he might as well loaf around in it all day, like he always did. And she's going to say Lotus Blossom is here. And he can talk with her, and——"

"Sakini," Fisby said quickly. "I think she's being a little hasty."

"She don't think so, boss."

"Well, look," Fisby said slowly. "If I find a half-opened bud of a chrysanthemum, will she send it?"

First Flower considered. "But, boss, there aren't any chrysanthemums around here. She look all over, and . . ." She seemed to catch herself. "That is, if you find one, boss, she might. She'll think about it."

So she had looked. Fisby hid his smile, then frowned. If she couldn't find a bud, how could he? Yet they really should have one. A man couldn't let a thing like this go on. Seiko should be here.

As he sat thinking, First Flower bowed. "She asks to be excused, boss. She has to get those guys back to work on the *cha ya*."

"All right," Fisby said. "Tell her I'll do my best to find the bud, but she shouldn't count on it."

First Flower smiled. "She knows it can't be found here, and she don't want you to worry about it. She'll just send a message."

Yet Fisby was worried. "Sakini, I'll try, yet if I don't have any luck is there anything else I can get in its place?"

First Flower hesitated. "No, there's nothing to get in its

place. But she says it might be nice if you could get some tea for the *cha ya,* boss."

"Tea?"

"She hates to ask you because you do so many things already. You give us permission to build the *cha ya,* and you get the reeds, and she hears how you show the guys how to make looms to weave mats for the floor. But she don't know if the tea in those hidden Japanese rations is going to be good or not. Maybe it was wet in the caves, and it all spoiled." She smiled and shook her head. "Boss, she say don't bother with it, because we can always make tea from the wild wheat that grows in the hills."

"Does that make good tea?"

Sakini glanced quickly at First Flower, and she whispered to him. "Oh, yes, boss. It's all right."

Yet Fisby knew that it wasn't. He felt that it was a tea used only when there was nothing else. Quickly, he straightened. "Sakini, you tell her Fisby never served bum coffee in his drugstore. Now he's not going to start serving bum tea in his *cha ya."*

The look of thanks in her eyes made Fisby beam. "Oh, yes," he went on, "and be sure to tell her to come back again for *kobiru* sometime."

Thirteen

WHEN FIRST FLOWER left headquarters, Fisby sank in the swivel chair to think over the situation. Perhaps he was rash in promising to supply tea for the *cha ya,* especially when he could think of no source of supply. Yet his jaw was set firmly, and he was determined to get it.

Glancing out the window, he could see the horse carts piled high with lumber, rolling in from big Koza. Apparently Lotus Blossom was successful with her swapping. He smiled, glad to be rid of the lumber problem.

At that moment, Hokkaido entered headquarters, and Fisby regarded him carefully. Though barefooted, Hokkaido was decked out in a new suit of target cloth, and Fisby nodded in approval. "Tell him he looks fine, Sakini," he said, then hesitated. Offhand, with Hokkaido's comfortable waistline perhaps a double-breasted model would be better, still—

However, Hokkaido wasn't interested in clothing just then. He was spouting excitedly in the Luchuan dialect, the tears began streaming down his cheeks, and Sakini turned solemnly. "Boss," Sakini said, "Hokkaido claims we have to do something about that police chief. Do you know what he do now?"

Fisby didn't have the remotest notion.

"Well, all the way over from big Koza, he sits beside Lotus Blossom on the horse cart loaded with lumber. Hokkaido says he's not supposed to do that, because when they tear down his house to start the *cha ya* one of the promises they make him is that the police chief can't sit beside Lotus Blossom."

Fisby nodded. "Yes, but that was only at geisha parties."

"But, boss, Hokkaido claim whenever you talk with a geisha girl, that's a geisha party."

Fisby had no desire of becoming involved in technicalities. "Now look," he said firmly, "I'm getting a little tired of these two trying to beat each other's time. He's the agriculture foreman. He should be out growing things."

"Growing things?" Sakini questioned.

"Sure. Chinese cabbage, and eggplant, and things like that. Does he think we're only going to eat sweet potatoes when we get the *cha ya* built? Why how is he going to know when spring is here if he doesn't see green peas on his plate?"

Hokkaido was a little confused. "He thinks he can tell, boss, if he just looks outside."

"I didn't mean it that way," Fisby said quickly. "You tell him to get out there and plant some stuff."

"Okay, boss. But he thinks it's going to be pretty hard."

"Why?"

"Well, he don't have any seeds."

"Oh." Fisby felt a little foolish.

"Now, boss, about the police chief—"

Fisby stood up. "You tell them to settle their own love affairs. I'm going to take a walk. I want to do some thinking."

As Fisby put on his helmet-liner, Miss Higa Jiga came trooping into headquarters. "Boss," Sakini said, "a little while ago she peek in the side door and see you talking with First Flower. She wants to know if you ask First Flower to build a *cha no yu* house for her?"

"I forgot about it," Fisby said, then added: "But don't tell her that. Just say I haven't gotten around to it yet."

"Okay, boss. But she wants to know if you mention to First Flower about teaching the Women's League the tea drinking ceremony and flower arranging?"

"Just tell her I'll get around to it. I'm busy right now." Quickly, he headed for the door. And as he walked through the village, he kept thinking over the tea problem. He remembered Sakini mentioning that First Flower always drank the best tea from China and the *ginseng* tea from Korea. China and Korea were out of the question now, of course. And apparently not much tea was grown here on Okinawa, else the people would drink it instead of substituting a tea made of wild wheat.

Suddenly he began smiling. From his Battery Commander days, he remembered a place where there was always a surplus of tea; remembered a place where if you served it any way but iced, they'd gripe. He would have to find the army messes, look up the mess sergeants.

As he rounded a corner, Doc McLean caught up with him. "Well, well, there you are, Captain. Did you finish your slingshot?"

"Slingshot?"

"Sure. Remember you were looking for inner tubes yesterday?"

"Yes, I found them, Doc. But I wasn't making a slingshot. I needed them to act as springs in the looms. By golly, they sure did the job. You should see those slats snap back."

The Doc seemed a little disappointed. "Well, what are you doing this morning?"

"A couple of things, Doc. First, I'd like to find the half-opened bud of a chrysanthemum."

A new interest crept into the Doc's face. "What do you want it for, Captain?"

"Well, we have to send for Seiko, and that's the signal."

"You mean like kids use when they're playing pirate?"

"Not exactly, Doc. This is a lover's signal."

"Between you and this Seiko woman?"

"Oh, no. Seiko's a man. This is between First Flower and Seiko. I'm just helping out a little."

Doc McLean was definitely disappointed.

"Is something the matter?" Fisby asked.

The Doc shrugged. "Well, for a moment there, I thought I had the beginning of a beautiful case history for the

Medical Journal, but—" He regarded Fisby sharply. "You sure the chrysanthemum bud isn't for yourself?"

Fisby was indignant. "Positive, Doc. Did you think I blew my top or something?"

"Well, Captain, there are certain indications."

"I'm all right," Fisby said quickly in self-defense.

Yet the Doc wore a skeptical, that's-what-they-all-say look, and Fisby decided to change the subject. "Doc," he went on, "do you know where I can get some vegetable seed?"

Doc McLean considered. "Back home, Captain, I always used to order mine through the seed companies. During the winter they'd send a catalogue, and I'd make my selection. Why?"

"In the first place," Fisby said, "we're building a *cha ya.*" Then he went on to tell about the kitchen, and Mrs. Kamakura, who used to cook at the Golden Dragon; about how First Flower liked to see the springtime, and the summer, and the autumn on the dishes before her. And the more he talked, the more engrossed Doc McLean became.

Finally, the Doc shook his head. "Captain, do you know what I always wanted to do?"

"What, Doc?"

"I always wanted to own a little farm. Yes, sir, someday when I retire from practice, I want to get away from the city. Maybe get a place up in Connecticut." The Doc's eyes had a remote look. "Not just an ordinary farm, you understand, but sort of a specialized farm."

"Specialized farm?" Fisby was puzzled.

"Sure, Captain. I thought I'd raise specialties for the restaurants. You know, globe artichokes, partridge, and squab. Maybe smoke my own turkeys and pheasants. Things like that."

To Fisby it seemed as if that was exactly what they needed around Tobiki village—a specialized farm, a teahouse farm that could supply food to Mrs. Kamakura in the kitchen. "Well, Doc," he said, "I don't know about pheasant and partridge. But do you know how to raise vegetables?"

The Doc chuckled. "Don't think I'm bragging, Captain, but everyone in our neighborhood at home says they never tasted greens like I raise in the backyard. Of course, the plot is small, yet I always manage to keep abreast of the latest developments in agriculture."

"Is that a fact?" Fisby was duly impressed. "Doc, I'd

like to start a restaurant supply place, like you mentioned, around here. Would you give me a hand?"

"It would be a pleasure, Fisby," the Doc said. His face grew intent, and he rubbed his forehead thoughtfully. "Now the first thing I need is a good piece of land."

Fisby indicated the fields surrounding the village. "You pick something out, Doc. I don't know anything about it."

"All right. Then I think I'll enclose the whole thing with a white fence. That sets it off, you know. Do you have any lumber for fencing?"

"We swapped with big Koza, Doc. I think there's some. Anyway, we can always swap more salt."

"Good." The Doc considered. "Next, I'll need some chicken coops. By the way, do you have any chickens, Fisby?"

"There's some Bantams in the village. Perhaps I can get you a few."

"Fine. I'll rig up my own incubators. I want a good-sized flock of chickens."

"What about goats?" Fisby asked helpfully. "I can get you plenty."

"Thanks, Fisby, but I was never much interested in goats. However, can you get me a good farm superintendent?"

"I'll talk with Hokkaido," Fisby promised, "maybe he has someone in his department." Then a thought struck him, and he said quickly, "Doc, you know we aren't going to sell any of this stuff to the *cha ya*. The economic system is shot completely. No one has money. This will all have to be for free."

The Doc nodded absently; he was engrossed in deeper problems. "Fisby, could you get me a horse? I'll have to ride over the farm, you know. A man needs a good horse to get around."

Fisby supposed he could get a cart horse for the Doc's private use. "But will you have time to do all this?" he asked. "I mean with your study and all."

"What study?"

"Your ethnological study."

"Oh. It slipped my mind for the moment. I have permission to remain as long as necessary, Fisby. The fighting's all finished on the island. There's nothing going on, so Colonel Purdy said . . . that is, he said I should just make a thorough investigation. I think I can sandwich this in all right." The Doc rubbed his hands. "Now we'll need some good seed. Burpee's is a reliable house, also Ferry, and—"

"You mean you're going to send back to the States for seed?"

"Certainly. A man's foolish not to get the best. And we'll need a soil testing outfit." The Doc held up a warning finger. "Always test your soil, Fisby. That's the first rule."

"But how are you going to get seed?" Fisby asked.

"Why I'll just send in an order," the Doc replied matter-of-factly. "Nothing to it. I know the approximate prices and varieties available—used to study the catalogues all during the winter. Now if I can borrow some paper and a pen—"

They retired to headquarters, and the Doc took over Fisby's desk. "Let's see, we'll start with asparagus—Martha Washington variety." As the Doc wrote, Fisby, leaning over his shoulder, watched. The Doc took the vegetables in alphabetical order, and Fisby nodded in approval—even though he had never heard of such things as celeriac, celtuce, and salsify.

At length the Doc looked up. "There we are, Fisby. That covers it."

But Fisby wasn't sure. "Have you got chrysanthemum seed down, Doc?" He wanted to be prepared for any future emergencies.

"Why, no, Fisby. I hadn't listed flowers. Do you want some?"

"You better get a few packs," Fisby advised. "I think the Women's League is going to take up flower arranging as a pastime. I might as well get ready."

Industriously, Doc McLean bent over the paper.

When he had finished, he quickly totaled the sum, then brought out his billfold. "Fisby, if you'll run me over to the post office, I'll get a money order for this invasion yen. I want to get the order out right away."

"Oh, no, Doc." Fisby held up a protesting hand. "I'm paying for this."

It developed into quite an argument. The Doc stating since it was his project, he should be allowed to pay. While Fisby insisted as village commander it was his duty. Finally, they flipped a dog tag, and Fisby won the honor. "But the next order is on me," the Doc made him promise.

After Corporal Barton returned from hauling reeds, they set out in the jeep. Their first stop was at the post office, then Fisby decided to investigate the tea situation, and pulled up at the mess tent of an ack-ack battery.

"I'd like to help you out, Captain," the mess sergeant, a veteran at the game, told Fisby respectfully, if not sincerely. "But you know how it is. The Quartermaster issues these things for the troops, and I can't give them away."

"But, Sergeant," Fisby protested, "you know as well as I do that you always have more tea than you can use. I commanded a battery for two years, I know."

The mess sergeant was sorry, but the troops were drinking a lot of tea now. Besides, there was a regulation governing the use of government rations. Why, the mess sergeant knew of a first cook back in the States who was court-martialed for taking home steaks.

Fisby knew that he wasn't getting anywhere. He took off his helmet-liner and mopped his forehead. The he remembered the *geta*, the wooden sandals he had put carpenters to work on making for the Women's League. "Sergeant," he began, "have you picked up any souvenirs yet?"

"Are you kidding, Captain? We got gun crews spread out all over the place. I have to run twenty-four trips a day out of here just to keep them fed. When would I have time to pick up souvenirs?"

The situation was exactly as Fisby suspected. "Well, I happen to have a few souvenirs on hand. Native wooden sandals." Fisby thought a moment. "Now we have the miniature size for children." Fisby crossed his fingers, hoping the carpenters could make them. "And we have the woman's size—"

The sergeant's eyes flickered shrewdly. "What are you asking for them, Captain?"

Fisby considered with the deliberateness of one who was in the proverbial driver's seat. Their eyes met. "Tea."

It was a perfect understanding. "But I wouldn't want you to get in any trouble because of government regulations," Fisby said in a face-saving gesture.

The sergeant thought it would be all right with the Quartermaster, being as how the day before he had scrounged two halves of beef and four hundred pounds of coffee from the Navy. "That will sort of make up to the government for the tea," he said by way of explanation.

Fisby fell in with the logic. "And I'll be around tomorrow with the souvenirs; I'll pick up the tea then," he said, knowing full well the sergeant wouldn't trust him with it. "Incidentally, Sergeant, what Battery is this?" It was A Battery, and Fisby went on, "Well, could you tell me where the other batteries of the battalion are located? Maybe their mess sergeants would like to do some swapping, too."

Unfortunately, the sergeant didn't know where they were located. But if the Captain had quite a supply of these souvenirs on hand, he thought he might be able to dig up a considerable amount of tea—one of the Quartermaster sergeants being a buddy of his, seeing as how they had soldiered together in Texas.

Fisby nodded, satisfied with the arrangement. It would save him chasing all over the island looking for mess halls. The excess tea of the other batteries and of the Quartermaster would be channeled in here. And A Battery, with an ample amount of souvenirs to swap, would do some fancy eating.

"You know, Doc," Fisby said, climbing back into the jeep, "you have to give these mess sergeants credit. They have more ways of getting their men fed than the government ever dreamed of." And he couldn't help but shake his head in honest admiration.

Fourteen

EARLY NEXT MORNING Fisby delivered the wooden sandals and collected a jeep load of tea from the mess sergeant. Returning to the village, he bumped along the cart trail outside little Koza; then spying two horsemen approaching, edged over, making room for them to pass. However, when one of the horsemen waved to him, he peered closer, then waved back.

Doc McLean was galloping toward him on a rawboned, dun cart horse, at least three sizes too large for him. The Doc had improvised a riding crop out of bamboo. He had dug up a pair of kid gloves somewhere. And he sat his saddle like an old colonel of cavalry riding out for morning inspection of the troops.

Reaching the jeep, Doc pulled up. "Whoa, *Uma.*" He patted the horse's neck, as if fully expecting it to dance nervously. But his expectations weren't realized. The horse sagged to a stop, dropped its head, and cocked a hind foot, resting. The Doc turned to Fisby. *"Uma's* a little skittish this morning. That's his name—*Uma*. It means 'horse' in Japanese."

"It does? Well what do you know," Fisby said. "How are you this morning, Doc?"

The Doc shook his head, his forehead wrinkled. "Busy, Fisby. Mighty busy. Sakini rounded up a permanent farm crew for me, like you told him, and I have them out building fences. But do you know how they plow around here?"

Fisby had only a hazy idea.

"Well, they use those iron hoes to break up the ground," the Doc explained. "It's like working up your garden back home with a pick. Imagine working a whole farm with a pick!"

"It would be slow," Fisby admitted.

"Too slow. Holy hell, Fisby, I have to get some plows."

"But where are you going to get plows?" Fisby asked.

"Why I'll just make them. I hear they have a good blacksmith over in Maebaru. He even makes his own forges. Now I figure if we set up a good-sized forge, he ought to be able to turn out plowshares for us."

Fisby was hesitant. "Doc, are you planning on moving him over to our place?"

"Why, certainly."

"Well, Doc, I think the village commander of Maebaru might get a little sore if you walk off with a skilled worker like that. I'd be careful."

"It's all right, Fisby," the Doc assured him. "I reconnoitered the situation, and this morning the Maebaru village commander is looking around Takaesu for carpenters. I figure we can slip in and slip out in no time. We need a good blacksmith to make those plows."

Fisby had to admit they needed a good blacksmith. "But where are you going to get the material for plows, Doc?"

That didn't stump the Doc for a moment. "If I can borrow your jeep afterwhile, I'll run up to the Engineer salvage dump. They should have some banged-up equipment that I can get a few sheets of metal from."

"You better take a few pairs of those wooden sandals for swapping purposes," Fisby suggested.

The Doc nodded. "Now, Fisby, the way I have it figured, we ought to be able to train those cart horses to pull the plows. And, of course, we can always use the jeep, there, to help out. Yes, sir, Fisby, I'd sure like to get my fall plowing done this month yet. I can still get a good-sized crop harvested before winter." He regarded Fisby intently.

"Say, can I have some of that fish we're catching. The ration chief tells me we have a surplus."

"Sure. But what do you want it for?"

"I have to swap it for water chestnuts."

"Water chestnuts?" Fisby questioned.

"That's right. Sakini and I had a talk with Mrs. Kamakura, the cook, this morning. Did you know her mother was a Chinese girl from Amoy?"

Fisby didn't have the slightest idea.

"Well, she was. And her mother left her a number of excellent Chinese recipes. You know . . . egg roll, sweet and sour duck, and things like that. And I'll teach her how to make chop suey. Yes, sir, Fisby, I always liked Chinese cooking. If we work it into the menu down at the *cha ya,* it should be a nice change."

"Oh, so you need water chestnuts for the Chinese dishes?"

"Right, Fisby. I intend to grow my own, but it will take time. So we'll just have to swap with the northern villages at present. However, Mrs. Kamakura feels that we ought to be able to raise the majority of things we need right in the village. You know, bamboo shoots, mushrooms, Chinese broccoli, and peas—the ones with the edible pod. By the way, Fisby, didn't you tell me you owned a pharmacy back in the States?"

"That's right, Doc. Why?"

"Do you think you could have some monosodium glutamate sent out?"

"I guess so."

"Good. That's the Chinese seasoning powder." The Doc raised a finger in reminder. "And this buy is on me."

"If you say so," Fisby agreed.

"Incidentally," the Doc went on, "do you know my farm manager Kamato, over there?" He pointed to the native boy astride the horse a few paces away.

Fisby knew Kamato, all right. He was one of Hokkaido's assistant agriculture foremen.

"He's a fine boy," the Doc said. "Doesn't speak much English, but he sure knows his bean sprouts." The boy beamed, proud of his new promotion to farm manager.

"Well, Fisby," the Doc continued, "I have to be going. Got a busy morning ahead. After I get the blacksmith, I have to get back to Tobiki and examine the food handlers. Then I have to give the kitchen a sanitary inspection."

"Sure, go right ahead, Doc. Don't let me keep you," Fisby said.

The Doc drew on his gloves, pulled up the reins, and looked at his farm manager. "Kamato. *Ikimasho!*" He turned to Fisby. "*Ikimasho* . . . that means 'Let's go' in Japanese."

"Hokay!" the boy called. And as Fisby watched, they went galloping up the cart trail toward little Koza, the Doc jauntily swinging his riding crop.

When Fisby reached the village, he sent the American tea down to Mrs. Kamakura, the cook, at the kitchen of the *cha ya;* then decided to walk down there himself to see how things were coming along. Before reaching it, however, he found a group of men building something else, something the likes of which he had never seen before. It was a raised platform of straw and earthen bales, about a foot off the ground, and about eighteen feet square. In the center of the platform a perfect circle was marked out. At each corner was an upright pole, supporting a canopylike affair.

"Sakini, what's that thing?" Fisby asked.

"That's a *sumo* wrestling place, boss."

"How come you're building that?"

"Well, yesterday, boss, you tell Hokkaido and the police chief to settle their troubles over Lotus Blossom between themselves. So Hokkaido challenge the police chief to a wrestling match tonight. Hokkaido says he's going to fix him."

It reminded Fisby of a couple of fellows going off to settle an argument by putting the gloves on. Something else caught his attention. They had taken strips of target cloth, dyed them, and were now fastening them around the upright poles. Fisby smiled. "So you're even decorating the goal posts, eh, Sakini?"

Sakini scratched his head. "Don't understand, boss."

"I was talking about the cloth they're winding around the poles there."

"Oh, we have to do that," Sakini said solemnly. "See the pole with the black cloth is to remind us of winter. The green reminds us of spring. The red, summer. And the white, autumn. And see that purple cloth around the edge of the roof, boss, that runs from pole to pole. Do you know what that reminds us of?"

"What?"

"The drifting clouds overhead. We start hanging the

cloth at the winter post, then we run it to spring, and summer, and autumn. That reminds us of how the seasons go round."

"I see. You like the seasons, and the outdoors, don't you, Sakini?"

"Sure, boss. If the seasons aren't any good, the sweet potatoes don't grow. Then, by gosh, we get pretty hungry."

For a while Fisby stood watching the men pound the earthen ring to harden it, watched as they spread a thin layer of sand over it for traction. Then he remembered something. "Sakini, what time do you stop work for your morning snack. What is it called—oh, yes, *kobiru*."

Sakini glanced at the sky and pointed. "When the sun's about up there, boss."

Fisby reckoned that the sun would be "up there" in about fifteen minutes. "Do you think First Flower is coming up to headquarters this morning?"

"I don't know, boss."

"Well, you better run over and invite her. I'll go up and put the coffee on."

Fisby made careful preparations. He washed the canteen cups twice and dusted the swivel chair with his handkerchief. After due consideration, he decided that C ration biscuits were not quite the thing to serve, so he opened a couple of K rations. Taking the crackers, he cut them in half, spread them with chopped-ham mix—added a few with eggs and shredded ham for variety—and carefully arranged the whole on a couple sheets of typing paper.

His preparations were careful, yet he was taken by surprise. This morning First Flower brought Lotus Blossom with her. "Well, well," Fisby said, rubbing his hands and smiling. "Come right in." Then quickly looked around headquarters, for he was short a chair. "Sakini," he whispered, "get off that bench and let Lotus Blossom sit down."

Scratching his head, Sakini arose. Fisby indicated that the bench was for Lotus Blossom, and saw her eyes widen. Puzzled, she looked to First Flower.

"Is something the matter?" Fisby asked.

"Boss," Sakini said, "they want to know if guys in America always give their chairs to girls like that?"

"They're supposed to. Don't they do it over here?"

"I never see anyone do it." Sakini shook his head. "First Flower, either. But she and Lotus Blossom say they think it's pretty nice. They'll have to have the guys around here practice that."

Fisby hoped he hadn't started something that would cause a kickback, and was flustered. "Well—" Quickly, he passed the coffee and K ration crackers with the ham spread. "By the way, Sakini," he said, attempting to change the subject. "How are things coming at the *cha ya?*"

"Boss, they say they don't want to tell you."

Taken aback, Fisby glanced at the smiling girls and saw the mischief playing in their eyes. He grinned. "They don't? Why not?"

"They can't tell you, boss. But tomorrow morning for *kobiru* they want you to come down there."

"All right." Fisby sipped his coffee.

"But you got to promise 'em something, boss."

"What?"

"You got to promise 'em that all day today you won't walk down there either. You can't go down there until tomorrow morning."

Fisby promised. Still he wanted to ask a question. "Did that fellow from Kishaba, who was to make the dishes, move to the village yet?"

"You mean Kiei, boss? He come yesterday. First Flower say this morning he find some good clay. And he's building some of those things to burn it in."

"Kilns?"

"I guess so. Only Kiei say it's a pretty hard job to make all those dishes by himself. He have to get some guys and kids to help him. They don't know much about it, but he thinks, after a while, he can teach them pretty good."

"Fine." Fisby glanced at First Flower. "And what about Seiko, who was to paint them? Has he arrived yet?"

At the mention of Seiko, First Flower flushed; and Lotus Blossom giggled. "First Flower hears he will arrive this afternoon, boss." Fisby saw her eyes drop.

Lotus Blossom glanced sideways, then tilted her head. "Boss, do you know what Lotus Blossom hear?"

First Flower whispered quickly, as if trying to quiet her, but Lotus Blossom's eyes were twinkling.

"What?" Fisby asked.

"She hears that Seiko even got a haircut."

The color spread up into First Flower's cheeks, and she seemed to be scolding Lotus Blossom.

"What does that mean?" Fisby inquired.

"Well, Lotus Blossom say she remembers when the Japanese police tell all the guys that they have to clip their hair short because those were the orders from Tokyo. Then

105

Seiko say nobody was going to tell him what to do, so he let his hair grow long. He say he's not going to cut it for anybody, no matter how bad it looks. But now he do it. And Lotus Blossom thinks she knows why, even though she wouldn't want to say anything."

First Flower was definitely flustered and glanced meaningly at Lotus Blossom, who giggled. Then First Flower drew herself up, in an effort to regain composure, and regarded Fisby. "Boss, she wants to know if they can build something else in the village?"

"What?"

"Well, down in Naha in the morning all the geisha girls use to meet at the public bath. She claim it was pretty nice to soak in the hot water. They use to sit there all morning and talk about different things. Now she wants to know if she and Lotus Blossom can build a bathhouse here?"

It was all right with Fisby. "But I don't know where they are going to get bath tubs," he said.

First Flower nodded solemnly. "She knows it's going to be pretty hard, but they try."

Fisby considered the problem, then snapped his fingers. "Say, Sakini, I read somewhere that the Swedes, or Norwegians, or someone used to heat stones in their baths."

"Stones?" Sakini questioned, and the girls were puzzled.

"Sure. They heat these stones, then sprinkle water on them. That gives plenty of steam. Then over on one side they have a bleacherlike affair, and you move up and down on the bleachers, depending on how much steam you want."

Sakini scratched his head. "Don't understand, boss."

Fisby attempted to explain, and while Sakini caught the general drift of the idea, still Fisby knew it was vague in his mind. "Tell you what I'll do," Fisby said. "If the girls want me to, I'll lay it out for them. All they need do is tell me where they want it."

The girls, impelled by curiosity perhaps, evinced a great interest in this new-type bathhouse. And Fisby, moved by their interest, promised that not only would it be first class, but the greatest thing ever devised on Okinawa. At that moment he heard a hoarse stage whisper that carried all through headquarters. *"Cha no yu,"* came the whisper, and he looked up in surprise.

But First Flower and Lotus Blossom were perfectly quiet. Fisby glanced at Sakini. But Sakini was helping himself to the K ration crackers. Puzzled, Fisby looked around. He spied the head then, peeking in the side door. Leaning over, he saw Miss Higa Jiga gesturing excitedly. *"Cha no yu,"* she whispered again, lifted her hand as if drinking tea, and pointed to First Flower and Lotus Blossom.

"Oh yes." Fisby forced a smile. "Sakini, would you tell the girls we have quite a problem here in the village. Now some of the ladies would like to take up tea drinking as a pastime, and we need some *cha no yu* houses."

When Sakini translated, Fisby saw First Flower and Lotus Blossom frown. Still he went on: "No one in the village knows how to build those things, and I was wondering . . ."

"Boss," Sakini interrupted, "they want to know if the *cha no yu* is for Miss Higa Jiga?"

"That's right. Why?"

"Well, they're pretty sore at Miss Higa Jiga and the Women's League right now."

"Oh." Fisby's eyebrows shot up in surprise. "Did Hiyoshi break loose again and get in their room?"

"No, boss, but they say Miss Higa Jiga and the Women's League for Democratic Action are all the time blocking off the streams to wash their feet. They keep the water from running down into the lotus pond. First Flower and Lotus Blossom don't like it."

"Well, I'm sure the ladies mean no harm," Fisby said. "But I was wondering, perhaps, if the girls would tell the carpenters how to build those little teahouses."

The girls discussed the situation, their inflection, tone, and speed in which they tossed the Luchuan dialect around told Fisby that they weren't happy about it. "Well, boss, they don't know. That Miss Higa Jiga gets 'em pretty sore sometimes."

Fisby was a little disappointed, and, no doubt, his disappointment was evident to the girls. They glanced at each other quickly, and First Flower spoke to Sakini. "Boss, she wants to know if you really want 'em to build the *cha no yu* houses?"

Fisby hesitated. "I would appreciate it."

The girls didn't even discuss the matter. Both bowed. "If you want 'em to, they'll do it," Sakini said. "But, boss, they want to know if you'll make the ladies stop washing their feet in the streams?"

"If they don't stop, we won't build the teahouses for them. By the way, is it much of a job?"

"Oh no, boss. The houses are real small. No windows or nothing in 'em. Easy to build. The hard part is the garden."

"Do you have to have a garden?"

"Sure, boss. It has to be fixed real pretty. It has to be just right so when you sit in it, you forget all about everything except how nice the earth, and trees, and everything are. But they fix it good."

Fisby held his breath. "Now some of the other ladies mentioned—"

"Do you want the girls to build *cha no yus* for them, too?"

"I hate to bother them, but it would be nice."

The girls bowed deeply. "Boss, they say they suppose they'll have to teach the Women's League the tea drinking ceremony and all that, because they think those ladies don't know nothing about anything."

"And could they throw in flower arranging?"

"They think so, boss, but that's going to be an awful job."

Fisby glanced at the grinning Miss Higa Jiga, peeking in the side door, and his face grew stern. "Sakini, tell them I'll make certain that the Women's League stops blocking the streams."

Though the girls bowed, Fisby noted that they hardly seemed to hear him. Something caught their eye and Fisby, following their glances, saw they were regarding the magazines piled over in the corner. "Sakini," he said, "would they like some of them?"

They were hesitant. "They don't like to ask, boss, but . . ."

Fisby went over and picked up an armful. "Here. They can take these along. If they want more, they should just come back. Even if they can't read English, they might like the pictures."

"They would like to look at them, boss."

Fisby watched as they sat there, their heads bowed as they turned the pages. Now and then they would show each other a picture and discuss it at machine-gun speed. Sometimes, they would gasp in awe.

"Sakini," Fisby said, "you know, they might even pick up some good ideas there. For instance—"

Just then a picture caught First Flower's interest, and

she tugged Sakini's sleeve. "Boss, she wants to know why this guy is choking this lady."

Fisby glanced at the illustration, done in a brilliant red and yellow. "Well, that's a murder mystery." He stood up quickly and went to the corner. "Maybe she ought to take some of these others."

Lotus Blossom had a question then. "Boss, she asks how can this guy fly through the air? He don't even have any wings." Sakini scratched his head. "And, boss, on that other magazine over there . . . why are all those cows chasing that guy on the horse?"

Fisby wiped his forehead. "Sakini, those are going to be too heavy for the girls to carry. Why don't they just leave them here. I'll send them over to their quarters later. Anyway, I'd like to look them over first."

When they had gone, Fisby began sorting over the magazines. But not before he gave Miss Higa Jiga and the Women's League a stern little lecture about washing their feet in the drainage ditches.

Fifteen

IT WASN'T UNTIL EVENING that Fisby learned he was expected at the *sumo* wrestling match between Hokkaido and the police chief. Sitting on the stoop of his quarters after supper, he watched as Sakini came trotting up the hill. "Boss," Sakini said, "everybody's waiting for you so we can start the wrestling match. You're supposed to be chief honorary inspector."

"I am? What is that?" Fisby asked.

"Well, boss, after the bout, suppose the inspectors talk it over. Suppose they can't decide who wins. Then you have to tell 'em."

Fisby paled. He wanted no part of this. "But I don't know anything about *sumo*," he protested.

"It's easy, boss," Sakini assured him. "Come on. I tell you all about it."

Still Fisby hesitated. Never having seen a *sumo* match, he feared making a bad decision if called upon, and did not want to be accused of partiality.

"But everybody's waiting," Sakini went on quickly. "We can't start until you get there."

Reluctantly, Fisby rose from the stoop. Over to one side of quarters, Doc McLean was seated before an improvised drawing board. The Doc had obtained a box of crayons from somewhere, and now he was working painstakingly over a multicolored chart, his tongue protruding between his lips.

"Sakini," Fisby whispered, "can the Doc be an honorary inspector, too?"

"Sure, boss. We make him assistant chief."

"Good. Hey, Doc," Fisby called, "let's go down to the wrestling matches."

The Doc waved a red crayon in negation. "I'd like to, Fisby, but I'm laying out the lower farm right now. And I'm just marking in my asparagus beds."

"But you're assistant chief honorary inspector," Fisby said.

"That's right, Mr. Doctor." Sakini nodded. "Didn't you know?"

"Besides," Fisby continued, "I'm not going to walk into this thing alone. Come on, Doc."

It took quite some persuasion before the Doc would put away his crayons; but, shrugging regretfully, he finally agreed. And they walked downhill into the village. At first glance, it seemed to Fisby as if the entire male population had turned out. They sat forty deep on the ground surrounding the raised platform. And right away he was called upon to make a decision.

Over to the right of the ring, an argument was going on. It was really a one-sided affair for Miss Higa Jiga, backed by the Women's League, was shaking an angry finger in the face of the cowering mayor. Seeing Fisby, the Women's League, en masse, gestured excitedly. "Boss," Sakini explained, "they want you to come over."

Fisby was deep in the crowd now, and it was too late to turn back. For a moment he looked to the Doc for moral support, then walked forward.

The League clustered around him, their dark eyes flashing, and Miss Higa Jiga sputtered excitedly. "Boss, she say the mayor is trying to kick them out of their seats."

Fisby regarded the mayor. "Is that true?"

Apparently relieved by Fisby's presence and the fact that Fisby was standing between him and Miss Higa Jiga, the mayor took on courage. "Boss, he say he and the village officials are supposed to sit in the front row. But these ladies just keep coming in and pushing 'em back so far, now they can't even see."

"Well, it seems to me," Fisby said thoughtfully, "the first ones here should get the front seats."

Sakini regarded him. "Boss, Miss Higa Jiga say they were the first ones here. Miss Susano come down real early, and she just save seats for everybody in the League."

"Oh." Fisby was stymied. But behind him, the mayor was getting braver. "Boss, he say they're not supposed to be here anyway. Ladies should stay home and weave, and sew, and wash clothes—not run around all over the place."

Fisby thought this was a rather tactless thing to say to a girl who was as sturdy as Miss Higa Jiga. She was edging toward the mayor now, blood in her eye. "Well," he said quickly, "I can't see any objection to some of the ladies of the village coming down to the wrestling matches."

The Women's League nodded happily, and Miss Higa Jiga made a face at the mayor.

"On the other hand," Fisby continued, "the ladies should act like the ladies they really are. They shouldn't try to take all the seats, just because one of them got here early."

Nostrils quivered, lips dropped, and there was a hint of tears in the Women's League. "Miss Higa Jiga say they didn't know that," Sakini explained, "because they never go to the wrestling matches before."

"Well it's all right this time," Fisby said benevolently. "They're excused. But I think we ought to let the village officials sit in the front row."

Apparently the Women's League thought so, too, for they opened a path. "All right, gentlemen," Fisby said, "this way." Then mopped his brow. "Sakini, where are our seats? Let's get out of here."

Their seats were on the other side of the ring. And as Fisby walked through the beaming crowd of men, they patted his shoulder, for hadn't he stood up to Miss Higa Jiga without flinching? When he, and the Doc, and Sakini reached the three homemade benches reserved for the honorary inspectors, the crowd began whistling.

"They call for Hokkaido and the police chief," Sakini explained.

But Fisby, a little nervous over the task ahead, was more interested in something else. "Where are the regular inspectors? The guys who are supposed to decide who wins, Sakini?"

Sakini pointed to one side of the ring. "Those six guys there in the kimonos, boss."

Fisby felt a little better. With six on hand they ought to be able to arrive at a decision without calling on him.

"And there's the referee," Sakini indicated another kimono-clad figure. "The guy with his face behind the fan."

"Oh, you have a referee, too?" Fisby relaxed. He was beginning to enjoy this. Leaning over, he asked: "How are you betting, Doc?"

"Wait till I see them, Fisby," the Doc said.

Hokkaido came in first, greeted by a nice round of applause. Yet Fisby noted that this was far from a partisan crowd. Hokkaido had discarded his white coat, that marked him as President of the Men's League, this evening. Tonight he wore a black loincloth, and the Doc shook his head.

"He looks flabby to me, Fisby. Look at that roll of fat around the midsection."

Fisby had to agree that Hokkaido was on the flabby side. But then the police chief, in a blue loincloth, came walking toward the ring, and Fisby turned. "Hokkaido's got the weight advantage though, Doc. I bet he outweighs the chief by forty pounds."

The Doc shrugged. "Maybe so. But the chief's wiry. He's got speed. Look at those legs."

The only outstanding features about the chief's legs, as far as Fisby could see, were that they were skinny and bowed. "The chief doesn't have a chance, Doc."

"No!" The Doc regarded Fisby. "How many of these Occupation yen make up a buck? I keep forgetting."

"Fifteen."

"All right, I have thirty yen that says the chief takes him."

"It's a bet—" Fisby started to say, then drew himself up, a picture of dignity. "Doc, you forget we're honorary inspectors. We have to be impartial."

Fisby had his first opportunity to be impartial in a moment. The police chief slipped along beside the platform and stood before them, gesturing excitedly. "Boss," Sakini said. "He wants to protest."

"About what?"

"About the inspectors over there. He says four of the six are from the agriculture department. And he knows they'll claim Hokkaido wins, even if he loses, because Hokkaido is agriculture chief."

"What does he want me to do?" Fisby asked.

"Well, boss, he thinks it would be pretty nice if you kick out a couple of guys from the agriculture department and put policemen in their place."

"I see." Turning, Fisby caught a glimpse of the protesting Hokkaido coming around the other way. "Sakini, now what's the matter with him?"

"Hokkaido say that wouldn't be fair, boss, because then the chief would have four policemen, and he would only have two agriculture guys on the board."

Silence hung over the crowd; and Fisby knew all eyes were on him, waiting for a decision. He moistened his lips. "Well, let's just kick the whole bunch off and let the construction department act as inspectors."

But that wasn't satisfactory to the police chief. "He say the construction foreman and Hokkaido are good friends," Sakini explained. "If the carpenters don't vote for Hokkaido, the police chief thinks the construction boss will give 'em all the hard work to do tomorrow. But if you want to let the sanitation department act as inspectors, boss, it's all right with him."

Hokkaido promptly raised a protest about the sanitation department, so Fisby decided it was best to consult his assistant chief honorary inspector. "What do you think, Doc?" he whispered.

"Well, Fisby, what say we put three inspectors on from the police department, and three from the agriculture crew. That ought to satisfy both."

Yet it didn't satisfy Fisby. He could see a split decision, a deadlock, and had the feeling that the whole thing would be dumped back in his lap again. Then he remembered something. "Sakini, does the referee have a chance to vote on the winner?" he asked.

"Sure, boss."

Fisby smiled. Here was the deciding vote, and he would be rid of the thing. "That's what we'll do then. They can each have three inspectors from their own department."

It was satisfactory to both Hokkaido and the police chief. So they went about their preparation for the match. Hokkaido stepped to one side of the circle, marked on the platform. Placing his hands on his knees, he began raising his legs high in the air and bringing them down hard on the ground, as if cracking walnuts with his heels. "What is he doing?" Fisby asked.

"We call it *siko,* boss. Hokkaido's showing the police chief how he's going to crush his skull with his feet."

Fisby's eyebrows arched. "Oh. Is that legal?"

"No, boss. But if it were, Hokkaido's showing the chief how he'd do it." Sakini leaned over and whispered confidentially: "Hokkaido's just scaring him a little bit, boss."

Across the ring, the chief was also scaring Hokkaido. He was stamping up and down, and Sakini explained: "It also makes their legs real loose."

The two contestants then walked over to the white-draped pole, representing winter. Bending, Hokkaido lifted a cup of water to his lips. "That's *tikara mizu,*" Sakini said, "the water that gives strength."

Apparently Doc McLean was unable to forget his partiality. "Hokkaido's going to need more than a drink of water," he pronounced.

"But he don't drink it." Sakini shook his head. "He just rinses his mouth. Now watch."

Sakini was right. Then Hokkaido wiped his lips with a piece of paper. "And that's *tikara gami,*" Sakini went on. "The paper that gives strength."

"He better use two pieces then," the Doc said.

Next, the police chief had to go through the same procedure, and Fisby became a little restless. "When are they going to start wrestling?" he asked.

"In a little while," Sakini assured him. "Now they have to throw salt over the ring."

This, Fisby assumed, was like throwing salt over your shoulder to ward off bad luck. And when the construction chief walked into the ring again, Fisby settled back to enjoy the match. But they had to go through another ceremony. They squatted on the balls of their feet, as if about to do knee bends, but instead began waving their arms.

"What are they doing, Sakini?" Fisby inquired. "Sending semaphore signals?"

"Semaphore—don't understand, boss. They got to purify themselves now with grass. They're being polite. See, when the police chief touches Hokkaido, he won't get his hands dirty, because he's purified."

The purification took some time; so Fisby reached in his shirt pocket, brought out cigars, and passed one to Sakini, and one to the Doc. Lighting up, they waited. Then it became evident that the match was about to get under way. Hokkaido began stamping his feet again and snorting —putting fear into the police chief. And Fisby, switching

114

his cigar to the side of his mouth, edged forward on the bench.

The referee, face behind fan, stepped to the center of the ring; and the two contestants came toward each other slowly. Assuming a crouch, like two opposing football guards waiting for the ball to be snapped, they stared hard into each other's eyes. "Now watch, boss," Sakini whispered. "When the referee drops his fan, they go."

At that moment, a voice came high and clear from the far edge of the crowd. *"Oii,* Hokkaido . . . Hey, Hokkaido!"

Hokkaido half-turned his head. *"Nani* . . . what?"

The referee dropped his fan. Springing across the ring the police chief caught Hokkaido with a series of machinegunlike, open-handed thrusts against the shoulders. And Hokkaido reeled backward into a half-sitting position, dropped lower and lower, and ended up on the ground outside the ring, sitting flat.

Fisby flicked the ashes from his cigar. Smiled. "Watch Hokkaido tear him to pieces now, Doc, when he climbs back into the ring."

"But he can't do that, boss," Sakini said quickly. "It's all over."

"Over! They haven't even started."

"Yes, they have, boss. In *sumo* when one guy pushes the other guy out of the ring, he wins. If you go out of the ring, you lose right away. So the police chief wins by *tukippanasi* . . . blowing Hokkaido out of the ring."

"But Hokkaido wasn't ready," Fisby began to protest. Yet he had no need to, for Hokkaido, tears in his eyes, was protesting for himself. "He say it's not fair that guy to yell at him like that," Sakini explained. "Now he wants you to do something about it, boss."

Having no desire to get mixed up in it, even though he felt Hokkaido had a good point, Fisby indicated the six inspectors. "What do they think, Sakini?"

The inspectors were deadlocked. The three from the agriculture department stating that Hokkaido was fouled; while the three from the police department claimed that since Hokkaido stepped out, he lost. It was as Fisby expected, and he turned to his ace in the hole. "What does the referee think, Sakini?"

The referee, face behind fan, promptly gave the decision to the police chief, while half the crowd applauded and half booed.

"Boss," Sakini said, "Hokkaido claim the referee is on the police chief's side. When Hokkaida was sitting outside the ring, there, he get a good look at him. Do you know who the referee is?"

"Who?"

"The police chief's Uncle Miyagi. But you got to make the final decision, boss, because you're the chief honorary inspector."

It was right back in Fisby's lap again. Hokkaido's supporters were calling for fair play, while the chief's supporters were yelling that Hokkaido was thrust out, hence he lost.

In desperation, Fisby turned to his asistant. "What do you think, Doc?"

The Doc eyed his cigar thoughtfully. "Well, Fisby, the chief's Uncle Miyagi would naturally be inclined to give him a break."

Fisby had to agree to that. "Yet technically, Doc, the chief won."

The Doc nodded, and put his cigar in his mouth. "I wouldn't know what to say. You're the chief honorary inspector, Fisby. I guess it's up to you."

The chief honorary inspector, at that moment, was sweating profusely. Running a drugstore back in Ohio was never like this. "Well—" he began, cleared his throat, and eyed the crowd, gathered round. "Well, Sakini, I think we'll call it no decision. That's it; by golly, we'll have to rematch them."

When Sakini translated, the crowd began to applaud, and Fisby gained confidence. "We'll rematch them tomorrow night at the same time."

"Joto. Joto . . . good," he heard and smiled. Then his face grew stern and he frowned. "But I can't say I'm pleased with the officiating here tonight. Tomorrow night we'll have some officials and inspectors who are impartial."

Sakini nodded. "Okay, boss. Should we get some guys from little Koza maybe?"

"I don't care who you get as long as they don't take sides." Fisby examined his cigar, then slipped it into his mouth. "Oh yes. And tomorrow night, Sakini, let's put some more bouts on the card. Say six or eight. I'd kinda like to see some wrestling."

Sixteen

THE FOLLOWING MORNING, being under strict orders from First Flower not to go near the teahouse until *kobiru* time, Fisby prowled restlessly through the village, glancing from time to time at his watch—for he was curious about the *cha ya*, was anxious to have his morning talk with the girls. Once or twice he was tempted to sneak down that way in order to look around, but decided against it.

For a while he stood watching a group of children playing some sort of a hopscotch game with stones. Next, he went over to the looms, set up in a banana grove, and watched the women, busy with their weaving. As near as he could figure, at least a hundred looms were in operation; and he could see a surplus of *tatami,* the thick straw mats, piling up. "We might need them to swap with the other villages," he told himself, and walked on.

The sun seemed to rise slowly in the heavens this morning. It seemed to Fisby as if the midmorning break would never come. Being near the old folk's home, he decided to drop in; he hadn't been there in several days. Entering the courtyard, he was surprised to find so much activity on the veranda. Usually, the old men just sat there, basking in the sun and smoking their long, bamboo-stemmed pipes. Usually, the old women crouched before the ever present pots of tea, chatting lazily. But this morning everyone was busy.

Curiously, Fisby approached. The men were making something. Over to one side, a group was sawing two by fours into small blocks. Another group was turning the blocks on what appeared to be hand-operated wood lathes. "Hey, boss," someone called, "what you doing?"

Fisby saw Oshiro, the spokesman for the aged, and waved. "Just looking around, Oshiro. What are you doing?"

Oshiro chuckled. "Fooling that damn fool mayor."

"You are? How are you doing that?"

Oshiro motioned, and Fisby walked over to where the aged one was sitting. "Boss," Oshiro whispered, "do you

117

know what that damn fool mayor use to do when we have geisha parties down here?"

Fisby considered. "Oh, you mean those first couple days just after First Flower and Lotus Blossom moved to the village?"

"That's right, boss."

"I see. What did he use to do?"

"Well, at the geisha parties he never use to like it because First Flower and Lotus Blossom bring us old guys tea to drink. He always want the girls to just sit beside him and sing songs. So when they talk to us, he get pretty sore. 'Grandpa,' he always say to me, 'it's eight o'clock. You guys better go to bed now.'"

"Is that a fact?"

"Yes. And the other day he tell us he don't think we can come down to the *cha ya* at night and sit around, because we need our sleep."

Fisby felt his anger rise. "You mean he's going to try keeping you out of the public teahouse?"

Oshiro chuckled again. "He thinks he is, but we fool him."

"How?"

"Well, boss, First Flower say, 'Grandpa, we need a lot of lacquer ware. Will you make it for us?' So I tell her what the mayor say, and do you know what she do?"

"What?"

"She gets pretty sore. She tells me to go ahead and make the lacquer ware; then if the mayor tries to stop us, she'll say, 'Well, Oshiro made lacquer ware. And what did you do to build the *cha ya*? What did you furnish? Oh, nothing? Well, I don't think you better come around this place any more.'" Oshiro's old eyes twinkled. "We fix that damn fool."

"I think you should be allowed in the *cha ya*," Fisby said, "even if you furnished nothing. Still I didn't know you could make lacquer ware."

"Make it sixty-five, maybe seventy years, boss," Oshiro declared proudly. "My papa start to show me how when I was just a little boy. And before that, his papa show him. You want to see some things I make, boss?" Oshiro's eyes were hopeful.

Fisby nodded, and Oshiro led him around to the other side of the building. Drying in the shade were long lines of blood-red trays that made Fisby's eyes pop.

"Now here's a *sake* cup, boss. See, it's thin as paper. I cut it out of a solid block of wood."

"Oh, is that what you use those hand lathes for?"

"Lathes?" Oshiro questioned.

"The machines out there those guys are turning."

"Yes, boss. I let them help so they can go to the *cha ya,* too. They don't know much about it, and I got to show 'em all the time. But they do pretty good." Oshiro put the cup in Fisby's hand. "Do you like it, boss?"

Fisby examined the cup closely, then could hardly take his eyes from it. It was thin as paper, true, but the blood-red finish, smooth as satin, and the great golden fish, etched in the bottom, were of such craftsmanship that Fisby whistled.

"You know how long it take me to learn to etch like that, boss?" Oshiro asked.

"How long?"

"Ten years. Every day I practice, and always my papa say, 'No, that's not right.' Then he show me a little bit more. But finally I learn. Now when you fill that cup with *sake,* boss, it looks just like the fish is swimming there."

"I never saw work like this before," Fisby said in all sincerity.

Oshiro smiled proudly. "Here, boss, here's a *kakeban.* See, it's got legs. It's a little tray, but it's a little table, too. We make them red on the inside and black on the outside. Sometimes, if we feel like it, we put in designs of gold."

Fisby saw that there were many *kakeban* drying there.

"And here, boss," Oshiro went on, "are the butterfly and cat-legged trays. Here are some without legs. And there are the lacquer bowls for soup and rice."

Fisby was amazed. "And you're going to let them use all of these things at the *cha ya?*"

"I give it to 'em." The old face grew sad. "Nobody wants Oshiro's lacquer ware any more, except maybe First Flower and Lotus Blossom."

"Nobody wants this work?" Fisby was puzzled. "I don't understand."

"Well, boss, a long time ago everybody want it." Oshiro's eyes had a dreamy look, as if remembering the past. "Then the great junks use to come across the China Sea into our harbor at Naha. Before the traders get a cup of wine, even, they come up to see me. 'Oshiro,' they say, 'we need some lacquer ware. The war lord of our province tell us before we do anything, we got to see you. And look what he sends you. Here are spices, and jasmine tea, and look at this silk.'" Oshiro shook his head. "Then, boss, everybody everywhere know about the lacquer ware from the Ryukyu Islands."

"I see," Fisby said. "But what happened?"

Oshiro shrugged. "Pretty soon there weren't any more war lords, boss, who send me presents. There weren't any more junks, either. The ships all burn coal. Instead of traders, some guys come who just get off the ships a little while to walk around before they go somewhere else."

"Travelers?"

"I guess so. Anyway, they look at the golden fish swimming in the *sake* cups and say, 'These are pretty good. How much you want for 'em? Twenty-five yen apiece? That's too much. Tell you what. We give you one yen.'"

"I don't understand," Fisby said. "Didn't you tell them that it took you ten years to learn to make that etching?"

"Sure, boss. But they say, 'We don't care about that. We got big machines in Kobe that can do that in a minute.'" Oshiro shook his old head. "So nobody wants my lacquer ware any more."

"Sure they do," Fisby said quickly. "Why I would like some myself."

Oshiro's eyes twinkled, and he bowed. "I thank you, boss."

The sun had risen in the heavens, and Fisby knew he was due down at the *cha ya*. "I have to go now, but I'll be back," he told Oshiro. "I want to see more of your work."

"You do?" The old face lit up.

"You bet I do." Fisby indicated the trays. "Those are really good. Now you just keep making them. First Flower wouldn't want your lacquer ware for the *cha ya* if it wasn't first class. You know that."

Oshiro considered. "I guess maybe you're right, boss." Then he frowned and pointed to a group of old women smoothing half-finished trays with bits of broken glass. "But I don't know if I can keep making 'em. I need those old ladies to help, and they get pretty grouchy sometimes. They say, 'Why should we do anything—just so you guys can sit around the *cha ya* and sip tea?' Maybe if I tell 'em that you get 'em something they really want, then they'll work."

"What do they want?" Fisby asked.

"I think they would like some of the good tea like you

get for the *cha ya.* You think maybe you can get some, boss?"

Fisby was ashamed of himself. He realized that during the past few days he had been thinking mostly of the *cha ya* and had neglected these old ones. "I'll see that mess sergeant this afternoon and pick up another load," he said quickly.

"Who you see, boss?"

"The guy who's got the tea. Only this time we'll distribute it to the whole village along with the regular rations."

Oshiro hesitated. "And, boss, do you think you could get us guys some tobacco for our pipes? We don't have much left."

Fisby started to say, "I don't know." Then seeing the old faces all along the veranda turned to him, he nodded quickly. "Sure, Oshiro. I'll get it somewhere."

He glanced at the sun again. He had to hurry now. But before he left, he held up a reassuring finger. "And, Oshiro, if that damn fool mayor tries to pull any tricks on you, just let me know."

Seventeen

SAKINI WAS AWAITING HIM at the door of the *cha ya.* "You're late, boss," he said. And Fisby nodded, his eyes on the teahouse. It stood low and sprawling in the grove of transplanted pines, its new thatch roof gleaming in the morning.

It consisted of a series of wings, each with its own covered veranda. And all along the verandas, the paper lanterns stirred gently in the breeze. In reality, it appeared as more of a framework than a building itself. The sturdy, lacquered uprights were clearly visible, but the siding appeared to be made of woven reed and the sliding doors of thin, almost transparent paper. "You have it finished, eh, Sakini?" Fisby said.

"Almost, boss. Except we got the wings on the other side to fix yet. And the carpenters are working to make it real strong for when the hurricanes come. They make sliding doors of wood that we just slip in the grooves, there, outside the veranda railings."

Fisby could see the whole thing would thus be closed tight as a box.

"Oh, yes, boss," Sakini went on, "we'll be all finished in about two weeks, and First Flower tell me to remind you that you and the Mr. Doctor are honor guests at the big *sukiyaki* party we have then."

"We are?" Fisby smiled. "Well, I'll be doggoned."

But Sakini was glancing at the sun. "We better go now, boss," he said. "I think First Flower is waiting for us." He led Fisby to the entrance, then held aside the strips of reed that served as a door. "Step in, boss."

Fisby entered, automatically taking off his helmet-liner. It was dark in here and quiet. The fine, clean scent of new-cut thatch reached him, and he breathed deep. Beside him, Sakini clapped his hands; and from somewhere a serving boy, clad in a target cloth jacket, hurried forward and bowed low on the steps above them.

"See, boss," Sakini explained proudly, "we do it just like in the big *cha yas* down in Naha. First Flower teach these guys how to bring tea and that stuff."

The serving boy held out a pair of reed sandals for each of them, and Fisby was puzzled until Sakini explained. "We never wear our shoes inside, boss."

"I didn't know." Quickly, Fisby bent and unbuckled his combat boots. "But where did you get those reed things, Sakini?"

"Those? Everybody can make 'em, boss. We just get a bunch of kids together and pretty soon we have enough."

Fisby's eyes were becoming accustomed to the darkness now. In his reed sandals, he followed Sakini up the three low steps and stood in the entrance way. Yet the maze of corridors, leading off in all directions, confused him, and he didn't know what to do.

"Wait just a minute, boss," Sakini said as they stood there. He gave rapid directions to the serving boy in the Luchuan dialect, and the boy disappeared down one of the corridors. "I send him for First Flower," Sakini explained. "See, that's her and Lotus Blossom's apartment down there."

Fisby was surprised. "Do they live here now?"

"Sure, boss. They got to be around to see that these guys keep the place clean and run it right."

Looking down at the bottom step, Fisby saw a number

of pairs of wooden sandals lined up. Here and there he could see serving boys hurrying along the corridors, carrying trays with steaming pots of tea; and he assumed the *cha ya* was doing quite a business. From somewhere in the maze of corridors came a faint tinkling, and he turned curiously. "What's that, Sakini?"

"Well, boss," Sakini explained, "First Flower take little pieces of bamboo and hang 'em in a cluster. When the breeze blows they hit each other and make a pretty sound. We call them wind bells. Nice, eh?"

Fisby nodded. He liked the faint tinkling off in the distance. It was the only sound in the cool darkness. And he liked this quiet. In a moment, however, he heard the shuffling of reed sandals, and looked toward the corridor leading to First Flower's apartment. He saw her coming toward them, smiling. At first, he stared at her, then peered closer because of the darkness, then his mouth flew open in surprise.

She wasn't wearing a kimono this morning. She was wearing something that looked like a slack suit made out of the white target cloth. At the bottom of each pocket was sewed a small patch of red, and even the straw ropes of her sandals were covered wth this same red.

Reaching them, she bowed, her eyes shining; then stood there before them, her feet apart, her hands thrust deep in the slanting pockets.

"Say, that really looks good," Fisby said. "Where did she get them?"

"Oh, she make 'em, boss. Remember the American magazines you give her? Well, she look at the pictures and see these. Then she has me read the English for her. It says American women wear these sometime during the day, so she thinks they'd be just the thing for her and Lotus Blossom. You see, boss, they'd kinda like to save their kimonos; because when the kimonos wear out, they believe it might be pretty hard to get some more."

Fisby grew uneasy. It would be hard, indeed. Those silk kimonos of theirs were imported, he knew. They came from the *Ginza,* the Fifth Avenue of Tokyo; but now, he understood, Tokyo was flattened, and he wondered, perhaps, if these weren't the last kimonos the girls would ever have.

Sakini interrupted his thoughts. "Boss," he said, "she wants to know how you like her hair?" Slowly, First Flower turned all the way around so Fisby could see. She didn't wear the elaborate coiffure of the geisha today. Her hair was fixed in an American manner.

"Why, that looks good," Fisby said, and First Flower flushed with pleasure.

"She see that in the magazines, too," Sakini explained. "The magazines say that's a rolled bob. You know what that means, boss?"

Fisby had to admit that he wasn't much of an authority on rolled bobs, but that First Flower could certainly wear one. "And did Lotus Blossom fix her hair the same way?" he asked.

"Sure, boss. You see, they have a picture of two girls, and Lotus Blossom don't want anyone to walk around saying she isn't toney."

Though Fisby felt there was a slight misinterpretation of the word, yet he hesitated to launch into a discussion of it for fear it would take hours. "Well," he began conversationally, "tell her the teahouse certainly looks fine, Sakini."

"She's glad you like it, boss. Come on. She show you around a little bit, then we have something to eat."

Frankly, Fisby was hoping she would take them down through her apartment, but she led them the other way. "Now on both sides of the corridor here, beyond the paper screens, are private rooms," Sakini explained as they walked along. And First Flower pushed back one of the sliding doors to show Fisby.

The floor of the private room was covered with the thick, pale-green reed mats. In the center stood a low, lacquered table with a china ash tray. It was simple, nothing ornate. Yet there was a certain beauty about its plainness that made Fisby nod in approval. "And see, boss," Sakini said, "each room opens on a covered veranda."

"Why is that?" Fisby asked curiously.

"Well, boss, even though the guys sit inside, First Flower don't want 'em to forget about the garden. She don't want 'em to forget the trees and shrubs. See, they sit in here and still see all that."

"But why do you have so many private rooms?" he asked.

"We got to have 'em, boss. Suppose some guy's got a big deal on, suppose he wants to talk it over. He say to his friends, 'Okay, let's go down to the *cha ya* and have a cup of tea.' They sit around a little while, boss. Talk about

124

this, talk about that, and pretty soon they settle everything."

"I see. And everyone in the village has his own room?"

"Well, boss, all he have to do is tell the chief serving boy to save one, and he can use it."

As they walked along, Fisby became aware that a good many conferences were going on at this moment, for he could hear low voices behind the screens. Sakini stopped for a moment outside one room, listened, then turned. "The mayor of little Koza come over to talk about being referee for the wrestling match between Hokkaido and the police chief," he explained in a whisper. "He tells our mayor that he's got a guy in little Koza who can wrestle better than anyone on Okinawa."

"Oh, yeah," Fisby said quickly. "What did our mayor tell him?"

"He say we got some pretty good guys around here ourselves."

"You bet we have." Fisby nodded. "Any time they want a match, just let us know."

First Flower, walking ahead of them, stopped suddenly to push back a sliding door. Then she stepped aside, bowing. "Boss," Sakini said, "this is your room. Nobody can use it but you."

Fisby was surprised. "I have my own private room?"

"Sure. Didn't you know, boss? First Flower pick it out for you, and she save the one right next door for the Mr. Doctor. She knows he's pretty busy out on the *cha ya* farm, but she thinks he would like a place to sit down when he comes to town."

Fisby agreed. The Doc ought to have some sort of office in town. Stepping inside his own room, Fisby saw that it was almost the same as the rest—only it was a little larger, the low lacquered table was a little better. And apparently First Flower had selected the best view in the place. He was right on the lotus pond. Across the railinged veranda, the garden—with its pines and shrubs, stone paths, and bridges arching over streams—extended back, shutting out all view of the bare potato fields and half-tumbled homes of the village.

But then Fisby noted there was something in his room, lacking in the others. There were pillows, here, covered with red silk, spread on the floor before the low table. He eyed them curiously.

"First Flower make the pillows for you," Sakini said.

125

"She have the silk put away, and she thought you might like them."

"But she shouldn't have done it," Fisby exclaimed. "Maybe she could have used the silk for a kimono."

Fisby saw her shake her head. "No, she say you're the best boss she ever have, and she wants you to have the pillows."

Fisby felt guilty, taking this silk away from her. "Now we eat," Sakini said, rubbing his hands.

First Flower clapped twice and in a moment a serving boy entered, bearing a tray. Bowing low, he set the tray on the floor. Taking it, First Flower began arranging the dishes on the low lacquered table. There was food that looked like small rice cakes to Fisby. There was something that looked like pickles. And there was a steaming pot of tea, with small, handleless cups.

"Boss," Sakini said, "First Flower asks you to excuse Lotus Blossom. She would like to be here for *kobiru*, but this morning she starts practicing the Women's League on the tea drinking ceremony."

"That's perfectly all right," Fisby said.

"And First Flower asks you to excuse the dishes. These are just old ones gathered in the village. Kiei don't have the new ones made yet." First Flower appeared rather wistful. "And even if he did have them made, they wouldn't have pretty pictures painted on them anyway."

"No?" Fisby tried to conceal his surprise. "Didn't Seiko arrive in the village?"

"He arrive, boss." Sakini shrugged. "But I don't think he's going to do any painting."

"Oh," Fisby said. "He isn't in the mood?"

Sakini hesitated. "Don't know how to tell you, boss, but he and First Flower have a fight again."

"That's too bad." Fisby was genuinely sorry. "I hope it's nothing serious."

"First Flower thinks it is. When she ask him to paint the dishes, he say, 'Aha, so that's why you want me to come here. You just want me to work, and make money, and spend it talking with you.' "

"But didn't she tell him differently?"

"No, boss. She figures if he wants to think that way, let him do it."

"You know," Fisby said, "I'd like to have a talk with that Seiko sometime."

First Flower tossed her head disdainfully. "She says just

126

let him go, boss, she don't care." But Fisby saw that she did care. "Besides, there are a lot of guys around here who say some pretty nice things to her. There's the mayor, and—"

"Did she tell Seiko that?" Fisby asked.

"Yep, boss."

"And what did he say?"

"She don't give him a chance to say anything, because she turn and walk away from him." Sakini shrugged. "Boss, she wants you to try the *sushi* there. It's vinegar spiced rice. We eat it all the time—between meals, sometimes at noon, all the time, if we have rice."

Fisby really wanted to talk a little more about Seiko, but First Flower was indicating the food on the table. He regarded it, then hesitated.

"Oh, she say you don't have to worry, boss. She knows how you Americans like sanitation, and she warn everybody who works in the *cha ya* that they must be real clean. Besides, the Mr. Doctor inspected them all and the kitchen, too. Everything's all right."

"It isn't that," Fisby said and pointed. "You see, Sakini, I never used chopsticks before. I don't know how to go about it."

"By gosh, boss, First Flower say she show you how." Quickly, she placed a pillow beside Fisby and knelt on it. "Now first, you take 'em like this—"

Though Fisby's fingers were clumsy and never meant for chopsticks, she did not laugh. Patiently she coached him, and now and then would say, "You use 'em real good, boss." And though Fisby knew he was the rankest amateur, he gained confidence. In a little while, he forgot his clumsiness and began enjoying the tart, spicy rice.

"See, it has shrimp in it," Sakini explained. "We got all kinds of *sushi*. First Flower say this is the kind they make real good at the Hiranoya restaurant in Maruyama Park, Kyoto. You like it?"

Fisby liked it fine. He ate rapidly of the first helping; but then, seeing such was not the custom, he slowed down on the second, took his time, gazed out at the lotus pond, exactly as First Flower did. He could tell they did not rush eating over here. They did not gulp their food; but took plenty of time, enjoying it, enjoying the quiet, peaceful surroundings in which it was served.

Especially did he like the variety of pickles, each served on a small, individual dish. They were called *tsukemono,* or "fragrant things," Sakini told him, and each variety offered a new taste between bites of rice. Yet it was the tea that surprised Fisby most. Though it was American tea, still it tasted like nothing he had ever experienced.

When he inquired, First Flower smiled furtively. "She have Mrs. Kamakura put a few drops of *ginseng* wine in it, boss. You see, they use to make it down in Shuri Castle. They have big distilleries. But just before you guys come, everybody knows the Japanese soldiers are going to defend Shuri, that there is going to be a big battle there, and maybe nothing will be left. So the people move away. They close down everything, and the distilleries bury all their wine."

"Oh, and you dug this up from the ground?"

"Yes, boss. First Flower knows where it is hid. One day Yamashiro San, who owns a big distillery, comes into the teahouse of the Golden Dragon in Naha and tells her all about it. So she sends some of the guys here in the village to dig it up."

"Won't Yamashiro San care?" Fisby asked.

First Flower was silent for a moment. "He didn't get away from Shuri Castle, boss. She hears he and his family were caught by the artillery. She thinks he would want her to have the wine, because he was almost like a papa to her."

"I'm sorry to hear about that," Fisby said.

First Flower glanced out across the lotus pond at the pines beyond. "But that is the way things must be," Sakini translated her words. *"Shikata ga nai . . .* it can't be helped."

No, it couldn't be helped, Fisby told himself. He glanced at her slack suit of coarse target cloth. Many things couldn't be helped, yet he ought to try making up for some things. For certain, he ought to see that plenty of target cloth was available, not only for First Flower to save her kimonos, but also for all the people. It wasn't much, yet it was clothing.

He thought of Mr. Van Druten, the young Ensign in charge of the Officers' Club. The Ensign had to improvise. Now Mr. Van Druten had plenty of mats for his Club, and Fisby tried to figure some things the Ensign would need; some things for which he would swap more cloth. Things he, Fisby, and the village could provide.

Sipping his tea, tasting the strange flavor, Fisby thought

he had it. "Sakini," he said, "could we make *ginseng* wine here in the village?"

Sakini consulted First Flower. "Don't think so, boss. We would need the *ginseng* root. It takes many years to grow. Besides, most of it comes from China and Korea."

Fisby knew of only one other drink. "Can we make *sake?*"

"Well, boss, First Flower say we can if you want us to. We have the rice from the Japanese military rations that we found in the caves."

"Do you have much?"

"Enough for maybe two months."

"Do you mean just using it here in the *cha ya?*"

"Yes, boss. If we gave it out to everybody in rations, it wouldn't last three weeks. But First Flower want to know if we should save it for *sake?*"

Fisby considered. He couldn't take this rice away from them. "No," he said, "I think we'll save it for *sushi*."

Both First Flower and Sakini seemed relieved. Then Sakini inquired, "What do you want *sake* for anyway, boss?"

"I thought I might be able to swap it for more white cloth. Maybe lay up a big supply here in the village for the future. The officers are usually short of potables—"

"Of what?"

"Something to drink."

"Do you think they'd like *shochu*, boss?"

"What's that?"

"It's a kind of brandy we make out of sweet potatoes. She's strong as the dickens."

Fisby nodded. "I think they'd like that." By golly, there were plenty of sweet potatoes in the fields, and if a man had a *shochu* distillery running—well, Fisby remembered a platoon sergeant of his up on Attu, who had made enough to buy a farm back home in Arkansas, simply by concocting some sort of drink out of corn meal. And he remembered a Pfc who was sending so much money home through the mail, because of a similar project, that the Inspector General sent a man in to investigate.

Fisby could see great possibilities with a little distillery going in the village. From his experience, common to every officer, of inventorying the Post Exchange, he knew there was always a surplus of certain items that the P.X. was glad to get off the shelves. Certain brands of soap, for instance, which never sold, but only lay there month after month. He snapped his fingers. Say, First Flower and Lotus Blossom would want some soap in their bathhouse. And there were always certain brands of tobacco and cigarettes that were almost impossible to give away. Perhaps it wasn't the best, yet it was good tobacco, just the thing for old Oshiro and his friends down at the home for the aged. Or for all the men in the village for that matter.

Fisby had no reason to worry about the demand for *shochu;* he could peddle it anywhere. In fact, they would probably be lining up at his door. Yet, at the moment, the supply bothered him. "Sakini, ask First Flower if she thinks we could build a little distillery here in the village. But remember," he held up a warning finger, "I want to turn out good stuff. I'll have none of the troops going blind because of the sweet potato hooch we make."

"She say we can make *shochu,* boss. She don't know how, herself, because it's a secret. You see, the families who make it, well, maybe that's all they do for five, six hundred years. The papas tell the sons, and they tell their sons. But they won't tell anyone else."

Fisby nodded. There should be no trouble at all with a product backed by five or six hundred years' experience. If it was good enough to last that long, it must be safe— and it must be palatable. "Do you have any of those families in the village?" he asked.

"First Flower don't know, boss. But do you want her to look around?"

"I would appreciate it. And if we don't have any, we'll try to move a family in from another village. Okay?"

"She say okay, boss."

Fisby felt good inside. "Well," he said, "I better be going, Sakini. I have lots of work to do. Ought to line up a few *shochu* customers, make a few contacts—"

"Boss," Sakini interrupted, "First Flower don't want you to move."

Taken by surprise, Fisby glanced at her. "Why not?"

"Because she's worried about you. She thinks you work too hard, and she wants you to rest."

"Worried about me?" Fisby couldn't keep the smile from creeping into his face. He tried remembering the last time anyone was worried about him and failed. "But I haven't been working hard."

"She say you have. Now she wants you to sit right there. She thinks if you go running around all over the place, you get all sick to your stomach. Then you can't eat *sushi* any more. And you won't be able to taste how good the pickles are. And the Mr. Doctor will have to give you medicine. She just wants you to sit right there and listen to the wind blowing through the pines, across the lotus pond. You can forget *shochu* and that stuff; she'll take care of it. And she wants you to listen real close. Maybe the pines will even sing you a song."

"But I have work to do," Fisby protested.

First Flower feigned severity. "Boss, she say she don't want any fooling around."

Pleased, Fisby rubbed his head. "Well, I might sit here a little while. How's that?"

"No, boss. She wants you to sit there a long time."

"Well—" Fisby hesitated. "Well, okay. I will for today."

First Flower and Sakini arose and went to the door. "Now she just wants you to sit there," Sakini warned again. "But if you want some more tea with *ginseng* wine, just clap your hands twice, boss, and tell the serving boy, '*O cha toh ginseng budoshu, wo kudasai.*' He'll understand."

Fisby repeated the words to make sure they were correct.

"That's right, boss. We go now. But First Flower say to be sure to listen for the song of the pine trees." Bowing, they left the room, closing the paper door behind them. Fisby heard the shuffling of their reed sandals as they disappeared somewhere into the teahouse, heard the shuffling grow fainter, until finally it faded, and all was quiet.

He felt a little foolish, sitting there on a pillow in the middle of the room. Then he glanced at the red silk pillows scattered about. Dammit, he told himself, he couldn't make a girl use what little silk she had saved for these. He ought to repay her. Slacks were all right, but what about when her kimonos were worn out?

Besides, he ought to get tea for the old women. And the old men, like Oshiro, shouldn't be worried about their next pipeful of tobacco. And this business of looking at the sun to tell when it was time for *kobiru*—Fisby shook his head. That was no good. Maybe he could pick up some dollar watches.

From the distance came the sound of horse's hoofs beating on the hard clay of the narrow streets. They came from beyond the garden of the *cha ya,* yet Fisby looked out across the veranda. That would be the Doc, he knew, busy on some project concerning the teahouse farm. Fisby could picture him swinging along on the big, rawboned dun.

Well, with everyone working he couldn't just sit there. He couldn't waste the rest of the morning. Standing, he edged toward the open door, leading out onto the veranda. Cautiously, he peeked up and down.

At the far end of the veranda, First Flower sat sewing in the morning sun with an American magazine propped before her. For a moment, Fisby watched, then she seemed to hear a noise and turned her pretty head quickly toward him. He ducked back just in time.

When First Flower said she wanted no fooling around, she meant business, Fisby reflected. Well, maybe he could sit around for a little while. Slowly, he walked back to the low lacquered table and sank onto a pillow.

A faint breeze, off the Pacific, blew across the lotus pond, and within the teahouse the wind bells began to tinkle. It was nice and cool in here, he had to admit that. And he liked the clean fragrance of the new-cut thatch. "Almost like new-mown hay," he told himself. Slipping off his reed sandals, he wiggled his stocking-footed toes.

Again came the breeze, rippling the pond, and the pines in the garden swayed gently. He leaned forward to catch their faint rustling. And the fading hoof beats of the Doc's horse drifted to him on the morning air.

It reminded Fisby of the bare feet of the people padding on the hard clay. This was an old land, he realized. Why, the very soil was packed by those bare feet treading over it since time began. And, in a way, it was a hostile land that must be torn at with heavy iron hoes, so that it would bring forth the sweet potato and soya bean.

The picture of Oshiro and the aged, sitting on the veranda of the old folk's home, came to him. He thought of the lumbering junks crossing China's sea and sailing into Naha's harbor, and wondered for how many centuries it had been thus.

Also, he wondered about those lumbering junks themselves. Did all come in friendship, merely to trade, or did some carry an invader? What could these people do against an invader? Why, they could only accept whatever was forced upon them. They were just a little people on a little island. Now, for the first time, he realized that he, too, was an invader placed over them. And he frowned.

The wind bells tinkled, and his frown deepened. He thought of Oshiro, whose lacquer no one wanted any more. He thought of his geisha girls, whose kimonos were wearing out and might never be replaced. And the term "invader" bothered him.

A serving boy—wondering, perhaps, if he wanted more tea—pushed back the paper door, just a bit; then quickly closed it. For the boss was looking out over the lotus pond. And the boss, the boy could tell, did not want to be disturbed. He was listening to the pines swaying gently in the breeze.

Meanwhile up in headquarters Sakini held the receiver of the field phone away from his ear. "Now you listen to me," Colonel Purdy was shouting at him, "you find that Doctor and tell him to call me."

Sakini scratched his head. "But the Mr. Doctor is busy this mornnig. He decide to make some *poi* so he's out looking for taro root."

"Poi!" Colonel Purdy exploded. "I sent him down there to act as a psychiatrist, not as a cook. By God, you tell him to get on this phone. I told him to report to me every day, not once every three months. I'm still commanding this team, and I want to know what's going on around that place!"

Eighteen

IMMEDIATELY AFTER LUNCH THAT AFTERNOON, Fisby fully intended to contact some of the P.X. officers and get a price list of slow-moving and surplus articles—things they would be glad to get off their shelves. First Flower had located a family skilled in making sweet potato brandy; and already carpenters were putting up the framework of a distillery; a group of workers, under the supervision of Kiei, was making large pottery fermentation jars; and the family, itself, was busy cutting up potatoes for their mash.

Expecting a rushing business from all ranks, and grades, and branches of service, Fisby did not want to be caught napping when the money began rolling in; he wanted to know what he could buy from the P.X.

But after lunch, he received an emergency call. Lotus

Blossom, her dark eyes filled with fear, came running into headquarters. "Boss," Sakini explained quickly, "she say that Seiko has left the village."

"No!" Fisby straightened at his desk. "What happened?"

"She don't know, boss, except that he and First Flower have that argument about painting dishes."

"Did Lotus Blossom see him leave?"

"No, boss. Miss Higa Jiga see him go. You see, Miss Higa Jiga thinks he's a pretty nice guy, and she's been planning on asking him over to the tea drinking ceremony at her new *cha no yu* house, just as soon as it's finished. But then she hears that Miss Susano and some of the ladies of the executive council of the Women's League are planning the same thing, so Miss Higa Jiga decides to get in her invitation early. Well, a little while ago she goes around to where he stays, and they tell her he packed all his brushes and paints. She looks; and sure enough there he is —heading across the fields toward little Koza."

Fisby considered. "What does First Flower think about his leaving?"

Sakini spoke briefly to Lotus Blossom. "She says that First Flower just tosses her head, boss, and says, *'Maa, let him go. I don't care.'* But First Flower don't fool Lotus Blossom. She can tell that when nobody's around, First Flower is going to cry, and maybe more than a little bit, boss."

"Gee," Fisby said, bracing his hands on the desk, "if he's fool enough to walk away from the most famous geisha girl in all Naha, we ought to let him go at that." But the thought of First Flower crying made his forehead wrinkle. "So he's heading toward little Koza, eh? Come on, Sakini. We'll take the jeep and cut him off."

They spotted Seiko coming across the sweet potato fields, carrying a small bundle under his arm. And Fisby stopped the jeep, waiting for him to reach the road.

Though Fisby had never seen Seiko before, still he recognized him from Sakini's description. He was tall for his race, with high cheekbones and a proud nose. He was dressed in a pair of old pants with a worn white shirt; and though he was on the thin side, he had the litheness of the natural athlete. But as he approached, it was the absent look in his eyes that caught Fisby's attention.

"Sakini," Fisby said, "tell him who I am."

Sakini spoke briefly, then turned. "He knows, boss. He sees you in Tobiki village."

"Good. Well, find out where he's going."

"He don't know exactly, boss. But he thinks maybe he go way up north to Kunigami country. He likes the rivers and the hills up there. And he thinks, maybe, he's going to build himself a little shack by the sea."

Fisby rubbed his chin. "Well, tell him I'm sorry he's leaving our village."

"He's sorry to leave, boss, because—well, he thinks we're going to have a good *cha ya*. And if there's anything he likes to do, it's sit around a teahouse."

"Well, does he have to leave?" Fisby asked.

"Yep, boss."

"If I were him," Fisby said, "I'd think it over carefully."

"Oh, he did, boss. All last night he couldn't sleep, and now he makes up his mind. He say no one's going to make a fool out of him."

"Is someone doing that?"

"He say First Flower is. She sends a message, and he thinks she wants to see him. But it was just a trick."

"A trick?"

"Yes. She just wants him to paint dishes, so he'll make money. Then she'll say, 'Why don't you sit and talk with me sometime.' And she'll charge him double to talk with her. Oh, he knows about those girls who just want money. His mama tell him all about that kind."

Fisby regarded Seiko. "But how is he going to make money painting dishes? No one has any to pay him with. Besides, the Japanese money used here, before, isn't any good now."

Seiko was a little puzzled. "He say he didn't know about that, boss."

Seiko's absent air convinced Fisby that he was the kind who would be at least six months behind in developments. "Well, it's true."

Seiko appeared to be turning this over in his mind. "By gosh, boss, he thinks, then, that she just wants the dishes. Maybe she's going to hide them or something, so when the money is good again, she can sell them."

"No," Fisby said, "the dishes are for the *cha ya,* not for First Flower."

Seiko shook his head. "Well, he wouldn't know why she wants him to paint then. But it must be some trick."

"Maybe there's no trick to it at all. Maybe she has good reasons for wanting him to paint."

Seiko eyed Fisby doubtfully. "But what could they be, boss?"

"Perhaps she sees that he has a great ability along those lines. Perhaps she wants him to use that ability instead of just wasting it."

Seiko shrugged. "He wants to know why she would feel that way?"

Fisby took his time in answering. "Maybe it's because she loves him. Tell him I know for a fact that she looked all over to find the half-opened bud of a chrysanthemum to send him."

For a moment Seiko's eyes widened; then he frowned. "But, boss, if she loves him, he wants to know how come every time he is around, First Flower make such a big fuss over the mayor? She pours his tea and laughs at the things he says, even though Seiko don't think they're so funny."

"Perhaps she's trying to make Seiko jealous."

When the meaning sank in, Seiko seemed to feel better. "Hey, boss, he thinks maybe you're right. Do you know what he thinks he ought to do?"

"What?"

"He ought to make her jealous. He says some homely girl's been following him all around the place. So he thinks if he starts talking to this homely girl, First Flower will get pretty sore, and——"

"Wait a minute." Fisby held up a hand. "Who does he mean by some homely girl?"

After questioning Seiko closely, Sakini looked up. "I think he means Miss Higa Jiga, boss."

Fisby mopped his brow. He didn't want an affair like that on his hands. He didn't want Miss Higa Jiga to come running into headquarters every five minutes, demanding the Okinawan version of a shotgun wedding. "Boy," he said solemnly, "you got the wrong slant on things. Making her jealous won't do you any good."

"But, boss," Sakini asked, "he says if she makes him jealous, why can't he make her jealous?"

"That's a woman's privilege," Fisby said, unable to think of a logical answer. "If I were him, do you know what I would do?"

"What, boss?"

"I'd just stick to my painting. Yes, sir, I'd paint morning, noon, and night."

"He don't understand, boss."

"Well," Fisby went on, "tell him I know that First

136

Flower is proud of his work. Tell him every time she looks at it, something catches in her throat. And she wants him to be the greatest painter on all Okinawa. She wants people to come from all over to see it. Then she can say her guy did that. Girls don't feel that way unless a fellow means a lot to them."

"He didn't know that, boss."

Frankly, neither did Fisby, but it sounded reasonable now that he mentioned it. "So you see," he continued, "it's better to make a girl proud, than to make her jealous."

Seiko gave this serious consideration, then bowed. "He thanks you, boss, for telling him these things."

Fisby nodded. "That's perfectly all right." He regarded Seiko carefully. "Well, Sakini," he said, "let's take a ride up through Maebaru, then we'll see if we can find some P.X.'s." He turned to Seiko. "Does he want a ride north?"

Seiko hesitated, looked at Fisby, looked at Sakini. "No, boss, he says he hasn't done any painting in a long time, and he thinks he'll go back and do some practicing."

As Fisby turned the jeep and headed up the road to the north, he glanced in the rearview mirror and saw Seiko, the small bundle under his arm, heading back toward Tobiki village.

Nineteen

SOME TWO WEEKS LATER, on the afternoon preceding the evening of the grand opening of the *cha ya,* activity in the village ceased. Out along the sea wall, the salt pits were untended, as were the fish nets offshore. No smoke arose from the *shochu* distillery this afternoon. But now and then when the wind shifted, Fisby could tell that the batch of sweet potatoes fermenting in the pottery jars, under the canopy of vines, was coming along fine.

The carts belonging to the agriculture department were parked in neat rows in a clearing, and the horses were picketed to one side. The clog makers had stopped work. Oshiro and his crew at the old folk's home had put aside their lacquer ware. Kiei and his helpers had forgotten their potter's wheels. Tobiki village was taking the afternoon off.

The only signs of life in all the village were the line of men making their way down to the Pacific to bathe, and, occasionally, a lone member of the Women's League heading toward the *cha ya* in an effort to find out what was going on, this being a stag affair.

For a while Fisby sat at his desk looking over the list of things that the P.X. officers said he could buy in quantity, without fear of taking necessities away from the troops. There were toothbrushes, pastes, and powders; combs and various assortments of hair tonics; both chewing and smoking tobacco; aftershave lotion; plus a host of things which made up an extensive list.

Yet he was stymied. The sweet potato brandy was hardly aged enough to sell, even though he had several orders on hand from units that would take the entire supply as it was. He had no money with which to make purchases—his own pay having been spent long ago on an ample supply of tobacco for the old men at the home for the aged.

As he sat there, his forehead wrinkled; for the Women's League was pressing him again for silk kimonos and lingerie, both unavailable at the P.X. And besides, he wanted to obtain a supply of silk, at least enough so that First Flower and Lotus Blossom would have no need to worry about their own kimonos wearing out for a long time.

But the problem of silk and lingerie was too much for him, and he arose. Tobiki village was taking the afternoon off, so he, too, may as well do the same.

Reaching his quarters on the hill, he found that Doc McLean, a towel wrapped around his mid-section, was also getting ready for the evening. The Doc, fresh from an oil drum shower, was laying out a set of sparkling khaki on his cot. "No use trying to get anything done this afternoon, Fisby," the Doc said, reaching for a blitz cloth to shine his brass. "They're too excited about tonight. Can't keep their minds on their work."

Fisby nodded and went about making his own preparations—shining his shoes, polishing his belt buckle and insignia, and filling the oil drum for his own shower.

Just before sundown, as Tobiki's thatched roofs caught and reflected the last golden rays, they began to dress. Then, knowing the party did not start until darkness fell, they sat down to a game or two of cribbage. It was a few minutes later that the nervous Sakini, clad in a blue cotton kimono with wide, flapping sleeves, came trotting up the hill.

"Son of a gun, boss," Sakini said, snapping his fingers. "I forgot to tell you. The party tonight is formal."

"Formal?" Fisby laid down his cards. "What do you mean?"

"Boss, everybody is supposed to wear kimonos. The committee decide nobody can get in unless they got 'em on."

"But we don't have kimonos, Sakini."

"You don't?" Sakini's eyes were wide.

"No. You see, we never wear them."

"Oh." Sakini hesitated. "Son of a gun, boss, I better run right down and tell First Flower. I don't know if we can change it or not, because it's pretty late. But maybe she can fix something for you, maybe——"

"Wait a minute," Fisby said quickly. He knew what First Flower would do. She would use her own kimonos for material in order to make something for them; and he wasn't going to have that happen. "Can't we go like this?"

"Well, boss, we been planning on this. Everybody have their kimonos washed and everything."

Fisby looked at the Doc. "What do you think?"

The Doc considered. "I'd sure hate to miss out on this party, Fisby. I've been looking forward to it for two weeks. Yet we should dress for the occasion, or we'll spoil it for everyone."

Sakini was apologetic. "Boss, I wish we know before you don't have kimonos. We could have changed it." He paused. "But you just come like that. It's all right. We want you and the Mr. Doctor there. We don't care what you wear."

Yet Fisby was uneasy in his own mind. The Doc was right—they would spoil it for everyone. All evening long people would be apologizing, people would be self-conscious, and the fun would be ruined. Suddenly, he looked up. "Sakini, I just remembered something. I have a bathrobe, how would that be?"

"A what?" Sakini scratched his head.

"Well, sort of a kimono. Wait, I'll show you."

The Doc, too, remembered that he had a dressing gown, and both went to their duffel bags and began rummaging through.

Fisby's was a blue woolen affair, perhaps a size too small, with a red wrap-around belt and red trimmings on

139

the collar and cuffs; while the Doc's was of red rayon with a swirling design in the same color.

Sakini's eyes were filled with admiration. "Oh, those are nice. I never see cloth like that before." And Fisby and the Doc smiled in relief.

"But how do we wear them?" Fisby inquired. "Over our uniforms?"

"No, boss. Over your underwear. And do you have some white socks, maybe?"

The Doc remembered the GI-issue cotton socks, and both went back to their duffel bags again.

"Now I'll run down to the village to where the guys make the *geta*," Sakini said, "and bring you a couple of pair. Then you'll be all ready."

When Sakini brought the wooden sandals, they slipped them on; and when darkness fell, they started down toward the *cha ya*. But Fisby wasn't used to walking around outdoors in his bathrobe, and now he was conscious of his legs. "How does it look, Doc?" he asked nervously. "Is it too short?"

The Doc, with the assurance of a man whose own dressing gown was a couple sizes too large, surveyed him critically. "Why no, Fisby, I wouldn't say so. It just covers your knees nicely."

Still Fisby was uncertain. However, when they fell in with a group of kimono-clad men and no one paid particular attention to his legs, Fisby felt better—even enjoyed the coolness of the breeze coming in off the sea.

The paper lanterns were being lit now, all along the verandas, all through the garden. The flickering rays fell on the still water of the lotus pond; and the teahouse, itself, glowed with a warm, amber light. As they walked along, they met laughing groups, who bowed deeply and smiled cheerfully, for everyone was in a holiday spirit tonight.

The chief serving boy, himself, had taken over the supervision of distributing reed sandals. As they entered, he was right there, waiting to take their wooden clogs.

Quite a crowd was gathered up in the entrance way. They stood in small groups, talking. And from the laughter it was evident to Fisby that someone was telling Okinawan jokes. Spying Fisby, Sakini, and the Doc—several hurried forward to greet them. While it was clear that the mayor was acting as official host, still it was roly-poly Hokkaido —a grin plastered all over his cherubic face—who reached them first and took them in hand.

"Boss," Sakini said, "as President of the Men's League for Democratic Action, Hokkaido greets you and the Mr. Doctor. He's glad you could come."

Both Fisby and the Doc assured Hokkaido that they were glad to be there, and Hokkaido beamed.

"Now boss," Sakini went on, "he wants you to come with him. He's going to introduce you to the mayors of little Koza and Maebaru."

Fisby was surprised. "Oh, are they here tonight?"

"Sure, boss. We invite all the big guys. Besides, they have some *sake* hid over at their place, and they bring it along."

As they followed Hokkaido, the President, through the crowd, the Doc whispered, "Say, Fisby, do you think we could slip into the bar for a quick one?"

"I'll find out, Doc." Fisby turned. "Sakini, do you have a bar?"

Sakini scratched his head. "A what, boss?"

"I'll explain later." Fisby regarded the Doc. "I guess they don't have one."

Their arrival, however, was a signal for something or other, because a corps of serving boys appeared with steaming cups of tea set on blood-red trays. After the first sip, the Doc's eyes widened. "Say, this is good. What kind of tea is it?"

Fisby, an old hand at the game, having tasted it once before, chuckled. *"Ginseng* tea, that is, tea with *ginseng* wine in it."

Even the mayors of little Koza and Maebaru were enthusiastic about it, never having drunk it before. And for a while they stood in a little group, cups in hand, discussing the merits of *ginseng*. Then the mayor of little Koza complimented them on the teahouse. And the Doc inquired about the crops over in little Koza. And things were moving nicely when the chief serving boy opened a sliding paper door, leading to the entrance way of one of the wings.

This, apparently, was the sign to come and get it. The crowd opened a path for the honor guests to enter the banquet room. And Hokkaido, chest thrust out, walking between Fisby and the Doc, led them in.

When Fisby saw the banquet room, he whistled to himself. "Say, Doc," he said, "this is pretty tricky. Do you know what they've done?"

The Doc didn't have the slightest idea.

"Well, you know those sliding doors they use. Anyway,

those divide the place into small private rooms. But when they give a party, they remove the doors and the whole wing becomes one big room."

The banquet room made quite an impression on Fisby, indeed. It was a long, low thing; and through the open doors on both sides of the room, he could look out at the railinged verandas with their paper lanterns swaying gently in the breeze. Across the verandas were the small gardens, and beyond these, other wings of the teahouse were similarly lit.

Within the room itself, lanterns of transparent paper hung from the varnished rafters. Low tables—covered with blood-red lacquered dishes, and *sake* cups, and huge trays of food—were arranged end to end all along the sides of the room. And Fisby realized that everyone was to sit with his back toward the outside and face in toward the open space of pale-green reed mats. Between every pair of tables was a squat pottery brazier, set in a box of sand, and filled with glowing charcoal.

It took Fisby but a moment to spot his place; for he saw the pillows of red silk spread on the mats, up at the head of the room. And sure enough, that's where Hokkaido was leading them.

Hokkaido indicated that they were to sit on the pillows, but Sakini said quickly: "Leave one pillow empty next to you." And Fisby nodded. Sinking down, he modestly drew his bathrobe over his knees and looked about. "Well, Doc," he said, "it looks like we're right up here with the big shots. Right up with all the mayors."

But the Doc was regarding the tray filled with cubes of raw beef, Japanese onions, shredded carrots and cabbage, and boiled bean curd. "Sakini," he said, "where did you get all this food?"

Sakini smiled proudly. "We have to trade like the dickens, Mr. Doctor. Go around to all the villages. Swap 'em salt, and fish, and mats for vegetables. Even get a cow from 'em for beef."

The Doc nodded. "Well, in a few weeks we'll be bringing all this in from our farm."

The serving boys were coming with trays again. This time they were loaded with small porcelain bottles. "What's that, Sakini?" Fisby asked curiously.

"That's the *sake,* boss. They have to heat it out in the kitchen. Now they pass it around to everybody."

142

Someone else was coming toward them, too, and the smiling Fisby tugged the Doc's sleeve. "Look."

First Flower and Lotus Blossom were dressed as geisha tonight. Their pretty faces were powdered and their lips red. Their hair wasn't in rolled bobs tonight, but arranged in an elaborate coiffure, and they walked with a mincing step.

"Well, well," Fisby said, rubbing his hands. "Good evening."

Their faces lit up, and they bowed deeply. Then Fisby saw what the pillows next to him and the Doc were for—the geisha sat next to the honor guests.

"Boss," Sakini said, "they say they never see you in a kimono before. You look nice."

Fisby pulled the bathrobe down over his knees again. "Well, I usually don't wear one around like this." Then remembering that the Doc had never met the girls, he made the introductions.

Lotus Blossom was kneeling beside the Doc, and First Flower was kneeling on the pillow beside Fisby. Taking the small porcelain bottles, the girls filled the lacquered cups with *sake* and passed them to the honor guests. Then all along the long row of tables the juniors began pouring for the seniors.

The Doc sipped the warm cup, rolled it over his tongue, and nodded appreciatively. "Very good. Very good." After another sip, he looked around the room. "Say, Fisby," he said. "This is a fine custom. We ought to have parties like this more often."

"Wait until you hear the singing, Mr. Doctor," Sakini said quickly. "We eat a little bit, then First Flower and Lotus Blossom are going to sing a lot of songs. They dance, too. We have lots of fun."

Fisby nodded. He liked this spirit of good-fellowship. All along the tables, the men were passing the cups back and forth in toasts. Arms were around shoulders, laughter was in the air. And he relaxed.

When First Flower placed a shallow pan over the brazier near their table, and Lotus Blossom broke a single egg into each bowl and began beating it lightly with chopsticks —it seemed as a signal. All along the line there was a stirring and a bowing. "We cook the *sukiyaki* now," Sakini said, and Fisby watched curiously.

Apparently each two tables cooked its own meal, and it seemed a deep honor to be named cook. The eldest, the

143

most revered, the one of highest social position, or something, was named; resulting in a series of protests and bowing, an "After you, my dear Gaston" procedure.

At their own table First Flower, the senior geisha, had taken over, as was the custom. The raw beef was carefully placed in a sauce of soy, sweet *sake,* and stock. Next the vegetables, one by one, were put in, and the Doc leaned forward. "I want to watch this, Fisby," he said. "I used to do a little cooking myself back home. You know, barbecues in the backyard. Things like that."

It was evident that things had been settled at the other tables. At each, the most honored, the most revered was bending over the various braziers, carefully measuring this and gravely measuring that.

At one table, however, quite a discussion was going on. It was down in the section reserved for the village officials, and Fisby whispered, "What's the matter, Sakini?"

Sakini listened for a moment. "I think they have an argument, boss. Hokkaido says he thinks the President should be allowed to cook the *sukiyaki.*"

"Oh?"

"But everybody else down there say Hokkaido can't cook nothing. They want the police chief."

Fisby grew uneasy. He hoped he wouldn't be called upon to name the cook. And as the argument grew stronger, Fisby decided to make conversation, to busy himself. "Sakini, will you tell First Flower that I noticed you're using all lacquer ware here tonight."

She looked up from the cooking *sukiyaki,* her chopsticks poised, and smiled. "She say lacquer ware is always used for formal parties, boss."

At that moment, Fisby decided to put in a plug for Seiko. "I thought perhaps you might use some painted dishes. You know, with flowers on them, or—"

"She say the other day somebody bring in something like that. But she don't think we could use them around here, even for informal parties."

"No?"

"No. She says she don't bother to find out who did the painting, but whoever it was is all out of practice."

Fisby knew she was fully aware that Seiko had done the work, yet was putting on a show of indifference. "By the way," he said, "I hear Seiko has come back to the village."

First Flower feigned surprise. "Oh, did he go away?"

Fisby had a sneaking suspicion that Seiko was going to do a little suffering for heading north that day. "Incidentally, is Seiko here tonight?"

First Flower tossed her head. "She say he wouldn't be here, boss. He wouldn't have the clothes. But how could you expect anyone to have a kimono who just sits around *cha yas*, chases girls, and roams all over the countryside." She reached for the small porcelain bottle of *sake* and refilled Fisby's cup. "Here, boss. She says—please, you drink."

Glancing down toward Hokkaido, Fisby saw that the argument had been settled. Outnumbered, Hokkaido was forced to turn the cooking over to the police chief; still that didn't prevent Hokkaido from offering suggestions, which he was doing at the moment.

When Hokkaido saw Fisby regarding him, he waved. Then an idea seemed to hit him, for his face began to glow, and quickly he struggled to his feet. As Hokkaido walked along in front of the tables, insecurity swept over Fisby. He didn't know what Hokkaido was up to, yet he did know he wanted no part of it.

Reaching Fisby's table, Hokkaido bowed deeply; and Sakini, his dark eyes filled with fear, turned. "Boss, Hokkaido wants to know if in honor of the occasion, and while the *sukiyaki* is cooking, you and the Mr. Doctor would like him to sing a song?"

Fisby noted that a hush had fallen over the party. All eyes were turned toward him now, and everyone seemed nervous and apprehensive. "Why I don't know." Fisby was hesitant. "What do you think, Doc?"

"Well, I always like to hear a song," the Doc said. "What do you think?"

Fisby wished he didn't have to do any thinking. It was clearly evident that a number of sarcastic remarks were being tossed at Hokkaido from the side lines for having dared make such a suggestion. Even First Flower, looking up from the cooking *sukiyaki*, seemed uneasy.

Fisby was about to suggest that Hokkaido might sing, perhaps, a little later in the evening. Yet Hokkaido's face, glowing in hope and anticipation, made him reconsider. "Why yes," he said slowly. "I think a song might be nice."

Sakini's eyes widened, as he regarded Fisby in disbelief. "Boss, you want me to tell him that?"

"Why, of course. We'd like to hear a song."

A groan arose in the room which made Fisby twitch

uneasily. But the pleased Hokkaido was rubbing his hands and beaming. Then Hokkaido grew solemn and professional. "Boss," Sakini said, "Hokkaido wants to explain to you and the Mr. Doctor that this song is four, maybe five hundred years old."

"Is that a fact?"

"Yes, boss. And it's all about a bunch of guys who come over from China and try to take the Castle of Naka-gusuku."

"I see," Fisby said. "It's a battle song."

"That's right. And in it, Hokkaido say he have to sing a lot of parts—the parts of the guys in the castle, and the parts of the guys who come over from China."

Though Fisby felt that Hokkaido was tackling a rather complicated number, he refrained from mentioning it.

"And boss," Sakini went on, "Hokkaido wants you to know that this is an awful hard song to sing, because in most places it don't have words."

The Doc eyed Fisby. Fisby eyed the Doc. "If it doesn't have words, how is he going to sing it?"

"Well, he sings the noises of the battle. Now he wants to know if you're ready?"

Fisby and the Doc were as ready as they would ever be. Pushing back the sleeves of his kimono, Hokkaido began. First, in a greatly exaggerated manner, he imitated a horseman astride a galloping mount. He galloped all the way down one side of the room. "See, boss," Sakini explained, "that's those guys from China riding up on their ponies."

Then, quick as a flash, Hokkaido ran across the room, put up a hand to shade his eyes, and Fisby understood that. "Look, Doc," he whispered. "See, that's a lookout on the castle wall. They're not going to be caught sleeping."

Quickly, Hokkaido changed again. The scene having been set, the characters introduced, Hokkaido was now ready for the action. He became the leader of the invaders, wheeling his horsemen into battle array. He rose on his toes, like a man rises in the stirrups, his face a picture of grim determination. Slowly, deliberately his hand came up. And the Doc leaned forward. "I think he's going to blow the charge, Fisby. Listen!"

Hokkaido took a deep breath, his cheeks puffed, and he blew.

The signal for the charge combined many qualities—one being, the loudest, most unearthly thing Fisby had ever heard. He jumped. The Doc jumped. And all along the

146

tables those, who had apparently heard the song before, brought their hands up over their ears.

After that, Fisby never did have a chance to gain his composure, for Hokkaido was many things. He was snorting ponies dashing up the hill at breakneck speed, their hoofs beating on the hard clay. He was lieutenants and sublieutenants urging their men on with lusty cries. He was individual soldiers, hurling blood-curdling challenges. He was the twang of a bowstring, and an arrow whistling through the air.

He was a flock of bleating goats caught in the charge and now fleeing for their lives. He was shrieking children, sobbing women, javelin shafts breaking, swords striking on armor. And apparently a dog that somehow had its tail cut off in the battle.

Here and there, people were slipping out onto the verandas. All had their hands clamped tightly over their ears, except the mayors of little Koza and Maebaru. Being more polite than the rest, they merely drained their *sake* cups, quickly refilled them, and drained them again.

"Holy hell, Fisby," the Doc whispered, "I hope someone wins that battle pretty soon."

For a moment, Fisby thought the Doc had his wish come true. The invaders, still hurling challenges at the top of their lungs, were slowly driven back down the hill, gradually the sound lessened, then the panting Hokkaido stood there in absolute silence.

Fisby was about to applaud the end of the number, but realized that there was more to it. Stealthily on tiptoes, Hokkaido was sneaking around in a great circle. "They're sending out a flanking party now, Doc," Fisby explained.

The Doc was pale. "Fisby, are you sure they don't have a bar around here?"

Fisby's answer was lost in the shouts of the castle defenders discovering the flankers. Hokkaido became heavily breathing, defiant re-enforcements, spears over shoulders, running from one wall of the castle to the other, in order to meet the thrust. That seemed to be exactly what the leader of the invaders wanted for again the main body of the invaders, as portrayed by a grim Hokkaido, came charging up the hill on the snorting ponies.

With a main attack and a flanking attack going on at the same time, Fisby lost track of the battle. But it was loud. And it was long. And it wasn't until the groups began drifting back in from the verandas and thankful smiles appeared on all faces in the room, that Fisby realized the fight was nearly over. He mopped his forehead with his handkerchief.

Then the winded, smiling, triumphant Hokkaido stood before him and bowed. "Boss," Sakini said, "he wants to know how you and the Mr. Doctor like his song?"

Fisby thought this was rather an unfair question to ask a man, yet a glance at the Doc convinced him that he better answer for both. "It was fine, Sakini. Very fine."

The doubtful Sakini translated, then said: "Hokkaido thanks you."

Fisby felt a word or two more was in order. "Yes, sir, Sakini, tell him it was the most realistic thing I ever heard. Why you could just hear those pack mules braying, you could just imagine——"

Sakini scratched his head. "But there weren't any mules in it, boss."

"There weren't?" Fisby's eyebrows arched. "Well, I swear something was braying. Maybe it was donkeys."

"But there weren't any donkeys in it either."

Fisby cleared his throat. "Ah, yes. Well, just tell him it was fine."

As Sakini repeated Fisby's words, Hokkaido's happiness was spread from ear to ear. Then it was Sakini who looked at Fisby in alarm. "Boss, Hokkaido says for his next song, he would like to sing about how the guys from China come back the next day and try to take the castle again."

Fisby hesitated. "That's fine, but maybe he can sing for us a little later." He looked around desperately. "I hate to have the *sukiyaki* get cold. I think it's almost ready."

"Oh, Hokkaido say that's all right, boss. Everybody should go right ahead. He'll sing for them while they eat."

Fisby wasn't going to be responsible for what Hokkaido did to people's digestions. Besides, the eyes turned to him from all along the line of tables were almost pleading. "Well, I think we'll wait a little while for another song."

Hokkaido's lip trembled. "Boss, he thinks maybe you don't like his singing."

"Why I thought—well, just tell him I've never heard anything quite like that before."

The tears were beginning to trickle down Hokkaido's cheeks. "Boss, he say he don't get many chances to sing, because the guys around this place don't appreciate good songs. Now if you won't let him——"

Fisby felt the perspiration break out on his forehead. It was then that First Flower took over. She spoke rapidly to Hokkaido, and Fisby asked: "What is she saying, Sakini?"

"Oh, she says Hokkaido should give the honor guests a chance to sing, too. She claims everybody would like to hear some American songs. And maybe see some American dances."

"But I don't dance," Fisby said.

For a moment First Flower seemed a little vexed, but then she smiled. "Well, she thinks maybe the Mr. Doctor does." She paused hopefully. "Maybe he would do a dance for us."

The Doc beamed. "Come to think of it, Sakini, I did do a little dancing in my time. Back in school I did a soft-shoe number, once, in our college revue. Let's see if I still remember it."

When Sakini made the announcement, the Doc drew a nice round of applause—whether it was because he was going to dance or because they were getting rid of Hokkaido, Fisby did not know. Drawing his dressing gown about him, the Doc swung into a step, then stopped and shook his head. "Can't do it, Fisby. It won't work with these reed sandals and mats."

Yet the Doc seemed reluctant to give up the floor. "But I'll tell you what, Fisby, I don't see why we couldn't sing them a song. What say we try a duet. Let's do 'The Sweetheart of Sigma Chi.'"

A duet was fine with Fisby, who liked to do a little singing himself. But then he caught a glimpse of Hokkaido, his lower lip sagging, doing the best he could to hold back the flow of tears. Fisby grew uneasy. "Wait a minute, Doc," he said. "Just a second."

He gave it careful thought, then had it. "I'll tell you what let's do. Let's make a trio out of it, and do the 'Whiffen-poof Song.' You take the lead. I'll sing harmony. And, by golly, we'll bring Hokkaido in on the 'baa . . . baa . . . baa.'"

Twenty

THE NEXT MORNING, sitting at his desk in headquarters, Fisby thought over the events of the night before. He was sorry that Seiko hadn't attended the banquet, for First Flower sang some wonderful songs, and her dancing was such that Fisby could well understand why she was the most famous geisha in all Naha.

But Fisby was especially proud of Hokkaido. Why, even the police chief had to admit that no one could put the realism into the "baa . . . baa . . . baa" quite like Hokkaido —even though the entire group at one time or other during the evening had tried it, both as soloists and during the community sing.

Outside, the village was quiet in the morning. In his closing speech of the night before, Fisby had told everyone, including Sakini, to sleep until noon—an announcement which brought down the house. In fact, Fisby would have been sleeping himself, except he was of the get-up-before-eight type and couldn't stay in bed.

A few women were prowling about here and there. And one, namely Miss Higa Jiga with the sleepy Sakini in tow, was heading toward the side door of headquarters.

When Miss Higa Jiga stood there before his desk, Fisby wished he had never gotten up; for Miss Higa Jiga was scowling just a little more than usual, and Miss Higa Jiga was pretty sore this morning.

"Boss," Sakini said hoarsely, "do you know what she thinks?"

"What?" Fisby asked. He was also hoarse from all the singing the night before.

"Well, she thinks we don't have any gentlemen around this place."

"No gentlemen!" Fisby was astounded. "Why, Sakini, you tell her that last night at the party, I never saw a finer group of—"

"But she's not talking about last night, boss. She knows what happened, because she was out in the garden peeking in." Sakini rubbed his sleepy eyes. "She's talking about this morning."

"Did someone do something wrong this morning?" Fisby inquired.

"Yes, boss. You see, this morning she decides to have the tea drinking ceremony down at her new *cha no yu* house. And she decides she ought to have a couple guys to practice the ceremony on."

"So?"

"So she goes around to some of the guys' houses, and wakes them up, and asks them to come over. And do you know what happens?"

"What?"

"Well, when the guys find out who's there, they won't come to the door. They just go right back to sleep."

"I think they're a little tired this morning," Fisby said, by way of explanation and justification. "You see, they—"

"But Miss Higa Jiga says gentlemen would get right up and say, 'Oh, how do you do. Why I'd be glad to come right over.' And they would."

While Fisby thought this was debatable, he kept it to himself, not wishing to enter into any debates with Miss Higa Jiga.

"And she ask Seiko, too," Sakini went on. "She always thinks he's a pretty good guy. But he just wants to paint dishes this morning. And she don't think it's very nice for him to do that when he could be drinking tea wth her."

"Well, what am I supposed to do about it?" Fisby asked.

"Well, she just thinks maybe you're the only gentleman around this place, so she's asking you to come over to the tea drinking ceremony."

While Fisby didn't know if he was the only gentleman around the place, or a gentleman for that matter, still he was one of the few men up, and she had him on the spot. What could he do but accept the invitation, or rather, the command.

"And Miss Higa says the ceremony is always formal, boss. So she wants you to wear your kimono, like last night. And she'll be ready in fifteen minutes."

Fisby arose from his swivel chair. Now he had to walk up the hill to put on his bathrobe. "Oh, Sakini," he said, "where will I meet you?"

Sakini turned quickly. "Do I got to go, too, boss?"

"Sure. If you don't, how will I know what's going on? Besides, don't you want to be a gentleman?"

151

•

Sakini scratched his head. "I'd rather sleep, boss. You say I can have the morning off."

Fisby rubbed his chin. "Well, after the ceremony's over, you can have the rest of the day off. How's that?"

While Sakini wasn't enthusiastic about the tea drinking ceremony, still he liked the idea of having the afternoon to himself, as he would like to go fishing. Then he left to put on his kimono.

After meeting in headquarters, Fisby and Sakini walked down to Miss Higa Jiga's house—a ramshackle, unpainted two-room affair set in a thick, boggy grove of textile bananas. Over to one side of the bare, grassless yard—packed by untold number of bare feet tramping on it—two women bent over a heavy stone mill, grinding soaked soya beans. "That's Miss Higa Jiga's mamma and Aunt Takamini," Sakini explained. "They're making bean curd." He pointed. "And there's Miss Higa Jiga's grandma, on her papa's side, telling them how to do it."

Fisby bowed to the ladies; and as they smiled at him, he could see they bore a strong family resemblance, even though related only by marriage. With their hunched shoulders, free swinging arms, and bowed legs, they all looked exactly like Miss Higa Jiga.

The grandma spoke quickly, and Sakini explained: "Boss, she asks you to excuse Miss Higa Jiga's papa for not being here to meet you, but he's out in back feeding the pigs right now."

"That's all right," Fisby said. "Perfectly all right. By the way, Sakini, ask how Hiyoshi is."

"Oh, you mean Miss Higa Jiga's best pig?"

"That's right."

Sakini made inquiries. And Miss Higa Jiga's grandma, who apparently did the speaking for the group when she was present, shook her head sadly. "She say he's not so good this morning, boss. Yesterday he break loose again, and get out in the fields, and eat too many sweet potatoes. Now he's got colic."

"That's too bad," Fisby said. "I hope it's nothing serious."

"They don't think it is, boss. They're giving him lots of tea to drink; and they put him under the house, where it's nice and cool, so he can sleep. And he'll be all right by tonight, they think. But they want to know if you would like to see him?"

Fisby drew his bathrobe about him. He had no desire

of crawling under the house to look at Hiyoshi. "I think maybe we better let him rest. Anyway, we're supposed to meet Miss Higa Jiga for the tea drinking ceremony, and I think it's about time now."

The group nodded brightly. "They say we should just walk out through the backyard, boss."

Yet they had trouble getting through the backyard. In fact, they never did make it, for the mud in the banana grove was knee-deep. Rather than get their sandals dirty, they walked out through the front, went down the street and around the corner, then slipped in between a bushy hedge. And Fisby's eyes opened wide in surprise.

Here was an area, perhaps 30 x 50 feet, set well behind Miss Higa Jiga's house and pigpen. It was a secluded area surrounded by spreading shrubs and sequestering hedges; an area, by itself, that had been carefully planned and landscaped to set forth the beauty and quietness of nature.

"Sakini," Fisby said. "Did First Flower plan this?"

"Yes, boss."

Fisby shook his head in admiration. "Say, this is a beautiful garden. She even has a pool, eh, and a stone walk, and—" Over to one side, Fisby saw the small plain building, with reed sides and a thatched roof, setting beneath the transplanted pines. "And that's the *cha no yu* house, eh?"

"Yep, boss."

Looking about, Fisby caught a glimpse of Lotus Blossom sitting quietly on a stone bench. "Well, well," he said, "look who's here. I didn't know she was coming."

Sakini scratched his head. "Neither did I, boss. Should we go over to see her?"

Lotus Blossom, in a beautiful blue kimono, greeted them with a smile and with a bow. And as she spoke to Sakini, Fisby noted that her voice was almost a whisper. "Boss," Sakini explained, "Lotus Blossom say First Flower is so busy lately with building the *cha no yu* houses for the Women's League and fixing the little gardens, that she has turned the teaching of the ceremony and flower arranging over to her."

Fisby smiled. "I see. So now she's here to see that Miss Higa Jiga does it right."

"Yes, boss."

"Good. And will you ask her to help me out on this, too. I never attended the tea drinking ceremony before, and I'll probably make a lot of mistakes."

"Okay, boss," Sakini said. "And I ask her to help me. I never go to one of these things before either." As he spoke to Lotus Blossom, her eyes twinkled, and she nodded with a smile, and her voice was still low. "She says she'll be glad to, boss. But she don't want you to be nervous about this, because it's just practice. Miss Higa Jiga will probably make a lot of mistakes, too."

Fisby felt better, and regarded her with confidence. "Well, Sakini, what are we supposed to do first?"

"First, boss, she don't know if Miss Higa Jiga tell you or not, but you're the *shokyaku*—that means the principal guest."

"I am?"

"Yes, boss. Now we all just sit here on the waiting bench." Lotus Blossom's voice grew lower. "And we forget about all the things that are beyond the garden. We just think about the trees and the bushes. We look at the hedges, and the shrubs, and the saplings swaying in the breeze. And we think how nice the skies and the whole earth are."

Drawing his bathrobe about him, Fisby sank onto the stone bench beside Lotus Blossom. Carefully, he looked about the garden. Here in the shade it was relaxing. He leaned over and whispered, "Say, this is fine."

Sakini's voice, too, dropped to a whisper as he translated; and Lotus Blossom, her eyes warm, whispered back. "She say you make a very good principal guest, boss, because you notice how nice things are. Not to notice and appreciate are the worst mistakes anyone can make."

Fisby made a mental note to notice and appreciate, then settled back to contemplate his surroundings. He breathed deep, looked at the small pines, looked at the *cha no yu* house resting beneath their overhanging branches, and nodded. Yes, sir, it was a fine thing, sitting around in the garden like this. If more people did it, there wouldn't be so many ulcers and nervous breakdowns. It did something for your system, it . . .

His thoughts were interrupted by a shout from beyond the hedges. "Hey, Fisby," someone called, "what are you doing?"

Glancing up, he saw the Doc, astride the rawboned dun, looking over the hedge. Quickly he put a finger to his lips, then whispered to Sakini. "Ask Lotus Blossom to excuse me for a moment. I want to speak with the Doc." He arose, tightened the belt of his bathrobe, and tiptoed over to the hedge.

"What's going on, Fisby?" the Doc asked curiously.

"Sssh. Not so loud, Doc," Fisby whispered. "We're meditating."

"You are? Well, I didn't mean to disturb you." The Doc scratched his head. "Say, this gives me an idea. I've been running short of material, and it's exactly what I need. Do you know, Fisby, that Colonel Purdy has been jumping me lately. Wants to come down here and prowl around. Why, he's just the kind who would monkey with my asparagus beds. I'm telling you, Fisby, I won't have it. If I have to keep doctoring every report I send in, if I have to make you the craziest—"

"Make me what, Doc?"

The Doc appeared rather sheepish. "Nothing, Fisby." He straightened in the saddle. "Well, I guess you want to get back to your meditating. See you later."

Fisby was puzzled. Then the thought of Colonel Purdy came, causing him to look at his bathrobe. Suppose the Colonel caught him sitting around like this? He winced. He had been so busy lately that he had forgotten all about Plan B, and the education program, and the new school. He'd have to get on that right away before the Colonel demanded another progress report. In fact, this minute. But Sakini was calling softly, "Hey, boss, aren't you going to sit down?"

Fisby turned, saw the garden. Well, maybe it could wait a little while. After all, when you were in the garden, you weren't supposed to think of outside things. You were supposed to commune with nature. Quietly, he went back to his place on the bench.

They sat there meditating for a few minutes, then Miss Higa Jiga slid back a small door in the *cha no yu* house, which apparently was a signal. Lotus Blossom arose and whispered, "Miss Higa Jiga is ready to receive the guests, now, boss. You're the *shokyaku,* so you go first, and we will follow in single file. You just walk along the *roji,* there, that's what she calls the stone path between the waiting bench and the *cha no yu* house."

"All right," Fisby said.

"And, boss, Lotus Blossom says along the path is the most beautiful part of the garden. Here everything's got to be just right, so the guest's mind is real calm, and he don't get all disturbed before he enters the *cha no yu*

155

house. Now everybody is real quiet, and everybody thinks only of the beauty of the garden."

"I understand," Fisby said. "Just walk right along the path."

"Yes, boss. But stop up by that rock before the *cha no yu* house. See, we're just practicing, and Lotus Blossom will tell you what to do next when you get there."

Fisby nodded, smoothed his bathrobe, and started along the path called *roji*. For a moment he was uncertain as to pace, then deciding the wedding march should be about right, he began humming it to himself. The garden path was simple. There was nothing ornate here. Yet each bush, each shrub, each sapling blended together in a perfectly balanced picture. And Fisby could well understand the hours of work, and experiment, and planning that went into making that picture.

Ahead was a large stone. Nearing it, Fisby saw that it had been painstakingly chipped into a basin, and the depression was filled with clear water. Close by stood a stone lantern, which made Fisby wonder how many hours of work had been required to fashion it. Here, near the basin and its lantern, the rocks and foliage were most carefully arranged. And here, Fisby assumed, was the pinnacle of the landscape architect's work.

He stood before the basin as directed. "Now," Sakini whispered. "Lotus Blossom say we must purify ourselves, boss. Take that little dipper, there, with the bamboo handle, hold your hand to one side, and pour water over it. Do it to the other one, too, boss, then rinse your mouth."

Squatting, as in a deep knee bend, Fisby did as he was told, and Sakini and Lotus Blossom went through the same procedure. "Now go to the rock before the little door of the *cha no yu,* boss," Sakini directed, "stand on it, remove your sandals, then crawl inside."

Crawl inside is exactly what Fisby did, because the door couldn't have been larger than three feet by three feet in size. As he came into the *cha no yu* house on his hands and knees, he looked up. On the floor were the pale-green mats, of which four and one half exactly covered the small, nine and one half by nine and one half room. The room, itself, appeared barren. There was a small brazier and a plain alcove; that was about it.

As Fisby regained his feet, Miss Higa Jiga was standing there waiting for him. 'Boss," Sakini said, rising off his knees, "Miss Higa Jiga asks you to excuse her kimono.

It's only of banana cloth. Now what she needs is a real nice one of silk, like Lotus Blossom is wearing, and she needs . . ."

But Lotus Blossom, laying a hand on Sakini's arm, stopped him, then whispered quickly to Miss Higa Jiga, who pouted.

"Is something wrong, Sakini?" Fisby asked.

"Yep, boss. Lotus Blossom tell her she shouldn't say things like that here. Here she is supposed to forget all about the outside world. Here is supposed to be a world by itself."

"Is that a fact?"

"Yes, but Miss Higa Jiga thought it would be a good chance to remind you that you haven't gotten the silk kimonos for her and the Women's League yet. And, boss, she says you can see how much they need them."

Fisby grew uneasy. And Lotus Blossom, noticing that the principal guest's serenity of mind had been disturbed, turned to Sakini. "Boss, she says we'll go on with the ceremony. Now we'll go over to the alcove and get on our knees to admire the scroll."

The hanging scroll was a piece of coarse white target cloth bearing characters of the Chinese ideographic script, called *kanji,* painted in black. "Lotus Blossom says it's an inscription from the ancient, classical literature," Sakini explained, "but I don't know what it means, boss. I can't read the ideogram. I read only the *katakana* and *hiragana* syllabaries."

Fisby hardly knew how to go about admiring a scroll that he didn't understand. Yet he did understand that if the inscription was from the classical literature it should, no doubt, be painted on a fine brocade, and not on target cloth. "Boss," Sakini went on in a whisper, "Lotus Blossom say that Seiko put the characters on it, and she wants you to notice them. See the sweep of them, see the flow; they're not like tight printed things. And they show the freeness of Seiko's spirit; they show he is not confined."

Fisby regarded the characters with a new light, and commented favorably on Seiko's lettering.

Next, they admired the incense holder, set on its small piece of silk, and Fisby learned that the contents of powdered aloe wood would be poured onto the hearth in his honor. When he inquired about the incense holder, itself, he learned that Kiei had made it. Then, the ceremony having been completed, they seated themselves on the straw mats.

It was Miss Higa Jiga who began speaking, and Fisby saw Lotus Blossom's mouth fly open in amazement. "What's the matter, Sakini?" he asked.

"Well, boss, Miss Higa Jiga say now she's supposed to serve the *kaiseki* meal, but she can't do it, because you let the guys down at the teahouse keep all the Japanese rations we find in the caves for themselves. Now she thinks it would be nice if you would take all that stuff away from the guys and give it to the Women's League. Then they could have the *kaiseki* meal."

The perspiration broke out on Fisby's forehead, and he was about to speak. But Lotus Blossom, her anger evident, was speaking for him. "Boss," Sakini said, "Lotus Blossom claim she never hear of such a thing. She never hear of the hostess speaking to the principal guest that way. By gosh, she's giving Miss Higa Jiga the dickens."

The pouting Miss Higa Jiga got the dickens for quite a while, then Lotus Blossom arose and bowed to Fisby. "Boss, she say now we must go out in the garden again. The first session is closed."

As they sat on the bench, it seemed to Fisby that things hadn't gone according to plan. By now, he believed, the guests should be in a peaceful state of mind, should be in a meditative, introspective mood. Frankly, he was a little upset over Miss Higa Jiga's reference to the Japanese rations, for he felt that a more equal distribution should have been made. And he could see that Lotus Blossom wasn't doing much meditating either. While it was plain that she was doing her level best to concentrate on nature, still she was having trouble keeping down the anger that seethed in her eyes and flushed her cheeks.

When the booming of a gong filled the garden, Lotus Blossom jumped, and in that instant lost her temper completely. "She say Miss Higa Jiga is supposed to ring it so the sound just floats out over the garden and mingles with the rustle of the trees, boss," Sakini said. "But she claims Miss Higa Jiga is hitting that thing as if she is running a lighthouse and is trying to warn all the ships at sea to keep off the rocks."

Lotus Blossom rose quickly and bowed. "She is sorry for getting angry. Maybe we better go in now."

They walked along the path, repurified themselves, entered the *cha no yu,* and seated themselves on the mats,

158

where all tried to get into an introspective mood. This session, Fisby learned, was to start with Miss Higa Jiga making *koicha,* a thick tea. And the guests were supposed to listen to the music of the boiling water which, Lotus Blossom stated, resembled the wind blowing through the pines. It was here, in this atmosphere conducive to rest and calm, that all were to arrive at the inner nature of the universe, and truth, and understanding.

Koicha, the thick tea, Fisby saw, was made by placing three spoonfuls of powdered tea in a bowl, filling it with one third of a dipper of boiling water, and stirring until it became frothy. This, Fisby imagined, was an art which required much practice. While Miss Higa Jiga wasn't very artistic, as least she was vigorous. The bamboo tea whisk flew round in the bowl at mile-a-minute speed, and it looked to Fisby as if she were whipping up a batch of lather in a shaving mug.

When she thrust the bowl toward him, Sakini whispered, "Lotus Blossom say to put the bowl in the palm of your left hand, boss, and protect it with your right hand. She claim we do that because some bowls are maybe three, four hundred years old, and we don't want to drop them."

Fisby nodded and looked at the tea. It resembled split pea soup with foam on it.

"Now," Sakini went on, "Lotus Blossom say to take one sip. Then we usually tell the hostess that it is fine, and just right, and stuff."

Fisby took one sip and said, "Now this is really good."

Miss Higa Jiga flushed with pleasure.

"Take a couple more sips, boss," Sakini continued, "then pass it to me, to do the same thing. Then I give it to Lotus Blossom."

The bowl went down the line, whereupon Fisby learned it was the custom for the principal guest to request the privilege of examining the bowl, of turning it upside down and scrutinizing it closely. Remembering that Lotus Blossom had said that some of these bowls were hundreds of years old, he handled it carefully. Yet the thing seemed new to him. "Sakini," he said, "may I ask a question about the bowl?"

"Yes, boss. That's what you're supposed to do. Then the hostess tells you all the stories about it, how it come into her family, what happened to it, and all that."

"I see." Fisby turned it upside down. "Well, how old is this, Sakini?"

Miss Higa Jiga, the hostess, scratched her head. "She say she don't know, boss."

"Oh." Fisby was stopped cold.

But Lotus Blossom broke in. "She say Kiei just make it," Sakini explained. "It don't have any stories about it yet, but someday it will."

"It will?" Fisby questioned.

"Yes, boss. Maybe four, five, six hundred years from now somebody in Miss Higa Jiga's family will have a tea drinking ceremony, just like this. Maybe the principal guest will inquire about the bowl, as he should. Then the hostess will tell all the things that have been passed down from grandpa, to son, to grandson. She will tell all about the guys who come from America in iron ships, and how they come running up on the shore. She will tell about you, who come to our village and give us cloth for the hanging scroll and clothes. She will tell how you build us a teahouse, when we never have one in the village before. How you build *cha no yu* houses. How you do a lot of things for us. And how you were the first one ever to sip from this bowl."

"Is that a fact?" Fisby looked more closely at the bowl.

"Yep, boss. May I see it now?"

As Fisby passed the bowl, he noticed that Sakini wasn't as careful as he might be. "Please, Sakini," he said a little tartly, "don't drop it." By golly, he wanted this thing to last six hundred years. It wasn't everyone who was going to be remembered that long; and he rather liked the idea that here, in this corner of the world, Captain Jeff Fisby of Napoleon, Ohio, was going down in history, even if he was forgotten everywhere else.

There was a rooting, grunting noise outside, and Miss Higa Jiga quickly went over and pushed back the door. Then she turned back to the room, all smiles.

"What's happening, Sakini?" Fisby asked.

"Boss, Miss Higa Jiga say that Hiyoshi come down to find out what's going on."

Fisby caught a glimpse of Hiyoshi's snout poked through the door. Then Miss Higa Jiga had him by the front feet and was helping him into the room.

Lotus Blossom gasped and jumped up quickly. Regardless of what language she spoke, her tone told Fisby that she was shrieking, "Get that pig out of here!"

Miss Higa Jiga looked up in surprise, then spoke quickly. "What did she say?" Fisby asked.

"Well, she says Hiyoshi likes tea, too, and she's just going to pour him a bowl. He'll lay over in the corner real nice, and he won't bother anyone."

Lotus Blossom's face was livid. She stomped her foot. She waved an angry finger. And fright actually appeared in Miss Higa Jiga's eyes. But Lotus Blossom was only warming up. She went on, and on, and Miss Higa Jiga pushed the protesting Hiyoshi back outside.

Then Lotus Blossom turned. "Boss, if you'll excuse us, she thinks we had enough of the tea drinking ceremony for today."

They arose, bowed, and took leave of Miss Higa Jiga, who promptly set off after Hiyoshi—who was heading for the sweet potato fields and another touch of colic.

As they stood in the garden, Fisby felt sorry for Lotus Blossom for the shame was burning in her cheeks. "Boss, she wishes to apologize. She thinks maybe she embarrassed you because she didn't teach Miss Higa Jiga so good. And she's sorry that she got angry, and——"

Fisby held up a hand. "That's all right. Perfectly all right. I understand."

Lotus Blossom, though still ashamed, seemed thankful. Then she hesitated. "Boss," Sakini continued, "she says it's a little late for *kobiru* and Mrs. Kamakura isn't working this morning, but if you would like to go down to the *cha ya,* Lotus Blossom will make us some grilled rice cakes and some tea."

Glancing at her, Fisby realized she was trying to make up for the tea drinking ceremony. "That would be fine," he said. "I'd sure like that."

Later, as they sat in the kitchen of the teahouse, Lotus Blossom looked up from the boiling rice on the hearth. "Boss," Sakini said, "she says you must not worry, because do you know what she's going to do?"

"What, Sakini?"

"She says she's going to teach that Miss Higa Jiga and the Women's League that when you pursue an aesthetic pastime, you shouldn't have pigs lying around in the corner. If it takes her ten years, she's going to teach them to appreciate that ceremony, and how to enjoy the trees, and the garden, and the out-of-doors."

Fisby smiled. "Why, that will be fine." But secretly he thought that Lotus Blossom had quite a job cut out for her. The Women's League as typified by Miss Higa Jiga, he felt, were hardly of the aesthetic type, given to meditation and introspection. They were a little more on the realistic side, concerned over the health of Hiyoshi and his species, which guaranteed the winter supply of pork.

Twenty-One

As THE DAYS PASSED, Fisby made constant inquiries of Lotus Blossom concerning the progress of the ladies, even volunteered his services as a guest to be practiced on. But while Lotus Blossom stated that the ladies were coming along pretty well; still she didn't quite think it was safe, as yet, for them to appear in a public performance. So Fisby fell into professional hands.

First Flower and Lotus Blossom had constructed their own *cha no yu* house in a secluded corner of the teahouse garden; and it was here, clad in his bathrobe, that he went at five o'clock every afternoon. Patiently, the girls coached him in the etiquette of the ceremony; and he became so proficient that he could sail right through it without giving a thought to details, concentrating only on the peaceful quiet and harmony of the surroundings.

Perhaps he did not understand the deeper significance of the custom; yet he knew it made him feel better after a day's work to sit in the garden and relax. It was good to leave all your problems there in the world beyond the hedges.

It was Doc McLean, however, who became the true *chajin,* or tea drinking man. Not only because it was the best ulcer preventive he had ever come across, as the Doc stated it, but also because as one became interested in growing things, he could better appreciate the hours of care and planning that went into the garden. Besides, the Doc had a deep interest in ceramics. He would bend over a small cup, much to the pleasure of the hostess, and observe with infinite care the skill and craftsmanship that went into it; then, with genuine interest, would seek its history.

Even Sakini had grown fond of the tea drinking ceremony, though his principal concern lay in the *kaiseki* meal, sent over from the kitchen of the teahouse.

So while the interests of the three varied, still First Flower and Lotus Blossom, much to their delight, had three steady customers at five each afternoon.

It was on one such afternoon that Fisby, returning to headquarters, found the hollow-eyed, restless Seiko waiting for him. As he entered, Seiko looked up, then his eyes turned back to the floor.

Fisby stopped quickly. "What's the matter, Sakini, doesn't he feel well? He looks as if he has a touch of fever."

Briefly, Sakini questioned Seiko, then regarded Fisby. "He feels all right, boss, only he just can't paint any more."

"Can't paint?" Fisby was taken by surprise. "I saw some of his work. It's fine."

"He don't mean that, boss. Oh, he can put pictures on dishes and things like that. But he means, he can't think about his painting. Even when he's got the brush in his hand, his mind won't stay on what he's supposed to do."

"That's too bad. Is there something I can do?"

"He says there is, boss, if you would."

Fisby sank into his swivel chair. "You tell him to name it, and I'll do my best."

"Well, boss, he wants to know if you'll act as his *nakodo?*"

"His what?"

"*Nakodo.* That means 'go-between.' You see, all the time Seiko just thinks of First Flower. And he says, boss, it's driving him crazy as the dickens."

"You mean he wants her to marry him?"

"Yes, boss."

Fisby considered. "Well, in that case, why doesn't he just go down and ask her?"

"But he can't talk to her like that, boss. He has to have a go-between do it. That's the custom. So he wants you to do it because you're his best friend."

"Well, in that case," Fisby said, "I'd be glad to. But what am I supposed to do?"

"First, boss, you must find out if it's all right to talk with her."

"I see."

"Then you tell her how much Seiko thinks of her, and what a good guy he is. And all that stuff."

Fisby nodded. "Give Seiko the old build-up, eh?" He looked at the boy standing before him, and his face grew stern. "But before I act as his go-between, Sakini, I want

163

to find out a few things. First, does he really love her?"

"He says he does, boss. He does!"

Regarding the boy, Fisby knew he had asked a foolish question. No one not in love could ever be as miserable as the red-eyed Seiko, standing there before him. It was plain that Seiko was eating his heart out—the uncertain, restless hands; the nervous, twitching lips; and the eyes filled with hope yet fear told Fisby that.

Slowly, Fisby arose, walked around his desk, and patted Seiko's shoulder. "Tell him to relax, Sakini. It can't be as bad as all that."

Seiko looked up pleadingly. "Boss, he wants to know if you will talk with her then?"

Fisby smiled. "Of course. Tell him I'll do my best. Now, let's see. Sakini, run down to the *cha ya* and ask her if I can speak with her tonight."

"Okay, boss. I'll make the appointment."

"Good. Then come up to my quarters and let me know." He patted Seiko's shoulder again. "Tell him we'll take care of everything."

The appointment, so Sakini stated, was to be at eight thirty that evening. First Flower had agreed to receive Fisby and Sakini, then, in her apartment at the teahouse.

As the Doc and Sakini sat down to a game of cribbage, Fisby began rummaging through his duffel bag. He was a little undecided as to just what a go-between should wear. Perhaps he ought to wear his uniform tonight; but then again, this was more of a formal call, and decided upon his bathrobe.

Slipping it off, he gave it a good brushing. If he knew he was going to be wearing a bathrobe so much, he told himself as he surveyed the blue woolen robe with its red trimming, he would have gotten something fancier before leaving the States. Maybe something in a satin or rayon. Then he laid out a clean pair of GI cotton socks, and went about scrubbing his wooden clogs in a bucket of soapy water.

Darkness had fallen when he and Sakini reached the *cha ya*. As the serving boy handed them reed sandals in the entrance way, Sakini spoke quickly to him. Bowing, the boy disappeared down the wing that was First Flower and Lotus Blossom's apartment. "He'll see if she'll receive us now," Sakini explained. And Fisby nodded.

There was quite a bit of activity in the *cha ya* tonight. Serving boys with lacquer trays hurried through the corridors. Laughter rose, filling the air with a spirit of cordiality. And Fisby turned. "Is something special going on tonight, Sakini?"

"There's a couple of banquets, boss. Hokkaido's giving one for the village officials of Awasi. The police are giving one for the police of Maebaru. And a bunch of the guys just come down, like they do every night, to sit around and talk."

Quickly, the serving boy reappeared and bowed. "He wants us to follow him, boss," Sakini said. And they started down the corridor.

Frankly, Fisby was a little curious about First Flower's apartment, never having seen it. As he shuffled along, he noticed it was shadowy down here. No lights hung in the corridor, the only illumination came from flickering candles beyond the thin paper doors, lining both sides of the hallway. From beyond the doors, too, came something else. It was the delicate aroma of burning incense that mingled with the scent of new-cut thatch. And he breathed deep.

Suddenly, the boy stopped, spoke in a whisper; and Sakini, too, whispered. "Boss, First Flower will receive us in her sitting room."

As the boy pushed back the doors, Fisby hesitated. He didn't know what to do. But apparently they were waiting for him to enter, so he walked forward.

First Flower was sitting before a low table, facing them. On the table a small candle burned in a silver holder, and by its light, Fisby saw the deep red of her lips and the dark shadowing of her eyes. She didn't rise to meet them tonight. Instead, she merely bowed from where she sat.

Her kimono was of the deepest blue with white flowers. Beyond her, the thin doors were pushed back. And on the railinged veranda a Japanese lantern swayed gently in the breeze, throwing its dancing light on the still waters of the lotus pond. Across the pond, other wings of the teahouse were visible, glowing warm and amber, beneath the dark branches of the pines. And the laughter from the banquet rooms floated across to them.

She indicated the silk pillows, spread before the table; and Fisby, a little uncertain now, sank down on one. Reaching over, she removed the lid from a black lacquered box, inlaid with mother of pearl. "Boss," Sakini said, "she wonders if, perhaps, you would like a cigarette."

Fisby waved a hand. "Thanks, but I only smoke cigars."

Sakini regarded him quickly. "Boss, you better have one.

165

These are the kind, I hear, that come all the way from Shanghai."

Though Fisby refused, the manner in which Sakini took one told him that they were something special. They were long, with a hollow end, and bore the imperial crown of Czarist Russia.

Fisby cleared his throat. "I guess we better get down to business. Now, Sakini, just say—"

They were interrupted by the serving boy, bringing a steaming pot of tea. Asking to be excused, First Flower poured each a cup. And Sakini was wide eyed. "Boss, this is jasmine tea from China."

"It is?" Politely, Fisby sipped it. "I must say this is good. Very good." After another sip, he set his cup down. "Now as I was saying, tell her that someone has asked me to act as go-between."

Sakini translated, and Fisby watched her face for reaction. However, she merely nodded, and spoke a few words, betraying no emotion.

"What did she say, Sakini?" Fisby asked.

"She wants to know if it is the ration chief who asked you to be the go-between?"

"Tell her no. It was someone else."

"She asks was it the construction chief?"

"Tell her it was Seiko."

Fisby heard her whisper: "Seiko? Seiko?" And she seemed puzzled. "Boss," Sakini said, "she don't remember this Seiko person. Who is he?"

Fisby became uneasy, for he realized that he wasn't talking with the girl he knew. He glanced at the silk pillows, caught the fragrance of incense, and looked into her dark, impassive eyes. Tonight, he realized, he was talking with the most famous geisha in all Naha. "Well, Seiko is an artist," he explained.

First Flower put a finger to her cheek, as if trying to recall. "Boss, she asks if that's the artist who is so out of practice?"

"Oh, no," Fisby said quickly. "He's been practicing regularly. Works every day. He's the one who has been painting the dishes for the *cha ya*."

"Yes. She has seen some of his work. But there don't seem to be any life to it."

"That's just the trouble, he can't keep his mind on his painting." Fisby paused. He wasn't quite familiar with the artistic temperament. "I guess he needs inspiration or

166

something. Now as go-between, I figure if he were married to a nice girl, he'd get back on the beam in no time."

Sakini scratched his head. "He'd get where, boss?"

"He'd get some inspiration. His pictures would come to life."

Sakini nodded in understanding. As he translated, First Flower brought the cup to her lips; and her impassive eyes, looking over the rim, fell on Fisby. "Well, boss, she says there must be several nice girls here in the village he could marry. For instance, there's Miss Higa Jiga . . ."

Fisby broke in quickly. "But he wants to marry her."

She shook her head a little sadly. "She claims she hardly knows what to say, boss. Why, just before we came, the go-between for the mayor was here to speak to her. And tomorrow morning a go-between for someone else is calling. So you can see she has quite a problem."

Fisby grew alarmed. "Sakini, did you tell anyone that Seiko asked me to be his go-between?"

"I tell a few guys, boss," Sakini said. "Not many though."

So that was it. The grapevine had spread the thing all through the village, and now everyone was putting in his bid lest he be overlooked. As go-between, Fisby really had to go to work. "Now about this Seiko," he said quickly. "There's a fine boy. Yes, sir, he'll probably be the best artist on Okinawa." He searched her face carefully but there was no reaction. "Why people will probably come from all over, just to see his paintings." He held up a finger. "Providing, of course, he has inspiration."

She spoke softly. "Boss, she wants to know if this isn't the fellow who one day decided he was going to leave the village and go up north?"

"Yes," Fisby said uneasily, then forced a chuckle. "But we all make mistakes, you know."

"She says he don't sound very reliable to her. If once he decided to leave, he might decide to leave again."

Fisby caught the aloofness of her manner. "No," he said, "I don't think he would. I'm sure Seiko loves her too much to ever leave. Tell her if I weren't sure of that, I wouldn't be acting as his go-between."

She glanced at the candle, watched its flame melting away the wax, then reached for her jasmine tea. "Boss, she say over here it is the custom to be married in the home of the groom. Does Seiko have a home?"

Fisby was stumped. "I don't know, Sakini. Does he?"

167

"Not that I know of, boss. He just lives with somebody here in the village. I think they let him sleep on one of their mats at night."

"I see. Tell her that," Fisby said, even though he felt certain that First Flower knew of this.

When Sakini translated, she spoke rapidly. Then Sakini turned. "Boss, she says it has always been that way with this Seiko—he has just slept on a mat that someone lent him."

Fisby felt the perspiration forming in his palms. He didn't like being on the defensive in this matter. "But Seiko was younger then. He's changed. He's turning over a new leaf."

"Well, boss, she don't see how she could accept a proposal from such an unreliable, undependable person. Not when a fine gentleman like the mayor has already sent his go-between; and other gentlemen are planning on sending theirs."

"But reliability isn't everything," Fisby said desperately.

"She says it's a lot, boss."

"Yes, but—"

"She asks you to excuse her."

"Wait a minute." Fisby rubbed his palms on his bathrobe. "Can't we talk this over a little bit?"

First Flower was rising from the table. "She is sorry, but she must go now. You see, she has promised Hokkaido that she will sing and dance at the banquet he is giving."

Fisby looked around quickly. "I thought maybe we could have another cup of tea, sort of discuss things for a while."

"She will tell the serving boy to bring you tea, boss. And you can sit here if you wish. But she must go. After singing for Hokkaido, she must sing for the police banquet, too. Now she will order you the tea." She raised her hands to clap for the serving boy.

But Fisby shook his head. "Never mind, Sakini. I guess we better leave." As Fisby rose to his feet, he regarded her. "Sakini, tell her I would like to say something—not as Seiko's go-between—but as—well, the boss."

"All right."

"Tell her I wouldn't do anything rash. I mean the mayor and the others are fine people, yet I wouldn't make any hasty decisions. I wouldn't make any promises until I thought it over carefully."

Her eyes grew impish. "She will see, boss. Now, please excuse her."

As Fisby and Sakini walked back toward the entrance, a serving boy slipped up. "He says Seiko has left a message that he is waiting outside, boss. He would like to know what First Flower say."

Fisby nodded, and they put on their wooden sandals.

Seiko was in the shadows by the entrance; and as he came toward them, Fisby noticed that he was trembling. Frankly, Fisby felt guilty. He felt that he hadn't quite done as good a job as a go-between might do.

Seiko, his eyes hopeful, peered at Fisby. "Boss, he wants to know if she says 'yes'?"

Fisby shifted uneasily. "Not exactly."

Seiko stared at the ground. "Then she says 'no'?"

Fisby thought it over. She hadn't come right out and said no. She had said she didn't know how she could accept a proposal from an unreliable, undependable person. And somehow Fisby wondered if, perhaps, she wasn't testing Seiko. Actually, the kid had been working. He was painting. Maybe she wanted to see if he would just give everything up now. "Look," he said, "she didn't exactly say 'no' either."

Seiko was definitely puzzled. "What did she say, boss?"

Fisby shook his head. "It's not what she said that counts. It's what she meant. Tell him he should just go right ahead with his painting, not to give it up under any circumstances, because I think he has a chance."

Seiko took on new hope. "You think so, boss?"

"I sure do." Fisby rubbed his head. "And do you know what I think we ought to do?"

"What, boss?"

"I think we better get the construction crew together tomorrow morning and start building Seiko a home. A home means a lot to that girl. He can just tell the carpenters what kind he wants, where to build it, and so forth."

When Seiko learned the meaning of Fisby's words, he hesitated. Once or twice he glanced at Fisby and seemed afraid to speak.

"What's the matter?" Fisby asked.

"Boss, he don't know how to explain. I told him how you think First Flower likes a home and all that, and he— well, he appreciates what you want to do for him. And he thanks you. But he couldn't have anyone build a home for him. He couldn't accept it."

"I see." Fisby couldn't blame a man for wanting to build

his own home. No man wants charity. "Well, look. Why couldn't we just swap the work he does on the dishes for the *cha ya* as a payment for his home?"

"I don't know, boss. Can we?"

"I don't know why not. Would that be all right with Seiko?"

"He say it would be fine, only he asks if you will promise him something?"

"What?"

"He wants you to keep real close watch of the painting he does. And he wants you to watch how much time and lumber the carpenters use. You see, boss, he don't want anything for nothing."

Fisby realized that here was an impossible situation. He would have to evaluate Seiko's art work, evaluate the carpenters' time, place a value upon the lumber. He rubbed his chin. Who owned the lumber anyway? They had swapped salt and fish for it. Yet he couldn't say no to the apprehensive Seiko. "Just tell him to go ahead," he said. "We'll work out something." He turned. "I think I'll take a walk, Sakini. I want to do some thinking."

He walked through the garden of the *cha ya,* along the lotus pond; and the laughter from the banquets floated across the water. Free rations, barter, and communal living were fine, he realized, but only in an emergency stage. Tobiki village was out of that now. What they needed was a system where a man could work and pay for his own home. He told himself that what they needed was a monetary system.

Twenty-Two

IT WAS MRS. KAMAKURA, the cook at the teahouse, who further pointed out the need for a change. One morning she came into headquarters, and her reddened face told Fisby that she had just come from bending over the fires in the kitchen. "Boss," Sakini said, "she say she don't know what we're going to do."

"What's the matter?" Fisby asked.

"Well, she say it's those guys down at the *cha ya*. All

some of 'em do is just sit around all day. They order rice and all the best things, and we don't hardly have any of those Japanese rations left."

"We don't?"

"No. Some guys eat six or seven meals a day. Then at night they give a banquet for their friends from little Koza, or Maebaru, or Awasi."

"And I suppose that means she has to work eighteen hours a day."

"It's not that so much, boss. But one of her sons works out on the farm crews. All day long he plants potatoes. Maybe digs potatoes. Bends over all day. Then at night when he wants a good meal at the *cha ya,* the loafers have all the rooms, and the only place he can find to eat is down in the kitchen."

Fisby realized that something must be done, and the best way to do it was with money. If a man worked, he could pay. And if a man worked, he was the one who should eat—not the hangers-on. "Well tell me," he said, "how long does she think those rations will last?"

"Maybe two weeks, boss."

"Is the doctor sending anything in from the farm?"

"Yes, boss. He's starting to send in vegetables, but no rice. He isn't growing any."

Fisby was surprised. "He isn't. How come?"

"She don't know, boss."

"I see." Feeling in the need for some expert counsel and information, Fisby rose from his chair. "Just tell her I'll look into it, Sakini." He reached for his helmet-liner. "I think I'll walk out to the farm and have a talk with the Doc."

The Doc had located his farm out past the farthest edges of the village. Nearing it, Fisby saw the white fences sparkling in the morning sun. Drawing closer, he saw that the place was bustling with activity. Hoeing crews were busy in the patches of green vegetables. Carpenters were raising some sort of a low structure. Another group was digging a series of holes down both sides of a narrow lane. And the Doc, himself, was bending over a drawing board —his horse tied to a nearby stake.

"Hey, Doc," Fisby called, "what are you doing?"

The Doc looked up. "Hello, Fisby. Just laying out some plans for housing my farm crew. It's too far to go back and forth every day, so I'm moving the whole bunch, with their families, out here."

"You are?"

"Yep. We're making tile for the roofing over there. See, where the smoke is rising from the kilns. We started making our brick. That marl down by the shore is just right. Now as soon as I can figure out something a little more lasting than lime mortar, we'll be ready to go. Fisby, do you think a ten-mat living room is about right for an average-sized family?"

Fisby was sure he didn't know. Besides, he had rice on his mind.

"We just can't raise it," the Doc explained. "In the first place, we don't have paddy land, Fisby. Only dry fields. In the second place, I'd hesitate. The yield is too low. Land is too scare to waste over here. Why if I put the whole farm into rice, I couldn't begin to supply the *cha ya*— even if I got forty bushel to the acre. I can get 150 bushels of sweet potatoes, 500 bushels of eggplant, and turnips, and onions to the acre. So why bother around with forty bushels of rice?"

"But who's going to eat 500 bushels of onions, Doc?" Fisby protested.

The Doc nodded. "I see what you mean. But look at it this way. The things I mentioned yield high, so all I need is a little patch of land in the corner of a field, and I'll have enough of, say, turnips to supply the kitchen of the *cha ya* for an entire year. See, they'll pickle them, Fisby, and that's good. Those pickles are packed with vitamins. With one acre of land I can produce a year's supply of twenty or thirty kinds of pickles."

"Yes, but you can't live on pickles," Fisby said.

"True. But over here the basis of the diet is sweet potatoes and soy beans. It always has been because of the high yield. Now we have to use those two as the nucleus of the teahouse menu. Then we supplement them with the fish and shell fish we pull in from the sea. And we add vegetables from the farm, here; and, of course, we supply eggs and meat, in the way of chicken, ducks, and other fowl." The Doc shook his head sadly. "I'd like to raise beef cattle and things like that, Fisby; naturally I would. But I can't spare the land for grazing, or fodder corn, or alfalfa. We're jam packed on this island and every inch counts. So I either give them variety in abundance or a few handfuls of rice. That's the choice, Fisby."

Fisby considered carefully. "I guess you're right, Doc. I suppose we better let the rice go then."

"Sure, Fisby. That's a luxury item, always has been. Besides, they'd only polish the hell out of it, which is no good."

"Well, whatever you say, Doc, is all right with me. I was just inquiring." Yet Fisby was troubled. When it came time for *kobiru* in the morning, that vinegar spiced rice, that *sushi*, tasted pretty good; and he was reluctant to give it up, for he knew that everyone enjoyed it.

"Fisby," the Doc said, "if you have time, I'd sure like to show you around the place."

Fisby had the time and was anxious to see the farm. Yet when the Doc called for a cart horse and Fisby learned he was expected to ride it, he hesitated. "Doc, couldn't we just walk?" he asked. "I'm not much good on those things. Besides, the exercise will do me good."

They went down a narrow lane, bordered by white fences, and the Doc pointed to a field. "There are my incubators, Fisby. Over there is my flock of chickens, and just beyond those, my ducks."

Fisby watched the flock of bantams, scratching industriously in the Okinawan dust, glanced at the waddling ducks.

"Here on the other side of the lane," the Doc went on, "I'm going to put my turkeys, quail, partridge, and pheasant. My smokehouse will go about here."

"But where are you going to get quail and those other things, Doc?" Fisby asked curiously.

"I'll have the eggs for hatching in a couple days. I had a talk with some of those transport pilots. They're a fine group. Most co-operative. They didn't see any reason why they couldn't pick up a few hundred eggs and fly them in on the next trip. Incidentally, could you get me a few sets of that hand-painted chinaware you're making over in the village? I'd like to give them a few souvenirs."

Fisby thought he could manage the souvenirs, but still he was puzzled. "How are you going to pay for those eggs, Doc?"

"I told the boys of a place up in Wisconsin, and they're going to pick them up. Told them to just charge it to my wife."

"Won't she care, Doc?"

"Well, she's not very good at keeping records, Fisby, so I think we can just slip the eggs in on her household account, and she'll never know the difference." The Doc turned. "Over there I'm raising the feed for my flocks. And

173

down the lane, here, where they're digging the holes, I'm putting in my persimmon and plum trees."

"Are the boys flying those in for you, too?"

"Certainly, Fisby. We have to have plums for pickling. And it's an old custom when a couple of friends get together for a visit to have persimmons or some fruit with the tea." The Doc held up a finger. "I want to have a first-class menu down there at the *cha ya*."

Fisby wondered if the Doc was going to charge the trees to his wife's household account, also. Yet not being a person who pried into the domestic affairs of others, he refrained from asking.

As they walked down the lane, the Doc indicated a field. "Here are my pickling greens, Fisby. You know, New Zealand spinach, chard, and so forth. I have about fifteen varieties."

"Can't you use those for salads, too?" Fisby asked.

"Nope." The Doc shook his head. "They just won't eat raw greens. Mrs. Kamakura says we have to pickle them, so next week we're putting on four women in the kitchen to handle the job. Now here's my plants of the cabbage family. They like cabbage over here, so I have plenty. But only a few ever tasted Brussels sprouts, broccoli, and cauliflower; yet I think they should go over big if they like the cabbage taste."

The Doc had quite a farm, Fisby had to admit. He had sweet potatoes, carrots, and just about every root crop listed in the seed catalogues. He had seed crops, his fall peas already having attained a good size. He had water chestnuts, the aquatic plant, growing in small water-filled beds. And he had taro, water mustard, edible ferns, and plants of the Orient which Fisby had never before seen.

It was the thatch-roofed, reed-and-bamboo fertilizer factory, however, that was the Doc's pride and joy. "Now you see, Fisby," he explained, "what we do is this. We run our horse carts around to the neighboring villages and pick up wood ashes from the hearths, and, of course, bones, too. We swap salt and fish for them."

Fisby was puzzled. "But what good are wood ashes and bones?"

"Well, wood ashes gives us about four per cent potash. Besides, they sweeten the land. That's exactly what we need. As for the bones, we grind them to a powder, and that gives us three per cent nitrogen and twenty-three per cent phosphorus. By mixing the two I can get a pretty fair

174

commercial fertilizer. It's not the best in the world, but at least we're not wearing out the soil. In fact, with a humus application now and then, we can build it up."

All this was too technical for Fisby, yet he could see that the Doc was doing a fine job. Not many people would worry about caring for the soil so that it would bear year after year. And he could see that the Doc was doing a fine job in many other ways, besides growing things for the *cha ya*. He liked the horse cart that went from field to field with steaming jars of tea for the workers. And he liked the grin and the wave that greeted the Doc everywhere they went.

When they returned to the Doc's drawing board and staked horse, Fisby explained the loafer situation at the teahouse and Seiko's desire to build his own home.

The Doc nodded solemnly. "We need a monetary system all right, Fisby," he admitted. "Holy hell, man, you ought to set one up."

"But I don't know anything about that," Fisby protested.

The Doc grew philosophical. "Well, Fisby, I'll be glad to give you a hand, that is, if you want me to. The way I look at it is: no one has set up a monetary system, starting from scratch like this, in the past, say, two thousand years. So we ought to be as expert as anyone else."

"Do you think so, Doc?"

"Certainly, Fisby. And you ought to know something about business. You owned your own pharmacy back in the States, didn't you?"

Fisby grew more confident. "I never thought of that. Naturally, I have had some experience."

"Good." The Doc rubbed his jaw. "You know, I never thought there could be too much to this economics business ever since the time, back home, I had that economics professor as a patient. Why, Fisby, every time I tried cashing his checks, they bounced, so we ought to be able to work something out." He scratched his head. "Now the first thing we'll need is money. Do you have any?"

"Well, not right now, Doc. I'll have some tomorrow though. We're selling our first batch of sweet potato brandy to the troops. I ought to have quite a bit of that invasion yen on hand."

"Very good. Very good." The Doc nodded authoritatively. "See, Fisby, the first principle is to get a sound currency in circulation, and we got one with the U.S. government behind it."

Fisby considered. "Maybe I ought to step up brandy production then, eh, Doc? Say triple the batches. We'll need plenty of money in circulation."

"A fine idea, Fisby. Very fine."

Yet Fisby was puzzled. "But, Doc, how are we going to get this money out to the people?"

"Simple, Fisby. We'll owe the family who made the brandy, won't we?"

"Yes, but when we pay them, they'll be the only ones with money. They'll have it all."

"But, Fisby, where did they get the potatoes for the mash? They'll owe for them."

"We just dug the potatoes out in the fields."

"And who owns the fields?"

Fisby had to scratch his head. "It beats me, Doc."

"The thing to do, then, is find out. I'd suggest setting up a claims department. Let the people reclaim the land. And get some old timers in the department, someone who actually knows who the land belongs to in order to verify the claims. Of course, these old-timers will know the approximate yield and can tell us how many potatoes were taken off for brandy production. Thus, it will be easy for us to settle with the owners, once we put a value on the potato crop."

Fisby was all in favor of this. The people should get their land back and should even be paid for the crops taken off it. Yet there were people who lost their land, the land used for the *cha ya* farm and the teahouse, itself.

"We'll just pay them off, Fisby," the Doc said. "See, we can set the *cha ya* and its farm up as a corporation. Sell stock. That'll take care of it. Besides, that will give us money for operating expenses until we start turning a profit —you know, running the farm, paying the serving boys and cook, paying off the workers for building the thing."

"Doc," Fisby said, "would you handle that angle, I mean, selling the stock, paying off the claims against the *cha ya,* and so forth?"

The Doc nodded. "I'd be glad to, Fisby. I'll set up my board of directors, organize it along business lines; then we'll figure out our operating expenses, and arrange the prices on our menu accordingly." He held up a warning finger. "But I want to give the stockholders a fair return on their money, say, six per cent. And I want to give the employees a paid vacation and, perhaps, a little bonus each year as a reward for service."

It sounded fair enough to Fisby. Besides, he was struggling with another problem. It was the people who lost their land and the people who were just shoved into the village, because of the invasion, that bothered him. He'd have to find some way for them to make a living. "Doc," he said, "we'll have to organize an industry of some sort."

"That shouldn't be difficult," the Doc said, "take that chinaware, for instance. Why not get Kiei to start a factory?"

Fisby nodded. "Sure, Doc. He'd need a few people to work for him." He scratched his head. "And we can get Oshiro to set up a lacquer-ware factory. And we'll set up a wooden-sandal factory, and a native-mat factory, and—"

"And you'll need shopkeepers to sell the farm products. Hell, Fisby, unemployment shouldn't give us any trouble. The big trouble will be marketing those products. And even that shouldn't be too difficult. Every American on this island is in the market for souvenirs. Lacquer ware, chinaware, clogs, and those things will go over big, just like that sweet potato brandy. Besides, you'll have a home and intervillage market."

Fisby grew cautious. Souvenir hunters were pretty sharp, and he was afraid that they might prove just a little too sharp for the new-made businessmen of Tobiki village. "Doc," hc said, "I'd kinda like to market those products myself. After all, they don't speak English, and they don't know the ropes, as far as the Army goes—" He stopped quickly. "Doc, if I handled the output for them, that wouldn't be socialism, or something, would it?"

"I don't see why it would, Fisby. We'll just put the thing on a voluntary basis, and designate you as the Tobiki Export Co."

Fisby thought it over. "Well, Doc, I'd like to import things, too. For instance, there's plenty of surplus items at the P.X. I could buy. See, then I could sell them to the local shopkeepers for resale to the people."

The Doc considered. "In that case, we'll just organize the Tobiki Export-Import. Let's see, we better make it a corporation just like the *cha ya*. Your sale of stock will give you money for operating expenses. You can be chairman of the board. And the corporation can act as a sort of clearinghouse for the village."

Fisby liked this idea of being in the import-export business. He lit a cigar, blew the smoke in the air. "Now, Doc," he began earnestly, "we're the only village with a monetary

177

system, and I don't want to lose out on this intervillage trade. What I'll have to do is set up a Swapping Division. Yes, sir, then I can barter and still give the items a cash value when I resell them, here, in the village." He examined his cigar carefully, then slipped it into his mouth. "Doc, don't you think it would be pretty nice if we organize—well, sort of a Businessmen's Association like we had back in Napoleon? Why we could meet down at the *cha ya*, say, on Tuesday noons, and we could have speeches and things. We might even ask the mayor of little Koza to drop over and give us a talk—"

Twenty-Three

ONE EVENING, some weeks later, Fisby lit his after-supper cigar and picked up a deck of cards. "Doc," he said, "how about a game of cribbage?"

The Doc, sitting at his drawing board on the other side of their quarters, barely looked up. "Not tonight, Fisby."

Noticing his worried look, seeing the frown on his face, Fisby asked, "Has something gone wrong out at the farm?"

The Doc regarded him. "Why, no. Everything's fine."

But the Doc was troubled, and Fisby knew it. Yet he hesitated to ask questions. The Doc, however, was ready to volunteer information. "Fisby," he said, "in all the days of my life I never saw such a damn fool as that Colonel of yours."

Fisby regarded him in alarm. "Oh, was Colonel Purdy in the village today?"

"No, Fisby. He phoned for me to come up to headquarters."

Fisby was puzzled. "How come, Doc? He doesn't have anything to do with you."

"Well, he's—he's interested in my ethnological study, and he wanted to talk it over." The Doc slapped his pencil on the drawing board. "Fisby, I don't care if he is the area commander. I won't have him coming down here and monkeying around with my farm. First thing you know, he'd be trying to tell me how to raise chickens and grow asparagus." His face twisted in a frown. "By God, if it's the last thing I do, I'm going to keep him away from here."

"Doc, did he say anything about me?" Fisby asked. "Do you know I haven't given a lecture to the Women's League in over two months."

The Doc cleared his throat. "Well, he did mention you, Fisby. But he was pretty upset this afternoon. It seems that someone up in headquarters got ahold of his latest issue of *Adventure* magazine and clipped out the climaxes of all the stories. Hell, man, he was ready for a strait jacket."

"He didn't say anything about the education program, did he?"

The Doc shrugged. "He was raving so much I couldn't tell. Well, Fisby, I got to get on with my report here or first thing you know he'll be down, prowling around the village."

As Fisby turned to put away the cards, he saw Sakini come trotting up the hill. "Boss," Sakini said. "I was sitting around the *cha ya* drinking tea with some guys when First Flower sent me a message. She would like to see you."

"Is something wrong?" Fisby asked.

"I don't know, boss. But she would like to see you right away in her apartment, if she could."

Fisby laid aside the deck of cards and slipped on his khaki shirt. "Well, I guess we better get right down there, then. Come on."

The *cha ya* was alive tonight. In fact, they were turning them away at the door. The talk had swept through the village that soon a monetary system would be introduced, soon the *cha ya* would start charging, and everyone was trying to get in as many free banquets as possible.

A serving boy led them quickly to First Flower's apartment. Again the aroma of incense hung in the air, but tonight First Flower wasn't sitting before the low table, nor was she dressed in the beautiful kimono of the geisha. She was sitting on the veranda. Her kimono was replaced by target cloth slacks—trimmed in blue, as were the ropes of her reed sandals—and her hair was arranged in the rolled bob of the West.

As she came to meet them, Fisby noticed that her eyes appeared fevered, and he tensed in alarm. "Sakini, is she sick?"

"No, boss."

Fisby breathed easier, relaxed.

"Boss," Sakini went on, "she wants to know if you would like to sit out on the veranda and talk?"

"That would be fine."

Quickly, First Flower went to an alcove in which small lacquered dishes, bearing food, were arranged as if in an offering. Taking the dishes, she placed them on a tray; and Fisby and Sakini followed her out through the open door.

They settled themselves on pillows with the tray of food before them. The night was cool. No paper lanterns burned along the veranda of this wing, yet the whole was bathed in a pale silver light from the rising moon. Fisby glanced at her, sitting there in the moon's light, clasping her crossed ankles with her hands. And he saw the trouble and concern in her dark eyes. "Sakini," he began hesitantly, "is there something I can do?"

"No, boss. But she would like to know if Seiko has said any more to you about being his go-between?"

"Why, no, he hasn't." Fisby stole a glance at her. "Has she made up her mind?"

For a moment she straightened, then her shoulders bent forward, and she shook her head. "Boss, she says she won't fool you. What's the use. When you love a guy, you just love him; and you can't do anything about it, even if at times he makes her pretty mad." She placed her hands flat on the veranda behind her, leaned back on stiffened arms, and looked at the sky. "Boss, she asks if you know what night this is?"

"No, I don't."

"Well, it's the night of the moon we call *meigetsu*. See it up there. It's the full moon that shines in the heavens on the eighth month of the lunar calendar. It's the autumn moon, the moon of August, and it makes her sad."

Fisby looked to the silver disc, floating high over the island of dark pines, saw its rays reflected there on the lotus pond. "Why does it make her sad, Sakini?"

"Boss, soon, she knows, it will be the moon of September. Then the moon of October. The year is dying, the people, and the land are dying. And now, no one must ever be alone."

Fisby saw the lanterns across the pond, heard the laughter rising from the banquet rooms. "But she isn't alone. She sings at parties. She dances. And the people around are smiling and happy. How could she be alone?"

"But she is, boss. And she says those people who go to the banquet rooms night after night are alone and afraid, too, or else they wouldn't be there. Maybe they don't know it, but the geisha girl sees. Oh, she smiles and jokes just like they do; but she knows why they laugh too much, and why they drink too much wine. They think they can keep the loneliness from creeping into their hearts. But she has seen them many, many times when the laughter dies like the flickering candles.

"They stand in the entrance way and say, 'Let's stay a while yet,' or 'where shall we go now.' They're afraid to leave the company of one another. And after the banquet, what is there for the geisha girl, boss? Just the thought of another banquet tomorrow; of grinning, empty faces looking up at her as she sings and dances. And the walk home alone through the dying world of the autumn.

"She says banquets are nice at first. It makes you feel good to hear guys whisper, 'Isn't she pretty.' Or it pleases you to have them come around in the afternoon because they want to talk with you. But she says when you get to be twenty years old, you begin to think of the springtime when the world is reborn. And you want to be of the springtime."

Fisby nodded. "I see. So Seiko's the one after all?"

"She says that's the way it is, and she can't do anything about it, even if he is kind of crazy." She shook her head and indicated the tray before them. "Boss, now she wants us to eat of the moon viewing food. See, there are the boiled *taros*, and green soy beans, and the fifteen little dumplings of rice flour. Please help yourself."

Fisby tried a rice dumpling, nibbled it absently for his mind was on Seiko. "Sakini," he said slowly, "tell her I think Seiko has changed. He's more realistic than he used to be."

"She asks if you think so, boss?"

"I certainly do. Does she know he's building a home?"

"No, she didn't know that."

"Well, he is. It's down by the sea. And tell her he's paying for it himself. No one is helping him."

"But, boss, she wants to know how he is doing that. Nobody uses money around here. There isn't any."

"Yes. But we're going to have some in a couple days. Soon as I can get it in circulation."

First Flower looked at the heavens. "Boss, she always wanted a hearth of her own; and now that it's come true, she can hardly believe." Then she glanced quickly at Fisby and seemed frightened. "Boss, she wants to know if you care if she gets married."

"Care? No, I think it's fine. Why?"

"Well, she's your geisha girl. Mr. Motomura give her and Lotus Blossom to you. You see, they owed him quite a bit of money yet for their training and kimonos. He'd never tell 'em just how much, though. He'd just say 'a lot.' So she thinks they owe you money, and—"

"They don't owe me a cent," Fisby said. "And from now on, they're no one's geisha girls any more, either one of them."

"You mean, boss, you let 'em be free?"

"Certainly."

First Flower couldn't believe. "She never hear of such a thing, boss. No geisha owner ever do that before."

"We're—we're just changing things around here a little bit, Sakini."

First Flower's appreciation was clearly evident. "Boss, she thanks you. She thanks you for Lotus Blossom. And she thanks you again for herself."

Fisby was embarrassed. "That's all right, Sakini. Tell her to think nothing of it."

Sakini regarded Fisby closely. "You know, boss, you're just like that guy you tell me about one time."

"Who's that?"

"That guy in America. You call him the Great Emancipator."

Fisby flushed. He wasn't an emancipator. He was just —well, he wasn't a Lincoln anyway. "You know, Sakini," he said, in an effort to change the subject, "tell her Seiko is going to have a mighty fine house, a tile roof, and everything."

First Flower grew troubled. "She says that's nice, boss, but she wants to know if you think he'll be able to pay for it all right?"

"I don't see why not. Why does she ask?"

"Well, you're going to have money in the village for sure, aren't you?"

"Yes."

"She thinks, then, that Seiko won't make any money at all, because the guys around this place aren't the kind who buy paintings."

Fisby considered. "What I'd suggest is that Seiko team up with Kiei, who makes the chinaware. The people always need dishes, and hand-painted work should bring a good price. Besides, I'm going to try selling that stuff to the

American troops. I think it will go over big. Tell her to mention to Seiko that he and Kiei get together."

First Flower seemed reluctant. "Boss, she asks if you would tell him. She don't want him to think that she's running his business."

"I'd be glad to."

Yet First Flower was still doubtful. "Boss, she thinks she better work after she's married, just in case the dishes don't sell."

"But will Seiko like that, Sakini? I mean, her singing and dancing at banquets for the other fellows."

"When she gets married, boss, she can't be a geisha girl any more."

"She can't? What kind of work will she do?"

"She thinks, maybe she'll start a school down at her house. There are still a lot of ladies who would like to learn the tea drinking ceremony, so she'll have classes in it."

"I see."

"That would be just in the morning, boss. Then there are a lot of awfully pretty little girls here in the village who would make good geishas. In the afternoon she could run a geisha school to train the girls."

Fisby looked across the pond at the banquet rooms. They did need a new group of geishas coming up. Here First Flower was leaving. The next thing you know, Lotus Blossom would find a fellow, and— Yes, sir, they certainly needed a new crop all right. Then he thought of Mr. Motomura, and his face grew stern. "Just one thing, Sakini. Tell her I'm not going to have any of those big syndicate owners operating around here. Motomura and his kind are out!"

"Oh, she don't want 'em around, either, boss. She won't charge much tuition and the papas can afford to send their own daughters to school."

"But who's going to set them up in business?" Fisby asked.

"Well, she thinks we better organize the geisha guild here in the village, and let the practicing geishas pay dues. Then when the new girls graduate, they can borrow money from the guild for kimonos and stuff."

"Very good." Fisby nodded. "Very good. But I think she better head the guild. We don't want any funny business going on in it."

As Sakini translated, First Flower nodded in agreement. "She'll be glad to, boss. And do you know some of the

183

other things she's going to do to earn money to help out?"

Fisby had no idea.

"She's going to teach classes in the *Ogasawara* etiquette. Then she'll start a school for guys who want to learn how to build *cha no yu* houses and fix the gardens. And maybe she'll even organize a troupe of actors and put on the *Kabuki* drama here in the village." Suddenly, her eyes grew wide. "Boss, she just thought of something. Do you care if Mrs. Yamashiro moves here?"

"Who's Mrs. Yamashiro?"

"She use to cook at one of the good *cha yas* in Naha. And many times Mrs. Yamashiro has told her that she would like to own a restaurant of her own. So First Flower thinks it would be pretty nice if Mrs. Yamashiro opened that restaurant here."

"But we have a *cha ya*," Fisby said. "Do we need a restaurant, too?"

"She believes it would be good if we had a place where married ladies could go with their husbands, boss. They can't do that at the *cha ya*." Sakini's voice grew confidential. "She says if you don't watch some of these geisha girls, they'll try to grab your guy just like that."

"They will?"

"Some will, boss. Not all."

"I don't think she'll have to worry about Seiko."

"It's not Seiko she's worried about, so much. Only he's a pretty good-looking guy, and some of these girls——" She shook her head sadly.

"I see. Suppose Mrs. Yamashiro does start a restaurant, does that mean geisha girls can't go to it?"

"Oh, she don't care if they go or not, boss. It's only that she'd kinda like to be around, too. You see, she was the most famous geisha in all Naha, so she knows just as much smart talk as they do, probably quite a bit more. And she'd like to be there just in case."

Fisby scratched his head. "I guess we better have Mrs. Yamashiro move over then. Tell First Flower to send her a message."

When Fisby glanced at her, he saw she was sitting with her hand to her cheek, her mouth wide open in amazement.

"What's the matter, Sakini?" he asked.

"Boss, she just remembers we've been talking about all these things, and Seiko hasn't even asked her to marry him again. What if he don't?"

Fisby thought it over carefully. "I don't think she has to worry about that, but I'll tell you what I'd better do. I'll casually mention that as go-between, perhaps, I'd better drop down and see her again."

"Will you do that, boss?"

"Yes, but don't you go spreading it all over the village."

"Oh, I won't, boss," Sakini promised. Then he explained to First Flower, whose eyes sparkled there in the moonlight, and whose smile turned into a glow. "Boss, she thinks that's a good idea. And when Seiko says okay, she wants you to just monkey around a little bit. Maybe go somewhere and have a couple cups of tea, and smoke a cigar, and let Seiko get pretty nervous. Then you go back and tell him, 'By gosh, First Flower says yes.'"

"I'll do that," Fisby said enthusiastically.

Then she laid a warning hand on Fisby's arm. "But, boss, she says—please don't monkey around too much."

Twenty-Four

ONE MORNING as Fisby sat in his private room at the teahouse—now the main office of the Tobiki Village Import-Export Corp.—Sakini came running for him. "Some guy's on the telephone at headquarters, boss," he explained. "I say, 'Hello, this is Sakini.' And he say, 'I don't care if it's Kanemoto. You tell Captain Fisby to get on this phone.'" Sakini scratched his head. "I think he's pretty sore."

Fisby laid his cigar in the china ash tray. "Who is it, do you know?"

"I think he say he's Colonel somebody. I talk to him once before."

"Colonel somebody?" Fisby edged forward. "Did he say he was Colonel Purdy by any chance?"

"I guess that's it, boss."

Fisby rose quickly from the pillow. Tucking his brightly printed sport shirt into his khaki trousers, he reached for his Panama hat, then handed Sakini a notebook. "Look, some of our agents are coming in. Will you handle them for me?"

"You want me to do it just like always, boss?" Sakini asked.

"That's right. Find out what they discovered the other villages have to trade and write it down."

"And should I put down what the other villages want for the things, too?"

"Sure. I have to beat it now." He hurried down the corridors, out onto the street, and dogtrotted through the village. He was puffing heavily when he lifted the receiver in headquarters.

"Fisby!" came the roar, "what are you doing down there? I've been waiting ten minutes."

"Oh, I've been expecting some of my scouts, that is, agents to drop in, sir, so I've just been sitting around having a cup of tea."

"Is that all you have to do?"

"Yes, sir."

Colonel Purdy's blast made Fisby realize that he had said the wrong thing. It was minutes later before the Colonel calmed enough to state what was on his mind. "Fisby, I talked with Major Enright this morning. He can look over from his village, and he tells me you've been hanging around the Officers' Club every afternoon. Don't you know you're confined to your area for observation?"

Fisby was puzzled. "I am, sir?"

"You most certainly are. Dr. McLean informed me and the public safety officer that he's keeping the closest watch over you. Did you break loose?"

Fisby scratched his head. "Not that I know of, sir."

"Well what are you doing running all over the countryside?"

"Why I have to tend the souvenir stands, Colonel."

"Souvenir stands? What are you talking about?"

"Oh, we have eight stands selling our products."

"What products?"

"The things we make in the village—wooden sandals, chinaware, lacquer ware, sweet potato brandy, reed cigarette cases, miniature Buddhist temples made from old tin cans, and things like that, Colonel. Mr. Van Druten, who runs the Officers' Club, let me put in a stand up there. And we're running the others in the backrooms of the P.X.'s. So you see, sir, I have to watch the stock and collect the money."

"What money?"

"The money from the sale of our products. And busi-

186

ness is fine, sir. We're taking in between five and six thousand dollars a week. If we could supply merchandise in greater quantity, we could make even more than that." Fisby smiled, a little proud of his accomplishment.

But the Colonel grew suspicious. "What are you doing with that money, Fisby?"

"I'm sending about half of it back to the States, sir, and—"

"Oh, you are. So you're exploiting the native population, eh? I suppose you're stashing that money away back home. I suppose you intend to retire when you get out of service. Does the doctor know of this?"

"Yes, sir. He's the one who suggested it."

"So you two are splitting it."

"No, sir," Fisby said righteously. "We're not getting a cent of it. Why, Colonel, you can examine the books if you wish. We have everything down in black and white, and—"

"A likely story," the Colonel cut in. "And where is that doctor this morning, doctoring the books?"

"No, sir. He's out at the agricultural experiment station. You see, he's running it along with the seed farms. I tell you, Colonel, we sure need a place around here where the farmers can buy young plants and seeds. They've never had a place like that before. Why the Doc is going to give them a complete line, every vegetable we have back in the States, and then some. And he's making commercial fertilizers; and he's giving talks on soil conservation. And he's even experimenting in growing plants and trees for drugs. We need those for local consumption, Colonel."

"Drugs!" The Colonel was horrified. It took him a moment to catch his breath. "Fisby, haven't you and that doctor any conscience at all. You're going to enslave those people in the opium habit, just to get their few possessions away from them!"

"We're not going to make opium, sir. We intend to make quinine for malaria. And, perhaps, digitalis, and . . ."

But the Colonel hardly heard. He was pounding his desk. "And while all this conniving was going on, just what progress has been made in the village, Fisby? Not that I expect any. I'm just curious."

Fisby considered carefully, then smiled, for he thought of some real progress. "Well, sir, we got Miss Higa Jiga a boy friend. You see, since First Flower is getting married all of her old boy friends have sort of been cut loose.

187

So they shifted their attention to Lotus Blossom, and some of the least eligible bachelors in that faction are being eliminated, and the Women's League is catching the overflow. Yes, sir, Colonel," Fisby said enthusiastically, "since Hokkaido found out Miss Higa Jiga likes his singing, he's been going over to the tea drinking ceremony at her *cha no yu* house quite regularly. I hear he's even taking her a box of sweet potato taffy this afternoon."

"Fisby," the Colonel roared, "this is a military telephone, not a party line. Have you started that education program?"

"Well," Fisby said, "we haven't done anything along the lines of formal education, sir. But we've been discussing it seriously."

"And all you've done is discuss it?"

"Yes, sir. You see, we have no textbooks, or blackboards, or chalk, or desks. But there are a number of private schools in operation."

"What do you mean by private schools?" the Colonel questioned.

"Well, Mrs. Kamakura is operating a cooking school that meets three afternoons a week. Some of the ladies of the village asked her to do it, because their husbands were taking all of their meals down at the teahouse. They just wouldn't come home to eat, Colonel. They liked the teahouse menu too well. So the ladies figured if they learned to cook like Mrs. Kamakura—"

"You call that education, Fisby?" the Colonel demanded.

Fisby wiped his brow. "I guess it's not exactly formal education, sir, but it's beginning to keep the guys at home. Anyway, First Flower has a school for flower arranging, and tea drinking, and sewing. Then we have some on-the-job training going on in the lacquer-ware shops, and so forth." Fisby considered for a moment. "Yes, Colonel, and we have our geisha school going, too. By golly, we have twenty-five of the prettiest little girls you ever saw lined up."

The gasp came plain over the line. "Fisby, do you know what those girls are? Do you realize what you're doing?" Colonel Purdy was shocked.

"Yes, sir. But we're only going to train twenty-five this year. You see, we don't want to overcrowd the field."

"Man," the Colonel's voice was a horrified whisper. "What will you and that doctor stoop to for profit?"

"Oh, but we're not taking any of the profit," Fisby said

reassuringly. "And we're not going to let any of those big syndicate owners in around here either. We're setting each girl up as an independent operator."

"Fisby," the Colonel shouted. "That's the last straw. I heard enough. Opium. Prostitution. I see it now. You and that doctor were trying to keep me away from there so you could carry on your low, conniving business."

"I don't understand, sir," Fisby said, puzzled.

But the Colonel paid no attention. "So you think I don't see through those phony medical reports that doctor has been sending in—delusions of grandeur, split personality, and all that hogwash."

"Medical reports?" Fisby asked. "What medical reports, sir?"

"Don't play so innocent, Fisby. I'll bet my last dollar you wrote them together. Keeping me out of my own area for the good of medical science, so you say. Well, I'll just show you two. Don't you dare move out of that village, Fisby. I'm coming down for a complete investigation. By God, I'm going to send both of you highbinders to Leavenworth if it's the last thing I do."

Twenty-Five

IN ALARM, Fisby slipped the receiver down into the leather case of the field phone. He didn't want to go to Leavenworth. Nor did he want to see the Doc sent up. It wasn't quite clear in his own mind as to what the Colonel was raving about, for he didn't understand this talk of opium and prostitution. Yet regarding this business of medical reports, the way he saw it was that the Doc was supposed to make reports on him for some reason, and apparently the Doc had falsified the reports to keep Colonel Purdy out of the village.

Well, he could hardly blame the Doc for that. The Doc didn't want anyone monkeying around with his asparagus beds, Fisby remembered him saying that. Come to think of it, the Doc liked to work solo on his projects. He didn't like a lot of free advice tossed his way. When the Doc

189

wanted advice, he asked for it. Fisby shook his head. You couldn't blame a man for that.

Looking down, Fisby tensed. The Colonel was always strict about uniform, and buttoned pockets, and those things. And his own uniform would hardly pass inspection. Taking off his Panama hat, he slipped his printed sport shirt over his head and replaced it with the regulation khaki. He found his combat boots over in the corner, blew the dust from them, and put them on in place of the reed sandals he was wearing.

And headquarters ought to be straightened up, too. There was a quarter-inch of dust on his desk and swivel chair. He hadn't been using the place much lately. He was just in the process of cleaning the room when the jeep screeched to a stop in front of headquarters.

"Fisby!" The roar floated across the quiet of the morning. "Come here!"

Clamping on his helmet-liner, Fisby ran out and threw a salute. "Yes, sir."

The Colonel didn't notice. His gray mustache was bristling, his face was a royal purple, and he stood pointing to the stones strewn about him. "Fisby," he demanded. "What did you do with your village?"

Fisby glanced at Colonel Purdy, towering over him. "Oh, we tore it down, sir," he said, then went on quickly before the Colonel broke an artery. "Now it's over in that grove of pines. You see, the Doc gave a talk before the Businessmen's Association a few weeks ago, and he thought it was the best thing to do."

"What's that doctor sticking his nose in this for?" the Colonel shouted. "Does he think he's running this area?"

"Oh, no, sir. But he said the village was a menace to the public health. Take those banana groves, for instance. They were just bogs, breeding places for malaria mosquitoes; and they'd never dry out unless the sun hit them. So he suggested we cut them down. Then he thought we better burn all the houses with their old thatched roofs."

"Burn the houses! What for?"

"To destroy the lice and rats, sir. The Doc was afraid of an epidemic."

"And you made these people homeless?"

"No, sir. After the Doc explained to the businessmen, they agreed with him. We even put it to a village vote and everyone backed the Doc one hundred per cent."

"I don't care what they did," the Colonel exploded. "Where are those people living?"

"Down there on the high ground, sir."

"I mean in what kind of houses?"

"Oh, in regular Japanese style houses. We all got together one day in a community house building project and put them up. Of course, those who want refinements have to take care of that themselves."

"Fisby." The Colonel's voice was like steel. "Can't you answer a simple question? I asked you what kind of houses. You just follow me. I'm going to find out for myself."

Colonel Purdy strode out, strode rapidly across the dusty sweet potato fields toward the grove of pines, and Fisby ran after him. "Sir," he said, "you're going the wrong way. That's the industrial area down there. The residential section is to your left."

But no one could tell Colonel Purdy that he was going the wrong way. He thrust his jaw forward, increased his stride, and Fisby of necessity increased his pace. They entered the pine grove on the far side of the village and immediately picked up a winding path of stones. For a moment the Colonel eyed the carefully landscaped surroundings with its shady quietness and dew-laden shrubs, then pushed on, his heels clicking.

"Sir," Fisby said, "would you be a little careful? I mean, would you be sure to stay on the walk. You see, we seeded the lawns here, and that grass is just getting a good start."

"Fisby," the Colonel snapped, "no one tells me where to walk."

He marched along the path, up and over an arched bridge, then regarded it. "What's the idea of building this thing?"

"Well, sir, First Flower—who's the village planner and landscape architect—thought it would be nice if we built this kind over all the streams. You see, we don't have any more drainage ditches, just these winding creeks. She says they fit in better with the pines."

The Colonel looked at the stream flowing slowly beneath the bridge. "Have you got any fish in those creeks, Fisby?"

"Not that I know of, Colonel."

"Hell, man," the Colonel said, "you're letting a lot of good water go to waste there." Through an opening in the pines, he spied the red tile roof of a building. Glancing

191

once more at the creek below him, he turned, and made for it.

The building was low and long. Its sides, beneath the overhanging roof that swept up at each end in the Chinese manner of the southern provinces, were plastered with a kind of white mortar. "That's the godown of the Tobiki Village Import-Export Corporation, sir," Fisby explained.

"It's the what?"

"The godown. That's what they call all warehouses over here."

The Colonel regarded him. "What the hell is the Tobiki Village Import-Export Corporation?"

"That's a local outfit, sir. I'm general manager and chairman of the board of directors. We handle the sale of all products outside the village. And, of course, we buy for the village from outside sources."

The Colonel examined the building carefully; and as they walked along one end of it, he ran his hand over the white mortar. "Fisby, where did you get the material for this building?" he asked.

"The Akiyoshi Brothers Building Supply Company makes the brick, the tile, and the mortar right in the village, Colonel. The lumber is imported from big Koza."

Rounding the corner, they came out on to a wide street of hard, blue clay, bordered on both sides by buildings similar to the godown, but varying in size. Along the front of the Tobiki Village Import-Export Corp., fifteen or twenty blue and red horse carts—each with a large white number—were lined up, their drivers dozing in the morning, while the shaggy Mongolian ponies ate from straw feedbags placed on the ground before them.

Colonel Purdy glanced at the carts, piled high with wooden tubs with tight-fitting covers. "What's in those things, Fisby?" he asked.

Fisby shook his head. "I don't know, sir. The cart drivers' co-operative just brings them in. Let's go up to the office and find out."

Up by the godown office, a cart was backed up and unloading under the watchful supervision of a group of natives. As they approached, the group looked up, then broke into broad smiles. "Gooda morning, boss," they said. And Fisby waved a hand in greeting. "Good morning, boys."

He turned to the Colonel. "Oh, this is processed sea food, sir. I can tell because there's Mrs. Kamakura's oldest son, Kenzo. He and his brothers run the fish processing business." Fisby regarded Kenzo, a short, stocky boy of about twenty-five who wore a perpetual smile. "How are things going, Ken?" he asked.

Kenzo patted a wooden tub, ran a finger across his forehead as if wiping away the perspiration, and shook his head in relief.

"Fisby, what does he mean?" the Colonel asked.

"Oh, he means they finally have the trouble settled, and he's sure glad of it."

"Trouble?" Colonel Purdy eyed Kenzo suspiciously. "What kind of trouble?"

"Well, sir, when Ken and his three brothers started their food processing plant, they contracted with the fishermen's co-operative to take all the surplus fish—that is, all the fish other than that marketed in the village each day. But for a while there, we didn't know if the fishermen had the right to sell their fish to Ken. As a matter of fact, they didn't."

Colonel Purdy grew stern. "Fisby, you mean to say a man can't sell the fish he caught?"

Fisby took off his helmet-liner and mopped his head. "The custom over here, Colonel, is that the fishermen can only wholesale their fish. That's right, sir. They have to sell it wholesale to their wives. Then the wives retail it, and the profit is theirs. Now the fishermen in the co-operative thought they could slip around that point and make a little extra profit by retailing directly to Ken." Fisby wiped his forehead again. "Gosh, sir, those wives sure raised the dickens."

Colonel Purdy straightened. "Those damn fool fishermen should have known they couldn't get away with anything like that. Tell me, how did you settle it?"

Fisby hesitated. "Why I stayed out of it, sir, figuring it was more or less of a domestic affair. But the women sure hopped on Ken, claimed he was using unfair business methods. Finally, sir, it got so bad he had to slip up to little Koza for a couple days rest. The Doc said he was on the verge of a nervous breakdown."

"Is that right?"

"Yes, sir. And things got so bad around home for the fishermen, they were afraid to land. They just sat out in their boats, until their food finally ran out. Then they had to give in. I'm glad that's settled, Colonel."

"You know, Fisby," the Colonel said, "that reminds

me of the time Mrs. Purdy claimed that I—" He cleared his throat. "Oh yes, now about those wooden tubs. What's in them?"

"Just a moment, sir. I'll ask Kamamoto, the godown manager. He's the one doing the weighing." Fisby pointed to a tub. "Kamamoto San. *Nani . . .* what?"

Kamamoto, a bushy-haired, lanky individual of about sixty-five, glanced at a pad of paper. "Paste, boss. Five carts. Got."

"That's fish paste, Colonel," Fisby explained. "It's like anchovy paste, only we have as many varieties as there are species of fish. Kamamoto San. *Nani; nani* else?"

"Four carts, cake, boss. Five carts salt *shiba-ebi.* Three carts salt bonito. Three carts *karasumi.*"

"I see." Fisby turned to the Colonel. "That means four cartloads of fish cake, five of dried and salted shrimp, three of dried and salted fish called bonito, and three cartloads of caviar."

"Caviar!" The Colonel's eyes flew open. "You have caviar?"

"Yes, sir. We're just starting to make it. You see, they use the roe of the gray mullet, and the mullet begins running offshore in the autumn. Mrs. Kamakura tipped her sons off on the processing method. First, you salt and dry the roe, then you press it—"

"Is it any good?"

"Well, I'm not much of an authority on caviar, sir. But the Doc says, while it's not the best, it's still of excellent quality."

The Colonel leaned forward. "And you have three cartloads. How much do one of those wooden tubs weigh?"

"About sixty pounds, American weight."

Colonel Purdy whistled softly, his mind, apparently, on the officers' mess up at headquarters. "What are you going to do with it?"

"Trade with the other villages, sir. First, the boys sell to the local merchants, then we take the surplus off their hands. So I guess everyone's pretty well stocked up in the village."

The Colonel could hardly take his eyes from the tubs of caviar. "And you have salted shrimp, too?"

"Yes, sir. You have to give these Kamakura boys credit, Colonel. They're real businessmen. Why, do you know what they've done? They picked up about five acres of marsh down by the sea wall. We thought it was just wasteland. And they converted it into a fish farm."

"What's a fish farm?"

"A place where they raise fish and shell fish, Colonel. For instance, oysters. They're going to put out about two acres. They take bamboo stakes and shove them into the ground; they need about 20,000 stakes to the acre. Then they attach old oyster shells to these as spat collectors. When the tide brings in the oyster larvae, it becomes attached to the old shells. Nourished by the tide, the oysters grow and in four or five months, the boys say, the stakes are hidden by clusters of oysters."

Colonel Purdy was skeptical. "You mean they grow oysters on bamboo stakes?"

"Yes, sir. They say the weight of oysters attached to each stake runs from 1½ to 2½ pounds. So we ought to get a yield of 60 to 100 thousand pounds of oysters. And, of course, they're raising lobsters, and crabs, and *sabahii.* That's milkfish. It's a Chinese delicacy."

"What are you going to do with all those oysters?" Colonel Purdy asked.

"The boys want to pickle them for winter use. But I don't know if I can get the rice for pickling mash, sir."

The Colonel's eyes turned back to the tubs of shrimp and caviar. "Fisby, you said you were going to trade these off to the other villages. What are you going to get for this stuff?"

Fisby brought a notebook from his pocket, leafed through it. "I need quite a few things, Colonel. For instance, the Minobe Mfg. Co., here in the village, has put an order into the Import-Export Corp. for 1000 pounds of goat hair, 500 pounds of pine soot, and a ton of red rocks."

Colonel Purdy's mouth flew open. "You mean you're going to trade caviar and shrimp for that junk?"

"But we need it, sir," Fisby said. "Minobe will manufacture the goat hair into bamboo-handled writing brushes, the pine soot into ink, and the red rock into polished inkwells. Those things go over big in our foreign trade. I can get rice for them. We really need that."

"Man," Colonel Purdy said, "you're crazy to let that shrimp and caviar get away."

"We can't use it though, sir. We have a surplus. And the Doc made a survey of the diet here in the village. While the people like fish, it only makes up one fifth of their diet. We need the five cereals, sir—rice especially,

195

then wheat, millet, sorghum, and panic grass. Without them, we can barely keep our heads above water by substituting sweet potatoes. For a while, the Doc thought we didn't need the cereals, either, but in checking he found that we really do. And we just don't have enough land to grow them."

Colonel Purdy was shaking his head. "I still think you're crazy. What other kinds of junk are you collecting?"

"I need limestone and travertine, Colonel. The Kamakura brothers put in a big order for both. They want to expand the fish farm next spring—grow their own seaweed for salting, raise shrimp and gray mullet. They're going to build a sea wall around the shallows, just offshore, so they need the stone for that. Then the Doc, up at the agricultural experiment station, wants some good Mongolian ponies for breeding purposes. We need them for working the land, and—"

"It seems like an awful waste of caviar," the Colonel said tartly.

"But I need lumber, too," Fisby went on quickly. "And I need reeds for our Panama hats. Those go good in the foreign trade. And I need clay for braziers, fermentation jars, and tile roofing. Also charcoal, and—"

Colonel Purdy was paying but little attention. He had the cover off a wooden tub and was sampling the salted shrimp. "Very good, Fisby," he said. "I think I better send a few tubs of this up to headquarters mess. Don't trade it off."

Fisby tried to keep the fear from showing in his face, for the smiling group of natives were watching them. He looked at the Colonel, looked at Mrs. Kamakura's boy, Kenzo, and Kamamoto, the godown manager. His hand was shaking as he slipped the notebook back into his pocket. He had to trade these things off, indirectly they meant cereals. And the health of his people depended upon his getting those cereals into their diet.

The Colonel finished his shrimp, then wiped his hands on his handkerchief. "Let's go, Fisby. I want to look around."

"Yes, sir." Fisby turned to Kenzo. "Ken. Slip. *Cha ya. Chekki.*"

The boy's grin widened. "Hokay, boss. Hokay."

"What did you tell him?" Colonel Purdy asked as they started up the blue clay street.

"I told him that after the warehouse foreman gave him

the weight receipt for the food, he should come up to the office in the teahouse, and I'll write him a check."

"What kind of a check?"

"An ordinary check, sir. You see, there was more to this business of economics than the Doc and I figured. We found a native up in Maebaru who used to work for the Yokohama Specie Bank. So we asked him to move here and set up a village bank for us. He knows his stuff, Colonel. Why, he put in a system of checks, trade acceptances, and promissory notes. And he even has a saving and loan department."

"What are you using for money?" the Colonel demanded.

"The invasion yen, sir."

The blood rushed to Colonel Purdy's face. "Fisby, you have no authority to do that."

"But, sir, we needed a sound currency. Besides, Seiko wanted to build a home, and—"

"I don't care who wanted to build a home. Don't you realize it'll take years for the experts to straighten out this mess you've made. Why, you've probably upset the whole economy of the American government."

Frankly, Fisby could hardly understand that. The invasion yen was pay for the troops, and they merely spent some of their pay on the island. What difference did it make who had the money in hand—an American soldier or a little Okinawan who had sold the product of his labor? What effect would that have on the American economy?

"Besides," the Colonel went on angrily. "We've already made plans for a monetary system up at headquarters. Do you think we're sleeping! We have our illustrations all made. We're putting Captain Blair's picture on the one yen note. Major Thompson will be on the ten yen bill; and, of course, I'll be on the hundred yen note. All we need is Stateside approval and someone to print the bills."

Fisby considered carefully, then regarded the Colonel. "But, sir, do you think Major Thompson is worth ten yen in the States? I mean could Peggy walk into a store in Seattle and buy something with that ten yen bill?"

"Peggy!" the Colonel shouted. "Who's Peggy, and what the hell does she have to do with it?"

"Peggy—that's Marguerite—she's the Doc's second youngest daughter, Colonel. She's a junior up at the University of Washington, and she and her sorority sisters are the American agents for the Tobiki Village Import-Export Corporation."

"Fisby," the Colonel regarded him. "What are you talking about?"

"Well, sir, we take that invasion yen up to the post office and convert it to money orders. Then we send them to Peggy, and—"

"So that's the way you're working it." The Colonel's face was purple. "And I suppose she's hiding that money away until you two get home."

"No, sir. The girls spend the money. Whoever doesn't have classes in the afternoon goes into Seattle shopping for us."

"Shopping?"

"That's right, Colonel. They buy the things we need here in the village—yard cloth, cotton dresses, skirts and sweaters, shoes, sport shirts for the men, slacks, and things like that. Then they mail them over. We have the sales slips from every purchase in case someone wants to audit us. But we're having a little trouble of late, sir. It seems the girls in the sorority are cutting too many classes to go shopping, and the University authorities are cracking down on them."

Colonel Purdy was aghast. "So you're upsetting the foreign trade of the United States, too. Fisby, do you realize that this is sabotage."

"But I wasn't destroying anything," Fisby protested.

"Not destroying anything. Fisby, you can just try explaining that to a congressional investigating committee." The Colonel leveled a stern finger. "I'm giving you a direct order. You stop that trading with the States immediately."

Fisby's heart sank within him. "But, sir. I have to buy at least clothing. These people cut down the textile bananas. We thought we could supply them through the Import-Export Corp. Now they won't even have banana cloth, because the source of raw material is gone. Besides, I have to see that First Flower and Lotus Blossom have silk for their kimonos. And Miss Higa Jiga—"

"See what your stupidity has done," the Colonel said. "Now everyone has to suffer."

Fisby stared at the blue clay of the street. His short, chubby body felt limp. His only hope now was that the stock of clothing in the godown would last the people for a long time.

"It certainly is fortunate that the proper authorities are looking after this operation," the Colonel went on. "Why, if they hadn't sent in relief supplies, these people would be starving right now."

Fisby looked up quickly. "Relief supplies, sir? Has someone sent in relief supplies?"

"Certainly, Fisby. Did you think the United States would leave these people on their own?"

Fisby was puzzled. "But we haven't seen any relief supplies."

"Of course, you haven't. We're holding them up at headquarters until we can work out an equitable system of distribution. I was going to ship them out to the villages, but Major Thompson warned me that you village commanders would screw up the operation. I'm glad I held them back."

Fisby grew curious. "What kind of relief supplies do you have, sir?"

"Rice, beans, cooking oil, canned fish, and things like that."

Something within Fisby quickened. "Do you have much rice, Colonel?"

"Enough to ration half a pound a day to each person."

Fisby decided to risk a question. "How long have you been holding back these rations, Colonel, if you don't mind my asking."

"About five months."

Fisby whistled to himself. According to his figures, about 75 pounds of rice for each person was stored away somewhere. The village had 375,000 pounds coming. His eyes flickered. The Colonel had rice, and he needed rice.

Twenty-Six

THEY WALKED down the street, and the Colonel surveyed the white buildings with their upswept Chinese roofs of red tile. The buildings here varied from the godown. They had wooden shutters, and now the shutters were removed on the street side, laying open the interiors to passers-by. The Colonel glanced at a sign, written both in English and the *katakana* characters, hanging over a doorway.

TOBIKI VILLAGE SOYBEAN PRODUCTS COMPANY
Bean Curd, Soy Sauce, *Miso* Paste

"Fisby," he said, "what the hell is *miso* paste?"

"It's a mixture made by crushing soy beans, then adding ferment, and salt, sir. After that, they let it stand for about two months to work. They use it for soup. You take a spoonful of paste, add hot water, and stir it up good. Everyone drinks it for breakfast." He regarded the Colonel. "Sir, are you going to send some of that rice down to the village soon?"

"I might. The Staff talked it over, and we agreed that a man should work for his rice, Fisby, otherwise it breeds an attitude of dependence in the population." The Colonel walked to the open side of the Soybean Products Co. and peered in at the women turning the stone grinding mills. Then he regarded the sign of the Nishimaru Bean Jam Factory across the street. "What's bean jam, Fisby?"

"That's something that looks like thick cream, Colonel. It's made by grinding together red beans and brown sugar. They harden it for use in native cakes. And they use it for filling rice cakes. That is, when they have rice. Colonel, just what kind of work does the Staff think a man should do to earn his rice?"

"Why, Major Thompson suggests we organize road gangs and put them to work."

"But, sir, the Engineers and the Sea Bees can do a hundred times more work with their heavy equipment than the people could do by hand."

The Colonel held up a finger. "You miss the point, Fisby. The point is we'll have them working."

Fisby looked to a little shop in which a group of men sat cross-legged on the mats of the floor. They were painstakingly fashioning *dahisens*, the Okinawan ukuleles. And it seemed to him that a man didn't have to work on a road gang to earn his rice. There were other ways. "Sir," he said, "would you sell that rice to the Import-Export Corporation?"

The Colonel was shocked. "Fisby, you should know that the government doesn't sell relief supplies."

Fisby was stumped. He could only follow the Colonel up the street past the Mat Weavers' Co-operative, where the hundred looms sat in the cool shade of the interior of the building; where a hundred gossiping, chatting women sat tending them; and the boiling kettles of water bubbled on the stone hearth, the water to make the ever present cups of tea.

They were deep in the heart of the industrial section

now, up by the big factories. They walked by the *shochu* distillery with its yard covered by a canopy of growing vines, under which the pottery jars of sweet potato marsh sat fermenting. They passed Seiko and Kiei's chinaware factory, the smoke from whose kilns filled the morning air with the fragrance of burning wood. From the doorway of the lacquer-ware office, Oshiro called, "Hey, boss. What you doing?"

Fisby stopped, and the Colonel walked on. "Just looking around, Oshiro." He smiled. "What are you doing?"

Oshiro took his long-shanked, bamboo-stemmed pipe from his mouth and indicated the long benches just inside the building. "Teaching these kids to etch, boss. I need good etchers."

Fisby looked inside the building at the old men turning the hand lathes. "Pretty busy this morning, eh?"

Oshiro shook his head. "Busy all the time now, boss." His old eyes rested on Fisby. "Boss, you don't forget that Fukahara is going to be seventy-seven pretty soon, do you?"

"No, I haven't forgotten."

"Did you get the rice yet?"

Fisby hesitated. "Not yet."

"You try though, will you, boss?" Oshiro said solemnly. "I promise I give Fukahara a longevity banquet at the *cha ya*, and we can't have it unless we got the tooth hardening rice to serve."

Fisby forced a smile. "I'll do my best. Don't worry. I have to go now."

"Won't you have a cup of tea?" the aged one asked.

"I'd like to," Fisby said, "but my boss is inspecting the place." He hurried away, but Colonel Purdy was nowhere in sight. Fisby went along the street, peering through the open windows, looking for him. He wasn't in the chopstick, or the Panama hat, or the cricket-cage factories. Nor was he in the godown where they were filling straw bags with coarse white salt. Fisby scratched his head, then heard the Colonel's voice. "You saw. You chisel. You sand."

The voice came from the wooden-sandal factory, and Fisby started off at a trot. Entering the building, he found a group of sorely perplexed, whispering natives gathered around the Colonel, who was gesturing wildly. "Is something the matter, sir?" Fisby asked.

The Colonel indicated the rows of workers sitting on the floor. "They're going about making these sandals all wrong,

201

Fisby. I'm just showing them how to set up a production line. Now if this first group saws out the rough forms, they can pass them over to the second group for chiseling, and—"

"But, sir," Fisby protested, "they can't work that way. Each man takes pride in his own work, tries to do better than the one next to him. Besides, they're supplying all the clogs we need, and they're working the way they like to. Anyway, they don't understand production lines."

"Well, it's about time they learned. There's too much wasted effort and motion here."

The group of natives looked to Fisby. "Nani, boss . . . what, boss?"

"Nochihodo. Nochihodo . . . later, later," Fisby whispered. "Sir," he said desperately, "is it all right if I set up a production line some other time? You mentioned that you wanted to see the houses in the village. Now the residential section is over to our left."

"Why not set it up now?" the Colonel demanded.

"Well, that's a pretty complicated idea to get across, sir, and I'll need my interpreter for that."

"You better get right on it this afternoon," the Colonel warned.

"Yes, sir." But as they left the building, Fisby shook his hand and whispered to the natives, "Never mind. Never mind."

Reaching the street, the Colonel looked back up at the line of buildings. "Fisby," he said, "it seems to me you could have gotten more variety in your construction. Why didn't you just use natural brick here and there instead of plastering everything up with that white mortar?"

"Well, sir, the natural brick is a faded yellow. It doesn't look good, so we thought—"

"You should have experimented, Fisby. Used different kinds of clay."

Fisby wiped his forehead and nodded. "Yes, sir."

The residential section lay back from the industrial section and was connected to it by stone paths. As they walked along, Fisby tried to explain the trees, and the shrubs, and the new growing grass. "In laying out the village, sir," he said, "First Flower tried to make the whole thing like a big park with the teahouse right in the middle."

But Colonel Purdy was eyeing the streams. "So you don't have any fish in those, eh, Fisby?"

"No, sir. Now you'll notice that there aren't many streets, just paths. That's because . . ."

"Fisby." The Colonel pointed. "What's that thing setting back in the bushes there?"

"That's a home, sir. We put them back like that so the families will have privacy."

Colonel Purdy left the walk, crossed the seeded area, and pushed through the bushes. The wooden, tile-roofed house sat beneath the pines. Its glass-enclosed veranda looked out over a small garden, and beneath the house were stacked the wooden shutters that would protect the glass when the hurricanes came. The Colonel surveyed it critically. "Fisby, why don't you get some of that white mortar and slap it on here?"

"We couldn't do that, sir," Fisby said. "The people want their homes of wood. They like the natural color of the wood, and they like—"

"You ought to teach them how a coat of white can set off a place. Now Mrs. Purdy and I had a home once back in Pottawattamie—" Something caught the Colonel's attention and his mouth flew open. "Well, I'll be damned," he whispered.

Fisby looked too, and saw the pink lingerie, hung on the clothesline, rippling in the breeze. "I guess it's washday, sir," he said.

"Where did they get that lingerie?"

"That's some of the stuff Peggy shipped in from the States."

"I'll be damned." The Colonel gave the lingerie another look, then straightened. "Let's get on, Fisby."

They pushed through the hedges and out into the park that was the village. It was shady, and quiet, and cool here. There was no sign of life except the pines stirring gently in the breeze from the Pacific. The wood smoke from the breakfast fires still hung in the air, and the Colonel breathed deep.

Down at the intersection of two paths, they met a group of smiling, slant-eyed kids, carrying an American football, who quickly ran up to Fisby. "We win, boss," they chorused and counted on dirty fingers. "We win 14-12."

"Good. Good." Fisby patted the shoulders beneath the green target cloth jerseys and turned to the Colonel with a smile. "Well, sir, I just took the Doc for twenty yen."

"You did? What team is that, Fisby?"

Fisby indicated the green jerseys. "That's Notre Dame.

They just beat Michigan. We have Minnesota and Purdue scheduled for this afternoon. Maybe you would like to see a game?"

The Colonel was looking at the green jerseys and frowning. "Fisby," he said, "I'll have you know that when Notre Dame steps on the field with Michigan, they won't have a chance." He cleared his throat. "By the way, does my alma mater, Indiana, have a team?"

"Yes, sir. The Big Nine is represented one hundred per cent."

"Tell me, how is my alma mater doing?"

Fisby shook his head. "Not so good, sir. They're in the cellar."

The blood rushed to Colonel Purdy's face. "Fisby, I hope you jumped that coaching staff!"

"No, sir. This is just sort of a sand-lot league—"

"I don't care what it is. Man, in a case like this you have to take action. Have you scouted up any good material for them?"

"No, sir."

"Fisby, what the hell have you been doing around here? I want that Indiana team built up. That's a direct order." The Colonel paused, as if to consider. "Say, Major Enright has a pretty husky kid working around his mess tent. I wonder if we couldn't move him over here."

"But, sir, these kids are just twelve years old."

"Well, the boy might be a little large for his age, but I'm sure he's not over eleven. I better phone Enright this afternoon."

"But, sir—" Fisby started to protest, then gave it up. "Would you like to see some more of the village, Colonel?" he asked instead.

They moved along the path; and coming to a hedge, the Colonel suddenly stopped. Doc McLean was sitting in the small garden, his dressing gown drawn about him; and the Doc was staring straight ahead. "Fisby," the Colonel whispered, "what's the matter with him?"

"Nothing, sir. He's just meditating."

"Does he always sit around in his dressing gown, meditating like that?"

"No, sir. First Flower is having the tea drinking ceremony this morning, and he's preparing to go into the *cha no yu* house."

Colonel Purdy's face was grim. "Fisby, I have a score

204

to settle with him. Sending me phony reports. I think I'll just go over there, and—"

"Please, sir," Fisby cut in, "couldn't you talk with him later? You see, he's having some domestic trouble back home, and he's trying to forget it."

"Oh?" The Colonel's eyes widened. "What kind of trouble?"

"It seems, sir, in checking over her canceled checks, his wife discovered she paid someone up in Wisconsin for 1800 eggs out of her household account. She found out the Doc charged them to her, so she wrote stating that if he didn't deposit that money to her account within one week, she was going to charge him one dress a day as interest."

"He sent the money, didn't he?"

"Yes, sir. But she didn't send her letter air mail, and he thinks she might have even held it back a few days. So the way he has it figured, he owes for twenty-three dresses right now, and his letter won't reach her for another week yet."

The Colonel was grave. "I'm telling you, Fisby, those household accounts are nothing to fool around with. Why, I remember one time, when I was a little short, I tried ringing in a car wash and oil change on Mrs. Purdy. In all the days of my life, I never saw a woman raise so much hell." He pointed. "Is that boy, there with McLean, having domestic trouble, too?"

"Oh, you mean Seiko. He's not married yet, but he's having some difficulty. He and Kiei are doing a fine business in chinaware, and First Flower is pretty sore at him."

"How come?"

"Well, Seiko wants to spend all his time painting dishes, but First Flower just won't stand for it. She says, by golly, if he can't take a little time off now and then to attend her tea drinking ceremony, he can just look around for another girl."

"And he gave in to her, eh?" The Colonel shook his head sadly. "Fisby, that boy is getting off on the wrong foot. He ought to lay the law down now. Let her know who's boss. That's the first thing I let Mrs. Purdy know, and we haven't had a bit of trouble in over twenty years of marriage." The Colonel considered. "Maybe we ought to let those two meditate. Domestic trouble can be a serious proposition. But remind me to have a talk with that boy. Oh, yes, and remind me to hop McLean about those reports and being out of uniform."

Fisby heard the clatter of wooden sandals on the stone

path and turned. "Well, well, Colonel, look who's coming."

The Colonel glanced up the path. "Who's that?"

"Miss Higa Jiga, sir. Say, Hokkaido was right. She doesn't look so bad with all that stuff on her face, does she?"

"What stuff?"

"The lipstick and powder that Peggy sent in."

Miss Higa Jiga came walking along with a mincing step, and she appeared almost girlish. Her hair was arranged in a Western manner. Her blue kimono was of nylon with large white flowers, and the *obi*—the Japanese sash—was of a brilliant red.

Fisby shook his head. "That girl's really got the money, sir."

"What do you mean—money?"

"We had quite a time with her at first, sir. When we introduced the monetary system, most all of the Women's League went into some kind of business. Miss Susano started a cosmetics shop. Various ladies started dress shops. But we just couldn't seem to fit Miss Higa Jiga in anywhere."

"You couldn't?"

"No, sir. And pretty soon all the business opportunities were snapped up. About the only thing left was the bathhouse I built here in the village. That wasn't much of a business, sir. First Flower and Lotus Blossom were the only two using it. But when Miss Higa Jiga took it over, she sure drummed up trade."

"How did she do that, Fisby?"

"She had her grandma, on her papa's side, and her Aunt Takamini circulate through the village. Whenever they'd get in a crowd, they'd whisper, 'Well, after all, ladies and gentlemen should take baths once in a while.' Colonel, you should have seen the business roll in. Right now it's reached a point where you have to make a reservation to take a bath." Fisby shook his head in admiration. "This free enterprise is a wonderful thing. There's no telling what people will think of to make a couple yen. Take Kanemoto. He just worked on the farm crews. But when we started establishing businesses, he grabbed off those caves up there in the hills. You should see the mushrooms he raises."

Miss Higa Jiga was before them now, and she gave them a walking bow. *"Ohayo gozaimas,"* she said.

Fisby tipped his helmet-liner and smiled. "Ohio."

Colonel Purdy regarded him. "What's this Ohio business?"

"Ohio means 'good morning' in Japanese, sir."

"It does? Well why don't you teach them some English?"

"They speak a few words, sir. They're learning. And I'm learning a little of their language."

Miss Higa Jiga interrupted by tugging Fisby's sleeve and pointing. "*Kami ii san,* boss. Hokay?"

"Okay."

Miss Higa Jiga grinned and went walking off in her mincing step.

"What did she say, Fisby?" the Colonel asked.

"She said 'hairdresser.' She means she's going down to the beauty shop to have her hair fixed, because she has a heavy date this afternoon. Hokkaido is coming over to her *cha no yu* house for the tea drinking ceremony."

Interest flickered in the Colonel's eyes. "You have a beauty shop here, Fisby?"

"Yes, sir. Lotus Blossom owns it. She has ten operators working for her."

"Well, well." The Colonel rubbed his hands. "Mrs. Purdy would certainly be interested in this. Let's take a look at it. If I can borrow a camera, I'll take a few snapshots and send them to her."

Fisby really wanted to show the Colonel the houses of the village, since he didn't like being accused of making the people homeless. He wanted to show him how the majority of people were hiring carpenters to add glass-encased verandas, and *cha no yu* houses, and other refinements. He wanted to explain the new stock laws which made it necessary to keep pigs and goats in the pens on the commons, just outside the village. But the Colonel strode rapidly in the direction which Fisby indicated was the uptown section.

The uptown section had a sleepy look about it. It was a wide clay street lined with trees and small shops, facing on limestone sidewalks. Here and there a few people moved leisurely about—some women wore American-made cotton dresses, others wore kimonos cut from American cloth. And most of the men wore reed sandals, cotton trousers, and printed sport shirts.

They passed the bank on the corner, hurried past the food stalls piled high with autumn vegetables, and cut over to the other side of the street. "There it is, sir." Fisby pointed to a small shop, covered with the white mortar and on whose plate glass window were pasted ads from various American magazines, showing the latest hair styles from the States.

"Well, well." Colonel Purdy glanced at the ads, then tried to peer through the Venetian blind of bamboo, covering the window. "Say, I want to see this." He went to the door, barged in, and Fisby followed.

It was evident that they were treading on sacred territory. The operators, in their smocks of white target cloth, looked up in surprise. The freely chatting ladies, in various stages of assembly, were suddenly stone silent. Eyes were cold. Stares were hard. And Fisby shuffled nervously.

"Look what we have here," Colonel Purdy said, walking behind the line of homemade chairs to a red-lacquered table on which were arranged various assortments of American cold creams, shampoos, home waving sets, and other such concoctions. Then he smiled. "I'll be damned —bobby pins!"

The whispering was starting over in the corner of the room. "Colonel," Fisby said, "don't you think we better get out of here?"

"No, Fisby." The Colonel shook his head. "I want to look around." He moved in front of a chair. "Fisby, this woman has a face just like Mrs. Purdy. I mean, it's oval in shape." He considered. "Now how did Mrs. Purdy say a woman with an oval-shaped face should part her hair— was it in the middle or to one side? Operator, try it in the middle once."

The smock-clad operator was confused. But the eyes of the woman in the chair, staring up at the Colonel, were unblinking. Her chin was thrust forward and her mouth drawn in a thin line.

Fisby's wrists felt weak. The whispering increased and it was evident that some pointed remarks were being tossed at the Colonel in both the Luchuan dialect and Japanese. Looking around desperately, Fisby spied an object on the lacquered table. "Colonel," he said quickly, "here's something you might be interested in."

The Colonel waved a hand. "Don't bother me, Fisby. I'm busy. Or did Mrs. Purdy say a woman with an oval face shouldn't wear a part at all? Dammit, I wish I could remember."

Frisby tried another tack. "Look at this, Colonel. Say, this would be a wonderful souvenir to send Mrs. Purdy."

"Oh?" The Colonel turned.

Fisby went on rapidly. "Yes, sir. It's a little item we're making here in the village." He held up an oblong box of highly polished wood with openings cut in the sides and top. "Just step over here, sir, and you can see it better. We call this a perfumed pillow. See, there's a drawer and little incense burner on the inside."

As the Colonel walked over, Fisby lit a pinch of aloe wood and let the fragrant smoke drift up. "Suppose Mrs. Purdy wants to perfume her hair. All she has to do is rest her head against this, and the job's done."

"That's quite a getup," the Colonel announced.

"And they're quite reasonable, too, sir. I think they sell for ten yen, that's about sixty-five cents."

The Colonel picked up the box, examined it, held it up in order to smell the burning aloe wood. "Fisby, I better take one of these." He thought for a moment. "No. You better give me two. If I don't send her mother one, there'll be hell to pay."

Fisby glanced at the belligerent ladies. "We have to get them up the street at Miss Susano's cosmetic shop, sir. Now if you'll just follow me—" He held aside the rush strips covering the door. "This way, sir." As Colonel Purdy walked out, Fisby turned and tipped his helmet-liner to the group inside the beauty shop.

They went down past Nakamura's home furnishing store, which was featuring pottery charcoal braziers and silk pillows in their window this week. Past the American Shop, which sold tobacco, soap, tooth paste, and other P.X. items. Past Gushi's, the men's tailor shop, and crossed the street in front of Mrs. Shimabuku's confectionery store.

As they walked along, the sound of gongs floated gently out on the morning; and the Colonel looked about quickly. People were coming out of the stores, both shopkeepers and customers. People were appearing from side streets. Drivers left their horse carts standing and walked away. "What's the matter, Fisby?" the Colonel asked. "Is there a fire?"

"A fire?" Fisby was puzzled. "Oh, you mean the gongs, sir. No. That's a signal that it's time for the midmorning snack. We call it *kobiru*."

"And everyone just walks away and leaves their shops?"

"That's right, Colonel. No one likes to miss *kobiru*. Would you care to go up to the *cha ya* for a bite? We'll get your souvenirs later."

"I might try it," the Colonel said.

At that moment a rather hefty, prosperous-looking gentleman in a white suit of American manufacture came out of a large, low building and started up the street ahead of them. He seemed to be talking to himself, and he seemed to be saying, "Baa . . . baa . . . baa."

"Fisby, what's the matter with him?" Colonel Purdy asked.

"Nothing, sir. That's Hokkaido."

"What's this baa, baa, baa business?"

"He's singing the "Whiffenpoof Song." I guess he feels good this morning. They just elected him president of the Junior Chamber of Commerce. And besides, he has a first-class card lined up for tomorrow night."

"What do you mean, a first-class card?"

"He promotes the wrestling matches in the village, sir. You see, he owns the sports arena and body building studio over there. He sure likes that business. It gives him a chance to get up and make the announcements and all that." Fisby glanced at the sun. "I think we better get down to the *cha ya*, sir."

When they entered the teahouse, Colonel Purdy stood for a moment in the darkness, then started up the three steps. But Fisby stopped him. "Please, sir," he said, "we always take our shoes off inside."

For a moment the Colonel seemed undecided, then reached down and unbuckled his combat boots. They slipped on the reed sandals, and the Colonel was definitely puzzled by the maze of corridors, leading off in all directions. "This way, sir," Fisby said, "I'd like to stop in at the office for a minute."

As Fisby slid back the paper door, Sakini and two agents for the Import-Export Corp. were just rising to go down for a cup of tea. Seeing him, Sakini smiled. "Got good news, boss. Tashiro, here, find the cinchona bark up in Itsumi village. And the people will take dried fish and tea for it."

Though Fisby forced a smile and said: "Good, good," still he was not smiling inside. They had looked all over for the cinchona bark, the raw material for quinine. But hadn't the Colonel said he should not trade off the fish to other villages?

"And Motoyama has found some more indigo plants and Japanese hawthorns to make our blue and red dyes, boss."

"That's fine." Fisby kept his own feelings from creeping

210

into his face. "Now I think all of you better take time out for *kobiru.*" He turned to the Colonel, who was looking around the room. "Sir, let's go down to the apartment. We'll eat down there."

"You have an apartment here?" the Colonel asked, as they walked through the corridors, lined by the sliding paper doors.

"Yes, sir. We added a few more wings on the other side of the building. We even put a tile roof over the whole teahouse. The Doc says it's more sanitary than thatch. Besides, it's a little more permanent."

The wings of apartments were also a little more permanent. The walls were of woven reeds, instead of paper, with the paper frameworks serving only as doors. Fisby's apartment was a three-room affair, one room right next to the other in a straight line, with each room opening onto the veranda and enlarged lotus pond. "The Doc has the apartment right next to me," Fisby explained. "And Mr. Van Druten is right across the corridor."

"Who the hell is Mr. Van Druten?" the Colonel asked.

"He's the Navy officer who runs the Officers' Club."

"Well, what is he doing living in this village?"

"He likes it here. And in his spare time he works for the Import-Export Corp. Of course, we don't pay him anything, but he works for us anyway."

"Fisby," the Colonel said, "where does that corporal of yours stay?"

Fisby shook his head. "Oh, Corporal Barton hasn't been with us for about three months, sir. He wanted a job tending bar up at the Officers' Club because of the extra pay, so Mr. Van Druten worked him in. I understand he's just about running the place now. And that's fine, for it lets Mr. Van Druten get away more often." Fisby pushed back the door of the middle room. "Just step right in the sitting room, here, Colonel. I think the serving boy left a menu for us."

The menu, written in romanized Japanese with an English explanation for Fisby's and the Doc's benefit, was lying on the low, lacquered table. Fisby shook the red silk pillows, placed them on the thick mats, and indicated that the Colonel should make himself at home. Sitting down, the Colonel looked about the room curiously, then his eyes fell on a single flower carefully arranged in a small vase in the alcove. "Where did you get a rose over here?" he asked.

Fisby smiled. "Lotus Blossom and First Flower think I should have flowers in my room. They bring them every day. Now, sir, if you'll notice, that's arranged according to the Ikenobo School . . ."

"I don't give a damn how it's arranged. I asked you where you got it."

"Peggy sent us in some flower seeds, and the transport pilots flew us in some bulbs and plants. You see, the girls own a florist shop together." Fisby picked up the menu and regarded the Colonel. "I'm sorry we can't offer you *sushi*, sir." He hesitated. "But we have no rice to make it."

The Colonel waved a hand. "I never did like rice."

Fisby considered. "You know, sir, I bet Mrs. Purdy would like *sushi*. If you would like me to, I'll get the recipe from Mrs. Kamakura, and you can send it—"

"No, Fisby. Mrs. Purdy doesn't like rice either."

"Oh."

The Colonel glanced at the menu.

Miso shiru . . .	bean paste soup.
Owan	clear soup with shrimp balls, dwarf cortinellus, and field peas.
Ichi no shiru . .	fish soup with two-colored bean paste.
Ni no shiru . .	soup with clams and young pepper leaves.
Shiru	soup with *Sanshu* bean paste, water shield, and water mustard.
Borsch	beet soup.

The Colonel looked up in surprise. "Say, Fisby. I didn't know they ate borsch over here."

"They didn't, sir, until the Doc introduced it. He's quite a cook you know. Barbecues in the backyard and that sort of thing. He had a surplus of beets on hand, so he thought he'd be able to use them up that way. And believe me, Colonel, borsch is really going over big."

The Colonel regarded the menu again.

Omuko-kaimori . .	shell-fish dish with clams, green peas, and white bean paste, served on the half shell.
Hachizakana . . .	Turbo roasted in the shell.
Gomama	dried young sardines.
Kazunoko	salted herring roe.
Kenchin jiru . . .	stew.
Ohira	covered wooden bowl — sea bream baked in soy, eggs, shrimp, butterfly-shaped yams, and kidney beans.

Mukozuke	. . . .	broiled bonito fish with grated horse-radish and soy.
Wanmori	. . . .	minced shrimp, lotus root, and citron flower.
Hachizakana	. . .	young broiled trout with salt and egg-plant.
Suppon	. . . . .	snapping turtle.
Imobo	. . . . .	red taro roots boiled with cod.
Nishin	. . . . .	herring flavored with eggplant and seasoned with green pepper.
Otsubo	. . . . .	small covered bowl, minced quail boiled with wheat flour.
Red flannel hash	. .	Navy beef with ground beets.

"Of course, Colonel," Fisby said, "this is only the menu for *kobiru*. Now at noon we have . . ."

The Colonel looked up. "What are you going to have, Fisby?"

"Well, I'd really like some *sushi*, sir. When you get used to eating rice, you feel hungry if you don't have it. But let's see—I think I'll have the minced quail bowl, maybe some pickles, and a cup of gardenia tea."

The Colonel nodded. "I'll have the same—and order me some of that caviar."

Fisby clapped twice for the serving boy, who took their order, and the Colonel looked about curiously. "Fisby, what's in those rooms?"

"In that one," Fisby pointed to the left, "is my bedroom. To the right, here, is my den. Would you like to see it, sir?"

The word "den" made Colonel Purdy perk up. "Let's take a look at it."

While the sitting room was plain, depending upon the natural color of the mats, and stained wood, and straight lines for its effect, the den was in the Chinese style. The walls were covered with target cloth, dyed a brilliant red, on which were painted white dragons. The ceiling was of blue target cloth, and the border of the room was made of long bamboo poles. To the rear, a reed blind, with blue drapes, covered a fake window. Metal Chinese lanterns hung down over a black-lacquer-topped bamboo desk. A three-shelved, red lacquer table—with double pieces of bamboo running up through each shelf and serving as legs —sat to one side. Homemade Chinese peel chairs with blue target cloth backs and pillows were carefully arranged around the desk.

The Colonel's eyes flew open. "Fisby, who fixed this den up for you?"

Fisby rubbed his bald head. "I fixed it myself, sir. Peggy always sends in a bunch of those women's magazines each month for the ladies of the village; and one day I happened to look through them, saw this room, so I built it. Of course, Seiko painted the dragons, and Oshiro lacquered the plywood for the table, and First Flower had the target cloth dyed. But I built the desk, and chairs, and put up the decorations myself."

"Well, I'll be damned." The Colonel sat down at the desk and looked out through the open door, looked out across the veranda at the lotus pond. "Say, Fisby, a man could really get some work done with a setup like this, couldn't he?"

"It's quiet here," Fisby said. "About the only noise is the tinkling of the wind bells. And the view of the pines and the garden across the pond is first class."

The Colonel reached up and touched the lanterns. "Where did you get these?"

"One of the blacksmiths hammered them out of old horseshoes. And we made the glass here in the village."

"I'll be damned. Fisby, do the Chinese go in for bright colors like this?"

"I don't know, sir. I just saw this room in an American magazine. They said it was modified Chinese, though."

The Colonel looked around. "If there's anything I like, it's color in a room. Now take my den back home. If Mrs. Purdy hadn't wanted to do it in knotty pine, why I'd have the brightest red and the brightest blue—" He stopped. "Say, do you have any more of these apartments?"

Fisby hesitated. "Well, we have a couple."

"Fine. Fine. You know, Fisby, I think I ought to get away from headquarters for a while. You have no idea what tension we're under up there. Why, any minute some congressman might fly in to inspect us."

Fisby grew uneasy. "You mean you're figuring on moving down here, sir?"

"Certainly. I'll just turn headquarters section over to Major Thompson, and I think the village commanders can get along without my help for a few days. Or a few weeks. Now about these apartments, would I have a den like this?"

Fisby grew desperate. He could see the Colonel barging in, modifying the tea drinking ceremony, which was hundreds of years old; replacing the native *sumo* wrestling with

214

catch as catch can; even setting himself up as an expert on hair styling at the beauty shop. "Well, I don't know, sir. I've already finished a den for the Doc and Mr. Van Druten. But Seiko and Oshiro both want one for their homes, and the teahouse corporation wants me to put in a whole wing of Chinese dining rooms, so I don't know if I would have time to build one for you."

"But, man," Colonel Purdy's face was solemn. "How can I work if I don't have a den? I'll have to spend long hours at my desk."

"You intend to spend most of your time at your desk, sir?"

"Of course." Colonel Purdy was grave. "Plan B and the supplement didn't quite live up to my expectations. We gave the supplement a trial run over in Major Enright's village, but Enright couldn't build bicycles, and he couldn't make brick, and . . . well, I sent Major Thompson over to show him how. But the Major reports that he believes our thinking is too advanced for the native population. So now I have to draw up Plan C and simplify things."

Fisby considered carefully. "If you're going to spend most of your time drawing up Plan C, Colonel, I think I could change priorities on the dens."

Colonel Purdy seemed relieved. "Fine, Fisby. Fine. Oh, yes, will my apartment be on the lotus pond?"

"I think we can arrange that, sir."

"Good. Incidentally, do all those streams in the village flow down into this pond?"

"Yes, sir."

"In that case, Fisby, if I were you, I'd just stock them." Fisby was puzzled. "I don't know what you mean, sir."

"Stock them with fish. First, I think you better get about 6000 blue gill fingerlings, and about 800 bass fingerlings to keep the blue gills down—"

"But where will I get fingerlings, sir?" Fisby wanted to know.

"Why any one of the State fish hatcheries in America would be glad to furnish them. What the hell is the matter with that Import-Export Corporation, can't they handle it?"

"But you told me, Colonel, that I shouldn't bring anything in from the States."

"I did?" Colonel Purdy's eyes widened. "But I was referring to nonessential items, Fisby. Now blue gills are something we really need."

"We do?"

"Of course. Those are essential for our indoctrination. Hell, Fisby, you ought to teach these people what it is to stand in a good pond or stream with the fish biting, the trees rustling above you, and the smoke from the breakfast fire still hanging in the air." The Colonel walked out onto the veranda and flicked his hand in a practice cast. "Man, when you stand out there, you can almost hear those pines singing you a song."

Fisby was taken by surprise. "I didn't know you were interested in the pines—that is, in fishing, and camping, and things like that, sir."

Colonel Purdy shook his head. "I always did like the out-of-doors. You know, someday I'm going to talk Mrs. Purdy into letting me build a lodge up in northern Michigan. I'm going to get myself a canoe and take off up those streams. Do you realize there's virgin forests up there never seen by white men?"

Fisby realized. Yet his mind was on his trade with the States, and he wanted to sound the Colonel out a little more. "Sir," he said, "don't you think I better have Peggy send in some fishing equipment—flies, reels, and so forth?"

"An excellent idea. Excellent."

Fisby considered carefully. "But I don't know much about those things. Would you mind drawing up an order for me? Now as I see it, we could fit fishing into the recreation program, and . . ."

"Very good, Fisby. I'd be glad to help out. I'll get right on it as soon as we have *kobiru,* or whatever you call it."

The Colonel stood on the veranda, flicking his hand in practice casts. And Fisby, convinced that there would be no interference with his Stateside trade as long as he could prove items essential, smiled in relief. "You know, sir," he said, "I think you might like it here in the village. Now on Tuesday and Thursday evenings we have wrestling." He regarded the Colonel. "Of course, they have their own rules, but once you catch on to them, it's interesting. Then after the bouts we usually drop into Mrs. Yamashiro's restaurant for a bite to eat. That's where the wrestling and theatrical crowds hang out."

"What do you mean by the theatrical crowd?" Colonel Purdy asked.

"The playgoers and First Flower's troupe. You see, she rounded up some of her old actor friends from down in Naha, and they're putting on the Kabuki dramas here in the village every Friday, Saturday, and Sunday nights."

Fisby shook his head. "I can't get us any tickets this week though, Colonel, because they're putting on one of Chikamatsu's love plays, and the Women's League bought out the house. But maybe next week I can fix things up."

The Colonel nodded. "Do that, Fisby. What else is going on?"

"This Saturday night the Doc and I are giving a stag party for Seiko. We got half a beef from one of the Navy supply ships, and the Doc is going to barbecue it." He looked up. "And, sir, before I forget, you better bring your bathrobe along. Seiko and First Flower are getting married Sunday afternoon. It's a formal affair and I wouldn't want you to miss out on it." He considered. "Incidentally, Colonel, would you like to go with them on their honeymoon?"

"Fisby," the Colonel said, "why the hell would they want to take me along on their honeymoon?"

"Mr. Van Druten is going."

The Colonel was indignant. "Fisby, doesn't he know enough to mind his own business?"

"But he has to sail the ship, sir."

"What ship?"

"The junk."

The Colonel eyed him. "Just what the hell are you talking about?"

"Mr. Van Druten wasn't very happy with his job of running the Officers' Club, even though the Admiral gave him a letter of commendation for fixing it up so comfortably by just using native mats, bamboo, and things like that." Fisby shook his head. "He told me all about it. He wants sea duty."

"What does that have to do with it?"

"One day, sir, he was down looking around the Import-Export Corporation. He got quite interested in the business, and he suggested that we open up the China coast trade. So he got hold of an old seagoing junk for us and repaired it, even put an auxiliary in her from one of those wrecked landing barges. He's good at shipbuilding, Colonel. He was studying marine architecture, had only a year to go on his course when they called him into service."

"You mean he fixed up a ship and he's sailing it over to the China coast?"

"He didn't exactly do all the work himself, sir. We found out there were quite a few shipbuilders on the island, so we moved some of them in here. But he did the supervising."

"I'll be damned," the Colonel whispered.

"Would you like to see the junk, sir?"

"Where is it?"

"She's anchored just offshore. Come around to the other side of the teahouse, and I'll show her to you."

They walked along the covered veranda, overhanging the lotus pond, and rounded a corner to where the teahouse faced the Pacific. Out upon the blue waters the junk, a white tarp hung over her afterdeck, rode easily on the swells. Her sails were furled now, and her decks showed no signs of life; but the great blue and white and red dragon, painted on her bow, glistened in the morning sun.

The Colonel shook his head as if unable to believe. "Tell me, Fisby, what are you carrying over to the coast?"

"Those goat-hair brushes for one thing, Colonel. And the native ink, and—oh yes—those inkwells of polished red rock. On the trip before last Mr. Van Druten found out that calligraphy is the highest of Chinese arts, so we have a big demand for those products. Then Mr. Van Druten says they practice moxacautery over there—"

"What?"

"Moxacautery. That's a system of curing. Suppose you have a pain in your shoulder, well, you set up a counter-irritation by burning powdered mugwort leaves on the flesh."

"And that cures your shoulder?"

"I don't know, sir. But there's a big demand for those mugwort leaves, and we're sending them in. And we're sending Oshiro's lacquer ware, bamboo cricket cages, dried and processed shark fin, fish cakes, soy sauce, and indigo dye."

"Is that right. Well, what are you getting for that stuff?"

"Oh, jasmine, gardenia, and *oolong* tea. *Oolong* is a kind of fermented green tea, sir. The people like it. And Mr. Van Druten is picking up some citron flower, *ginseng* root, and rice—I hope."

The Colonel laid his hand on the railing of the veranda and looked out at the junk. "*Ginseng* root and jasmine tea, eh?"

"And rice, sir."

The Colonel shook his head. "I don't see why you bother with rice. It takes up too much cargo space."

"But we need it, sir. It's more than a question of getting rice into their diet. For instance, Oshiro needs it for the longevity banquet he is giving for one of his friends. And they need it to make the sweet wine for offering on the feast of the ascension of the god of the hearth."

"But why cart it all the way from China? I have a whole warehouse full up at headquarters," the Colonel said. "What else do you need, besides citron flower and *ginseng* root?"

"We need sesame and perilla seed to press for cooking oil."

"Sesame and perilla seed, eh?"

"Yes, sir. Now about this rice. If I could get a few truck loads, Colonel, I wouldn't have to bring it in from China."

But the Colonel was eyeing the junk with the great dragon painted on her bow. "Tell me, Fisby, are you smuggling?"

"No, sir. Mr. Van Druten comes from one of the oldest and finest families in New England. I'm sure he wouldn't think of such a thing, sir."

"You're not?" The Colonel ran a hand through his bushy gray hair. Ramrod-straight, he was drawn up to his full height, and Fisby noted that he seemed a little disappointed. "Well, what flag are you flying?"

"I don't know, sir. But Mr. Van Druten is getting through all those destroyers out on the East China Sea all right. Why on the last trip out, he blinked to one, asked them if they wanted to search. And they flashed back: 'The war's over, Mac. Just batten down your hatches and look out for hurricanes.'"

The Colonel had a remote look in his eye. "The East China Sea, eh? Fisby, you ought to be a little careful of hurricanes. Now I don't think it's a good idea to anchor her offshore like that." He turned, his eyes earnest. "Don't you think we ought to find a little cove to run her into, some place that's overhung by trees, and vines, and a good growth of bamboo. She'll need protection . . ."

"I never thought of that, sir. I might speak to Mr. Van Druten. Now about this rice—"

"Maybe I ought to hunt up a cove, some place that's well concealed," the Colonel said. "See, we'll use one of those Chinese dens you built here in the teahouse as a headquarters." He turned suddenly. "Incidentally, what do you call this place?"

"The Teahouse of the August Moon. You see, sir, it

was on the night of the August Moon that First Flower decided—"

"Fine. And we'll run out, without lights, from The Teahouse of the August Moon." Colonel Purdy's hand clenched the railing of the veranda, his shoulders were back, and his face bore a daring look. "We'll slip over and down the China coast. We'll pick up our cargo in some inlet, dodging the river patrols. Fisby," he said, "I think we ought to arm her. I read in *Adventure* magazine how they build cannons out of metal pipe. We'll put a scatter gun up on her bow, load it with nails, train a good crew to man it."

Fisby was certain that the Colonel had an entirely wrong slant on the China trade. "But, sir, Mr. Van Druten just goes into Wenchow. The custom inspectors are friendly. No one bothers him, in fact, they're glad to trade. So I really don't think we should arm her." Yet looking at the Colonel, somehow, Fisby was sorry he had said it, for he realized he had broken a long-held dream of the China coast. A dream that was, no doubt, built up on many a winter night as the Colonel sat in his knotty pine den with *Adventure* magazine on his knee. The Colonel's hand loosened on the veranda, his shoulders slumped a trifle, and his eyes seemed dead.

Slowly he turned to Fisby. "I was thinking—well, tell me, you mentioned rice. How much do you need?"

"As much as you can spare, sir." Somehow, Fisby wanted to make up for this disillusionment. He felt a little sorry for the Colonel, standing there, his shoulders bent, and he went on quickly. "You know, sir, I was just thinking. If you let me sell the rice to the people, I can take the money and use it for the public welfare. I can hire carpenters and get those schools built. And we can circulate over the island and find some good teachers. Also, the Doc would like to start a hospital here in the village, and—" He searched the Colonel's face for reaction, but there was none.

The Colonel was gazing out toward the junk. "All right," he said. "I'll phone the supply officer and tell him to release it to you."

Though Fisby wanted to smile because of the rice, still no smile was in him. For the Colonel, with his gray hair and mustache, seemed like an old man. Gone was his swagger, gone was the ramrod posture. "Sir," Fisby said, "the people will really appreciate this. I just can't tell you how much that rice means to them. And to me, too. So I want to thank you for all of us."

The Colonel merely nodded, and Fisby went on slowly. "But just because we have rice, sir, doesn't mean we're going to stop the China trade."

As the Colonel half-turned, Fisby watched his face carefully. "No, sir. We'll need lotus root, and water chestnuts, and fine brocades for the hanging scrolls in the *cha no yu* houses, and a lot of things."

"You will?"

"Certainly." Fisby noted a new interest creep into the Colonel's eyes and felt relieved. "And now that I think of it, maybe we better use one of those Chinese dens as a headquarters. You see, we are getting a little cramped for space at the Import-Export Corporation." He hesitated. "Colonel, would it be all right if we used, say, the den I'm going to build for you?"

"That's perfectly all right, Fisby."

"I mean, we wouldn't be crowding you or anything?"

The Colonel waved a reassuring hand. "Not at all. Not at all."

Fisby saw the smile cross his lips. "Sir, why don't you go out with Mr. Van Druten on the next trip?"

The Colonel hesitated. "If First Flower and her husband are going on their honeymoon, they wouldn't want me tagging along."

"But Mr. Van Druten will be going, he has to captain the junk. And the crew will be along to man it. I'm sure you wouldn't interfere in any way, sir."

"You don't think so?"

"Not at all, sir." Fisby paused and glanced out at the junk. "Besides, I think it might be a good idea to have an extra hand on board. We've been pretty lucky so far, but I don't know. If Mr. Van Druten should run into river pirates—" He held up a finger. "A good man comes in handy."

"River pirates, eh?" The Colonel's shoulders came up, and he smoothed his gray mustache, that gave him a somewhat rakish appearance. "Do you think I really ought to go?"

Fisby nodded. "They could certainly use a good man, sir."

The Colonel's hand tightened on the railing of the

221

veranda. "I think you're right, Fisby. I'd hate like hell to lose a cargo of gardenia tea, citron flower, sesame seed and—and—"

"And *ginseng* root," Fisby added.

SIGNET Short Stories You'll Enjoy

THE BLACK PRINCE
and Other Stories

Shirley Ann Grau. An exciting collection of stories by one of today's most talented young writers. "One reads these haunting, strikingly original stories with pleasure and excitement . . ." — *New York Times.* (#S1318—35c)

KNIGHT'S GAMBIT

William Faulkner. Six short stories by the Nobel Prize winner. Lawyer Gavin Stevens investigates crimes of passion and baffling murder. (#1315—25c)

THE GRASS HARP and A TREE OF NIGHT and Other Stories

Truman Capote. Two brilliant books in one: an enchanting novel about a man, two women and a boy who rebel against the humdrum life of a small town, plus a collection of haunting stories that explore the terror and wonder of modern life. (#S1333—35c)

GOODBYE TO BERLIN

Christopher Isherwood. The extraordinary best-seller about wild, impudent Sally Bowles, personality girl *extra-ordinaire* and her madcap adventures in corrupt pre-war Berlin. (#S1252—35c)

THE HUMOROUS SIDE OF ERSKINE CALDWELL

A treasury of laughter from Caldwell's best stories and novels, with introduction by Robert Cantwell. (#899—25c)

NINE STORIES

J. D. Salinger. Brilliantly penetrating and dramatic stories of life in our times by the author of *The Catcher in the Rye.* (#1111—25c)

A GOOD MAN IS HARD TO FIND

Flannery O'Connor. Colorful, passionate. and perceptive short stories about the South, by an author who has been favorably compared with Faulkner, Caldwell, and McCullers. (#S1345—35c)

FRENCH GIRLS ARE VICIOUS

James T. Farrell. Compassionate - and dramatic tales of Americans here and abroad seeking love to fill the void of loneliness. (#1349—25c)

THIS THING CALLED LOVE

Edited by Marc Slonim and Harvey Breit. Ten superlative stories about the ecstasies, delusions, and confusions of men and women in love, by Aldous Huxley, William Faulkner, Sean O'Faolain, James Thurber, and other outstanding writers. (#1234—25c)

ADVENTURES IN THE SKIN TRADE and Other Stories

Dylan Thomas. Brilliant and fantastic tales by the great Welsh poet, who writes of sinners and lovers, nature and madness, "in wild, leaping language that comes at you from the page."—*Saturday Review Syndicate.* (#S1281—35c)

THE SOFT VOICE OF THE SERPENT and Other Stories

Nadine Gordimer. Finely wrought, perceptive stories probing behind the barriers that separate one human heart from another. (#S1266—35c)

THE UNHOLY THREE and Other Stories (The Injustice Collectors)

Louis Auchincloss. In these urbane and striking stories, one of America's most gifted writers gives a candid picture of frustration and rebellion among the well-to-do. (#1255—25c)

Other SIGNET Books of Interest

THE GIRL HE LEFT BEHIND
Marion (See Here, Private) Hargrove. The rollicking story of the life and loves of a wisecracking peacetime draftee in the "new look" army, by the author of World War II's bestseller funnybook. (#S1364—35c)

NO TIME FOR SERGEANTS
Mac Hyman. America's laugh bestseller, about a drawling, easy-going Georgia cracker whose misadventures with officers, KP, latrine duty. and the induction center psychiatrist upset the whole United States Army! (#S1285—35c)

DIRTY EDDIE
Ludwig Bemelmans. A spicy novel by one of today's wittiest writers about the frenzied actors, writers and directors who live and love in the glaring spotlights of glamorous Hollywood. (#1278—25c)

THE CATCHER IN THE RYE
J. D. Salinger. The captivating novel about a sixteen-year-old boy who runs away from school to spend a wild, hilarious, and desperate week-end in New York. "A rare miracle of fiction."—*Clifton Fadiman.* (#1001—25c)

A MANY-SPLENDORED THING
Han Suyin. A lovely Eurasian woman doctor tells, with honesty and delicacy, of her love affair with a British newspaperman in the seething, war-ravaged colony of Hong Kong. (#D1183—50c)

HEART OF DARKNESS and THE SECRET SHARER
Joseph Conrad. Two masterfully written novels by one of the great modern novelists tell of embattled, lonely men who are drawn into violent adventures. (#S1254—35c)

NECTAR IN A SIEVE
Kamala Markandaya. The widely acclaimed novel about a farmer's wife in India whose love for her husband and children gave her the courage to triumph over disaster and misfortune. (#S1336—35c)

NIGHT FLIGHT
Antoine de St. Exupéry. A beautiful, unforgettable novel of the breath-taking feats and adventures of the intrepid men who gave their lives and hearts to bring the mail through in the early heroic age of aviation. (#1354—25c)

A DEVIL IN PARADISE
Henry Miller. In this brilliant new book, the dynamic author of *Tropic of Cancer* tells the tense story of an eccentric visitor, a strange man who attempts to dominate everyone in his orbit. (#1317—25c)

TOO LATE THE PHALAROPE
Alan Paton. A magnificent novel of South Africa by the author of *Cry The Beloved Country*, about a young white police lieutenant who violates the strictest laws of his country when he falls in love with a Negro girl. (#S1290—35c)

TO OUR READERS: We welcome your comments about any Signet, Signet Key or Mentor Book, as well as your suggestions for new reprints. If your dealer does not have the books you want, you may order them by mail enclosing the list price plus 5c a copy to cover mailing costs. Send for a copy of our complete catalog. The New American Library of World Literature, Inc., 501 Madison Avenue, New York 22, New York.